Active Database Systems
Triggers and Rules
For Advanced Database Processing

The Morgan Kaufmann Series in
Data Management Systems

Series Editor, Jim Gray

Active Database Systems: Triggers and Rules For Advanced Database Processing
Edited by Jennifer Widom and Stefano Ceri

Joe Celko's SQL for Smarties: Advanced SQL Programming
Joe Celko

Migrating Legacy Systems: Gateways, Interfaces, and the Incremental Approach
Michael Brodie and Michael Stonebraker

The Object Database Standard: ODMG-93 (Release 1.1)
Edited by R. G. G. Cattell

Database: Principles, Programming, and Performance
Patrick O'Neil

Database Modeling and Design: The Fundamental Principles, Second Edition
Toby J. Teorey

Readings in Database Systems, Second Edition
Edited by Michael Stonebraker

Atomic Transactions
Nancy Lynch, Michael Merritt, William Weihl, and Alan Fekete

Query Processing for Advanced Database Systems
Edited by Johann Christoph Freytag, David Maier, and Gottfried Vossen

Transaction Processing: Concepts and Techniques
Jim Gray and Andreas Reuter

Understanding the New SQL: A Complete Guide
Jim Melton and Alan R. Simon

Building an Object-Oriented Database System: The Story of O_2
Edited by François Bancilhon, Claude Delobel, and Paris Kanellakis

Database Transaction Models for Advanced Applications
Edited by Ahmed K. Elmagarmid

A Guide to Developing Client/Server SQL Applications
Setrag Khoshafian, Arvola Chan, Anna Wong, and Harry K. T. Wong

The Benchmark Handbook for Database and Transaction Processing Systems, Second Edition
Edited by Jim Gray

Camelot and Avalon: A Distributed Transaction Facility
Edited by Jeffrey L. Eppinger, Lily B. Mummert, and Alfred Z. Spector

Readings in Object-Oriented Database Systems
Edited by Stanley B. Zdonik and David Maier

Active Database Systems
Triggers and Rules
For Advanced Database Processing

Edited by

Jennifer Widom
Stefano Ceri

MORGAN KAUFMANN PUBLISHERS, INC.
SAN FRANCISCO, CALIFORNIA

Sponsoring Editor Bruce M. Spatz
Production Manager Yonie Overton
Production Editor Cheri Palmer
Editorial Coordinator Marilyn Uffner Allen
Cover Design Patty King
Icon Design Lori Margulies, Lori Margulies Design
Final Formatting/Output Mary Miller Associates
Printer Edwards Brothers, Inc.

This book has been author-typeset using LaTeX macros provided by
the publisher.

Morgan Kaufmann Publishers, Inc.
Editorial and Sales Office
340 Pine Street, Sixth Floor
San Francisco, CA 94104-3205
USA
Telephone 415 / 392-2665
Facsimile 415 / 982-2665
Internet mkp@mkp.com

Library of Congress Cataloging-in-Publication Data
Active database systems : triggers and rules for advanced database
  processing / edited by Jennifer Widom, Stefano Ceri.
      p.   cm.
    Includes bibliographical references and index.
    ISBN 1-55860-304-2
    1. Database management.   I. Widom, Jennifer.   II. Ceri, Stefano,
  1955-
  QA76.9.D3A333   1996
  005.74–dc20   95-23101
                                                          CIP

ISSN   1046-1698

Contents

7   The HiPAC Project   177

Umeshwar Dayal, Alejandro P. Buchmann, and
Sharma Chakravarthy

8   Active Database Facilities in Ode   207

Narain Gehani and H. V. Jagadish

Preface

Active database systems enhance traditional database functionality with powerful rule processing (or "trigger") capabilities, providing a uniform and efficient mechanism for database integrity constraints, views and derived data, authorization, statistics gathering, monitoring and alerting, knowledge bases and expert systems, workflow management, and many other database system features and applications. The field of active database systems has been one of the most prominent areas of database research during the late 1980s and early 1990s. Active database capabilities are now finding their way into many of the most popular commercial database management systems, and it is anticipated that active database technology will become a central component of next-generation database management systems and their applications.

This book is the first single source to cover the vast research literature and commercial advancements in the area of active database systems. It is intended to provide developers, researchers, and other computer professionals with a comprehensive guide to and reference for the field. In an educational setting, this book could be used in a course specifically covering active database systems, or in a course on advanced topics in database systems (see "How to Use the Book" below). This book also is useful for researchers or developers embarking on projects in active database systems, or on projects in related fields such as expert systems, knowledge-base systems, deductive database systems, extended relational database systems, or object-oriented database systems.

Structure of the Book

The book begins with a comprehensive introduction to the field of active database systems. The introduction provides motivation and history for the area, it defines the fundamental concepts of active database systems, and it discusses the most important issues in the field—both theoretical and practical—highlighting trade-offs in active rule language design, system implementation, and usability. The introductory chapter also provides a survey of research activities and commercial efforts in the field.

The next seven chapters of the book cover seven of the most prominent research projects in active database systems. Four projects based on relational database systems are covered first, followed by three projects based on object-oriented database systems. The projects covered are: *POSTGRES*, *Ariel*, *Starburst*, *A-RDL*, *Chimera*, *HiPAC*, and *Ode*. These projects were chosen because of their maturity and completeness, and because each one has contributed to the field in a major way by advancing important aspects of active database rule languages and their implementation. Most of the projects are backed by a full experimental prototype; all of them are at least partially implemented. Together, the seven project chapters give a broad overview of the entire area. Each project is covered in detail by the project leaders themselves.

After the project chapters, the book includes a chapter on standards and commercial systems. Because active database (trigger) capabilities have not yet been standardized in commercial systems (although ANSI/ISO standards are underway), and because commercial products evolve quickly, this chapter necessarily provides only a "snapshot" of the current state. However, based on standards activities and product release information, we feel that this snapshot is representative of the direction of commercial work in active database systems. The next chapter describes active database applications, covering both specific applications as well as general tools and techniques for active database application development. The final chapter ties together the previous ten chapters, pointing out both commonalities and differences among the projects covered, analyzing and predicting trends in active database systems, and outlining our vision for the future of the field.

How to Use the Book

This book should be accessible to any reader with a solid grounding in the field of database management systems. The book is geared towards working professionals and educators in the database area, as well as graduate students or advanced undergraduates who have taken at least one database course. (References to books covering foundations of database management systems are given in Chapter 1.) As described earlier, the book consists of five distinct parts:

1. A comprehensive introductory chapter

2. Seven chapters covering active database system research projects

3. A chapter on standards and commercial systems

4. A chapter on active database applications

5. A concluding chapter that summarizes and outlines future directions

We strongly recommend that all readers carefully cover the introductory chapter. However, beyond the first chapter readers may "pick and choose." With the background provided in the introduction, each of the project chapters can be read independently. Each project chapter includes a description of the system's rule language syntax and semantics, a number of examples, a discussion of the system's architecture and features of its implementation, a description of relevant applications, and plans for future work. The chapter on commercial systems and the chapter on applications also can be read independently, since they rely mostly on concepts provided in the introduction. The concluding chapter will of course make the most sense to readers who have covered the majority of the earlier chapters of the book, however the conclusions may be interesting as well to those who have covered only selected portions of the book.

A graduate course focusing exclusively on the field of active database systems should be able to cover most if not all of the book during a single term. A course on advanced topics in database systems should certainly cover the introduction, along with a selection of the project chapters. Depending on the focus of the course, the last three chapters of the book may or may not be covered.

If not all of the project chapters are to be covered, we suggest reading about one of *POSTGRES*, *Starburst*, or *Ariel* as representative of a mature relational active database system, reading about *HiPAC* for its comprehensive ideas and its position as a pioneering project in the field, reading about *Chimera* or *Ode* as representative of a mature object-oriented active database system, and reading about *A-RDL* for its unique relationship with deductive database systems. Needless to say, we feel that all of these projects are very important, there is only marginal overlap across project chapters, and readers are encouraged to cover all of them for a complete understanding of the field.

Acknowledgments

Jennifer and Stefano would first like to thank their colleagues, students, and families for their help and understanding during the long and arduous process of putting together this book. They also thank their editor Bruce Spatz at Morgan Kaufmann for his encouragement and especially his patience during the process. Umesh Dayal provided significant help in the organization of the book, as well as comments on a number of chapters. Jim Gray provided comments on the book outline and early draft material. Anthony Tomasic provided comments on the introductory chapter, and Roberta Cochrane provided comments on the standards and commercial systems chapter.

Jennifer was supported in her book efforts by the IBM Almaden Research Center, by the Anderson Faculty Scholar Fund at Stanford, and by equipment grants from Digital and IBM corporations. Stefano was supported by Esprit project P6333, "Idea." Some of Stefano's work reported in the applications chapter was supported by grant ENEL-POLI, VDS 1/94, and the following people are thanked for contributing to this work: Elena Baralis, Leonardo Dalle Rive, Piero Fraternali, Gabriella Monteleone, Stefano Paraboschi, and Letizia Tanca.

In addition to the authors of the project chapters, a great many people contributed to the research projects covered, and to the chapters describing these projects.

- **Ariel:** Eric Hanson would like to thank Yu-wang Wang, Anjali Rastogi, Min Zhang, Y. Satyanarayana, Michael E. Carey, and Indira Roy.

- **Starburst:** Jennifer Widom would like thank Roberta Cochrane, Shel Finkelstein, and Bruce Lindsay.

- **A-RDL:** Eric Simon and Jerry Kiernan would like to thank Eric Dujardin and Christophe de Maindreville for contributions to the system, and Rakesh Agrawal, Francoise Fabret, Allen van Gelder, Francois Llirbat, Philippe Picouet, and Patrick Valduriez for comments on the chapter.

- **Chimera:** Stefano Ceri, Piero Fraternali, Stefano Paraboschi, and Letizia Tanca would like to thank Elena Baralis, Elisa Bertino, Stefano Crespi-Reghizzi, Christoph Draxler, Ulrike Griefahn, Giovanna Guerrini, Rainer Manthey, Danilo Montesi, Giuseppe Psaila, and German

Rodriguez for contributions to system design, and Paola Abbi, Annalisa Apicella, Andrea Bassani, Davide Berveglieri, Elena Bianchini, Antonio Bossi, Michele Campriani, Carlo Capellini, Stefano Castangia, Lanfranco Colella, Oscar Croci, Paola De Prati, Pier Paolo Merli, Roberto Penzo, Francesco Ronsivalle, Paolo Rossetti, Daniele Roda, and Renato Ronconi for implementation.

- **HiPAC:** Umesh Dayal, Alex Buchmann, and Sharma Chakravarthy would like to thank Jose Blakeley, Barbara Blaustein, Michael Carey, David Goldhirsch, Meichun Hsu, Rajiv Jauhari, Rivka Ladin, Miron Livny, Dennis McCarthy, Richard McKee, and Arnon Rosenthal.

- **Ode:** Narain Gehani and H.V. Jagadish would like to thank Bob Arlein and Dan Lieuwen for contributions to the system, and Oded Shmueli for comments on the chapter.

Jennifer Widom   Stefano Ceri
Stanford University   Politecnico di Milano

1

Introduction to Active Database Systems

Jennifer Widom and Stefano Ceri

A database management system is a facility for storing large volumes of data and allowing multiple users to manipulate the data in an efficient and controlled fashion. This text assumes that readers are familiar with the basic concepts of database management systems as described in, e.g., [EN94, KS86, Ull89].

Conventional database management systems are *passive*: data is created, retrieved, modified, and deleted only in response to operations issued by users or application programs. Recent trends in database technology have focused on extending conventional database systems to enhance their functionality and to accommodate novel and more advanced applications. One important and useful enhancement is transforming database systems to be *active*: the database system itself performs certain operations automatically in response to certain events occurring or certain conditions being satisfied.

Active database systems are significantly more powerful than their passive counterparts:

- Active database systems can efficiently perform functions that in passive database systems must be encoded in applications.

- Active database systems suggest and facilitate applications beyond the scope of passive database systems.

- Active database systems can perform tasks that require special-purpose subsystems in passive database systems.

Several examples are described to motivate and illustrate these facets of active database systems.

Examples of functions that can efficiently be performed by active database systems, but that in passive database systems must be encoded in applications, are *general integrity constraints* and *triggers*. Integrity constraints specify conditions that must hold over the data in the database, usually stipulating that the data is a valid representation of the real world. Conventional passive database systems support limited forms of integrity constraints, such as the specification that certain data items must take on unique values (*key constraints*), or that certain data items must contain references to other data items (*referential integrity constraints*). However, many applications require constraints well beyond these simple forms, such as the specification that all values must be within a certain range, or that an aggregate function on the data must produce a certain value. In addition, in conventional passive database systems, integrity constraint checking is restricted to immediately after each update or at the end of each transaction, and the response to a constraint violation is to roll back the transaction. Active database systems support the specification and monitoring of general database integrity constraints, they allow flexibility in the time of integrity constraint checking, and they provide execution of compensating actions to rectify a constraint violation without rolling back the transaction.

Database triggers, sometimes referred to as *alerters*[1] or *monitors*, specify that certain actions should be invoked whenever certain conditions are detected. For example, an inventory control trigger might detect when stock is low and automatically reorder items. Active database systems support triggers, and in fact are based on the triggering concept.

Consider how integrity constraints or triggers would be encoded in applications. There are two reasonable approaches. In the first approach, every modification to the database in each application is followed by code that checks the constraint or the trigger condition and then, if appropriate, performs the associated action. (In the case of a constraint violation, the action would be to undo the modification or abort the transaction; in the case of a trigger condition, the action would be to invoke the trigger's procedure.) There are several disadvantages to this approach: (1) adding, changing, or removing a constraint or trigger requires finding and modifying the relevant code in every application; (2) the correct constraint-checking or triggering behavior is guaranteed only when every application implements it correctly; (3) additional application-to-database communication is required after every modification.

The second approach is to add a special application process that periodically polls the database to check each constraint and trigger. While solving some of the problems with the first approach, this approach has the disadvantage that if the polling is too frequent then there is significant performance overhead, while if the polling is too infrequent then a constraint violation or trigger condition may not be detected in a timely manner. Active database systems support constraints and triggers without the disadvantages of either of these approaches.

Examples of applications that are suggested or facilitated by active database systems, but that are beyond the scope of passive database systems, are *data-intensive expert systems* and *workflow management*. Expert systems typically are programmed using an artificial intelligence (AI) rule

---

[1]Note that the term *alerter* sometimes is used to mean a trigger whose action is a simple notification.

language such as OPS5 [BFKM85], where the data operated on by the expert
system is stored in main memory. If an expert system is data-intensive, i.e.,
the data exceeds main memory, then the expert system must store its excess
data in a database or file system, moving data back and forth to main memory
as needed. Active database systems use a rule processing paradigm similar
to AI rule languages, so active database systems provide a convenient and
efficient platform on which to build data-intensive expert systems.

Workflow management is an area of emerging importance associated
with controlling interconnected computational tasks, in office procedures or
hospital management for example. Workflow management systems typically
monitor the state of certain tasks and, when appropriate, automatically invoke other tasks, passing related data between the tasks as needed. Because
of the monitoring and action invocation behavior provided by active database
systems, and because many of the tasks in workflow applications are performed on database systems, active database systems provide a convenient
and efficient core for workflow management systems.

Examples of tasks that can be performed by active database systems,
but that require special-purpose subsystems in passive database systems, are
simple integrity constraints, authorization, statistics gathering, and *views.* As
explained earlier, conventional passive database systems include a component
for managing simple forms of integrity constraints—these constraints (along
with more general integrity constraints) could instead be managed by an active
database system.

Conventional passive database systems include an authorization component that associates privileges with users and checks these privileges each
time a data manipulation operation is performed. Many active database systems can perform exactly the same tasks without requiring a special-purpose
subsystem. Furthermore, active database systems can enforce more complex authorization policies than those enforced by conventional authorization
components. (For example, active database systems can enforce semantically-
oriented or data-dependent authorization policies.)

Conventional passive database systems may include a statistics gathering component that monitors data access and modifications, recording information about frequency of data values and frequency of access to particular
data. Again, these same tasks can be performed by active database systems
without requiring a special-purpose subsystem.

Finally, many conventional passive database systems include a view component, allowing the definition of virtual data that is derived from other (base)

data. Views usually are implemented by a special-purpose subsystem that, for each view, either modifies queries that reference the view or maintains a materialization of the view in the database. Here, too, active database systems can provide this functionality without requiring a separate subsystem.

While these examples illustrate only some of the uses of active database systems, they should be sufficient to convince the reader that active database systems add considerable power to conventional passive database systems, and active database systems can be used to perform a wide variety of tasks. Further details of these examples, along with additional applications of active database systems, are discussed in Chapter 10.

In developing an active database system it is necessary to consider a number of issues:

- An active database system must provide all the usual functionality of a conventional passive database system. Meanwhile, it is desirable that the performance of conventional database tasks is not degraded by the fact that the database system is active.

- An active database system must provide some mechanism for users and applications to specify the desired active behavior, and these specifications must become a persistent part of the database.

- An active database system must efficiently implement any active behavior that can be specified; it must monitor the behavior of the database system and, when appropriate, automatically initiate additional behavior.

- An active database system must provide database design and debugging tools similar to those provided by conventional database systems, extended to incorporate active behavior.

The focus of this book is on how these issues are addressed in current active database systems and how active database systems can be extended and improved in the future.

This introductory chapter provides a brief history of active database systems in Section 1.1. Next, in Section 1.2, the paradigm of *active database rules* is introduced; this paradigm forms the core of all active database systems. General issues in the design and execution semantics of active database rule languages are discussed in Sections 1.3 and 1.4, while system architecture and implementation issues are discussed in Sections 1.5 and 1.6. The problem of application development is discussed in Section 1.7, although details of specific applications and application development techniques are deferred until Chapter 10. Section 1.8 provides a broad overview of a large number of research projects on active database systems; Chapters 2–8 cover seven of these projects in detail. Section 1.9 contains a brief discussion of commercialization of active database systems; this topic is covered further in Chapter 9.

The purpose of this introductory chapter is to present the concepts underlying active database systems and to motivate and discuss the various issues and alternatives. Consequently, many aspects of active database systems are discussed here in relatively broad and speculative terms. This introduction provides a useful basis for Chapters 2–8, in which the details of seven specific active database system prototypes are presented. Note also that, although numerous examples of general concepts are given in this introductory chapter, few specific examples are provided. Chapters 2–8 include many specific examples for each system.

1.1
History

The area of active database systems did not become widely recognized until the mid to late 1980s, with the emergence of the pioneering *HiPAC* project (described in Section 1.8.2 and Chapter 7). However, several active database features and proposals did appear in the 1970s and early 1980s, and are described briefly here.

The *CODASYL* data manipulation language, defined by the *Data Base Task Group* (DBTG) in the early 1970s and often referred to as the DBTG language, includes a mechanism for automatic procedure invocation in response to specified database operations. The declaration of DBTG sets and record types can include one or more *ON* clauses:

ON ⟨command list⟩ CALL ⟨procedure⟩

The ⟨procedure⟩ specifies an arbitrary procedure in the DBTG data manipulation language, which includes the full power of the programming language COBOL. For a DBTG set S, the ⟨command list⟩ specifies one or more of INSERT, REMOVE, and FIND. The ⟨procedure⟩ is invoked automatically immediately after one of the specified operations is executed on set S. For a DBTG record type T, the ⟨command list⟩ specifies one or more of INSERT, REMOVE,

FIND, STORE, DELETE, MODIFY, and GET. The ⟨procedure⟩ is invoked automatically immediately after one of the specified operations is executed on a record of type T. Details on this active database feature in CODASYL can be found in [COD73].

Query-by-Example (QBE), a screen-oriented query language for relational database systems developed in the mid 1970s, includes a trigger facility for integrity constraint checking. A QBE user can define conditions associated with data modification operations **insert**, **delete**, and **update** on particular tables or tuples. When an operation that has a trigger condition is executed, the condition is checked—if the condition is false then the operation is undone. QBE trigger conditions include a feature for referencing both the old and new values of modified tuples. Details on QBE can be found in [Zlo77].

A "trigger subsystem" was suggested for the *System R* relational database research project in the late 1970s, but this feature did not become part of the relational database products that evolved from System R. Proposals for the trigger subsystem can be found in [EC75, Esw76]. It is interesting to observe that many of the features suggested in these proposals reemerged to be improved and extended when active database systems finally became popular ten years later. For example, [Esw76] includes discussion of active database language features, concurrency control, and protection; it also outlines the use of active database systems for integrity constraint maintenance, authorization, and views.

As a last historical note, in the early 1980s a paper appeared motivating and describing a general active database system framework [Mor83]. Although many features in this proposal are quite different from current active database systems, it was in this paper that the term "active database system" was coined.

1.2
Active Database Rules

Active database systems are centered around the notion of *rules*. Rules in active database systems are defined by users, applications, or database administrators; they specify the desired active behavior. In their most general form, active database rules consist of three parts:

- **Event**: causes the rule to be *triggered*

- **Condition**: is checked when the rule is triggered

- **Action**: is executed when the rule is triggered and its condition is true

A wide variety of alternatives are possible for events, conditions, and actions, and other rule components also may be included. These issues are discussed in Section 1.3.

Once a set of rules is defined, the active database system monitors the relevant events. For each rule, if the rule's event occurs then the active database system evaluates the rule's condition, and if the rule's condition is true then the active database system executes the rule's action. (The execution of a rule's action sometimes is referred to as *firing* the rule.) The details of rule monitoring and execution are quite a bit more complex than this simple description—and the details vary considerably from system to system—but this is the general paradigm used by all active database systems.

Many other terms may be used synonymously for rules in active database systems, for example *production* or *forward-chaining rules* (indicating the relationship to AI rule languages), *ECA rules* (for Event-Condition-Action rules), *situation-action rules*, *triggers*, *monitors*, or *alerters*.

1.2.1   Other Database Rules

Active database systems are not the only context in which rule processing has been added to database systems. Rules also form the core of *deductive database systems*. In deductive database systems, declarative logic programming style rules are used to add the power of recursively defined views to a conventional database system. Much of the focus in deductive database systems is on developing efficient strategies for processing rules in response to queries on recursively defined views. Unfortunately, many of these strategies are not applicable to active database systems since the rule processing paradigm in active database systems is quite different. However, there has been some work in extending deductive database systems with active capabilities [BJ93, dMS88b, SKdM92], in implementing deductive database systems using active database systems [CW94], and in integrating the two approaches [HD93, PT94, Zan93], so the two types of extended database systems are not entirely distinct. Details on deductive database systems can be found in [CGT90, Min88, Ull89], and a discussion of the relationship between deductive and active database systems appears in [Wid93].

Rules also can be used in database query optimization. For example, the *Starburst* prototype database system employs two separate rule processing systems during query optimization [HCL$^+$90]. The first rule system specifies how a query can be rewritten into an equivalent but more efficient form, while the second rule system specifies the execution plans that are valid for a query. Rule processing is used in query optimization primarily for extensibility: new rules can be defined when new query language constructs are added, when new query evaluation methods become possible, or when new equivalences are discovered. Currently, most rule processing systems used for query optimization are built into the database query processor and are highly specialized, so they do not provide the user interface or generality provided by active database rules.

1.3
Rule Language Design

The desired behavior of an active database system is specified using an *active database rule language*. Clearly, what can be specified in the rule language has a direct impact on the power and on the complexity of the active database system. This section discusses the wide variety of features possible in active database rule languages. Certainly no active database system provides all of these features in its rule language, however each feature discussed is supported or suggested by at least one system.

1.3.1   Events

In an active database rule, the *event* specifies what causes the rule to be triggered. Useful triggering events are:

- **Data modification.** In a relational database system, a data modification event might be specified as one of the three SQL data modification operations—**insert**, **delete**, or **update**—on a particular table. In an object-oriented database system, a data modification event might be specified as the creation, deletion, or modification of a particular object, or of any object in a particular class; it also might be specified as the invocation of a particular method that modifies objects.

- **Data retrieval.** In a relational database system, a data retrieval event might be specified as a **select** operation on a particular table, while in an object-oriented database system it might be specified as the fetch of an object, or as the invocation of a particular method that retrieves objects.

- **Time.** A temporal event might specify that a rule should be triggered at an absolute time (e.g., *1 Jan 95 at 12:00*), at a repeated time (e.g., *every day at 12:00*), or at periodic intervals (e.g., *every 10 minutes*).

- **Application-defined.** Application-defined events might be specified by allowing an application to declare a name E as denoting an event (e.g., *high-temperature, user-login, data-too-large*, etc.) and allowing active database rules to specify E as their triggering event. Then, each time an application notifies the database system of the occurrence of event E, any rule specifying E as its event is triggered. Using this approach, the application may perform any monitoring or computations it desires (with or without accessing the database) to detect when event E should occur, i.e., to detect when the rules associated with E should be triggered.

In addition, while the default in most active database systems is for a rule to be triggered *after* the occurrence of its triggering event, sometimes it can be useful for a rule to specify that it is triggered just *before* its triggering event.

The examples given so far are single events. Triggering events also might be *composite*, i.e., they might be combinations of single events or other composite events. Useful operators for combining events are:

- **Logical operators.** Events might be combined using Boolean operators *and, or, not, implies*, etc.

- **Sequence.** A rule might be triggered when two or more events occur in a particular order.

- **Temporal composition.** A rule might be triggered by a combination of temporal and non-temporal events, such as "*5 seconds after event E_1,*" or "*every hour after the first occurrence of event E_2.*"

Very complex composite events are possible if an event specification language is based on regular expressions or a context-free grammar.

Some active database systems allow events to be parameterized. When a parameterized triggering event occurs, values related to the event are bound to the event's parameters, and these parameter values can then be referenced in the rule's condition or action. For example, a method call event in an object-oriented active database system might bind as event parameters the identifier of the object on which the method is invoked along with certain parameters of the method call. As another example, an **insert** event in a relational active database system might bind as a parameter the values of the inserted data (although sometimes this information is provided to the rule's condition and action without explicit binding—see Section 1.3.5).

Finally, some active database systems allow the event to be omitted altogether. The issues associated with including events versus not including them are discussed in Section 1.3.4 below.

1.3.2 Conditions

In an active database rule, the *condition* specifies an additional condition to be checked once the rule is triggered and before the action is executed. Useful conditions are:

- **Database predicates**. The condition might specify that a certain predicate holds on the database, where the predicate is defined using a language corresponding to condition clauses in the database query language (e.g., a relational active database system might allow as rule conditions anything corresponding to an SQL **where** clause). For example, a condition expressed as a predicate might state that the average value in some set of values is below a certain threshold.

- **Restricted predicates.** The condition might specify that a certain predicate holds on the database, where the predicate is defined using a restricted portion of the query language's condition clauses. For example, a relational active database system might restrict its rule conditions such that comparison operations are allowed but aggregate operations and joins are not allowed. Restricted predicates generally are used instead of arbitrary predicates only for performance reasons—condition evaluation can be the most expensive aspect of rule processing.

- **Database queries.** The condition might specify a query using the database system's query language. For example, a condition specified as a query might retrieve all data whose value is below a certain threshold. The meaning can either be that the condition is true if and only if the query produces an empty answer, or that the condition is true if and only if the query produces a non-empty answer. Like predicates, conditions that are queries may use a restricted language to guarantee efficient evaluation. Note that since most database query languages include conditions as one component, there may be no difference in expressiveness between predicates or queries as rule conditions: a rule with any predicate P as its condition is equivalent to a rule with query $Q(P)$ as its condition, where $Q(P)$ retrieves all data satisfying predicate P.

- **Application procedures.** A rule condition might be specified as a call to a procedure written in an application programming language (e.g., *max-exceeded()*), where the procedure may or may not access the database. If the procedure returns *true* then the condition holds; if the procedure returns *false* then the condition does not hold. Similar to the difference between predicates and queries, procedures might return data instead of returning a Boolean value. Here too, the meaning can be that the condition is true if and only if the procedure returns data, or that the condition is true if and only if the query does not return data.

In all of these cases, if the rule language allows parameterized events, then the condition language probably includes a mechanism for referencing the values bound to the event's parameters.

In some active database systems, values related to the condition can be passed to the action, either explicitly through a parameter mechanism or implicitly through other rule language features. Most commonly, if the condition is expressed as a query or as a procedure that returns data, then the values returned by the query or procedure are passed to the rule action. If the condition is expressed as a database predicate, then data satisfying the predicate may be passed to the rule action.

Most active database systems allow the condition part of a rule to be omitted, in which case the condition always is true.

1.3.3   Actions

In an active database rule, the *action* is executed when the rule is triggered and its condition is true. Useful actions are:

- **Data modification operations.** A relational active database system might allow rule actions to specify SQL **insert**, **delete**, or **update** operations, while an object-oriented active database system might allow rule actions to specify object creation, object deletion, or method calls that modify objects.

- **Data retrieval operations.** A relational active database system might allow rule actions to specify SQL **select** operations, while an object-oriented active database system might allow rule actions to specify object fetches, or method calls that retrieve objects.

- **Other database commands.** A rule action might allow any database operation at all to be specified. In addition to data modification and retrieval operations, most database systems support operations for data definition, operations for transaction control (e.g., **rollback**, **commit**), operations for granting and revoking privileges, etc.

- **Application procedures.** A rule action might be specified as a call to a procedure written in an application programming language, where the procedure may or may not access the database.

In all of these cases, if the rule language allows parameterized events, then the action language probably includes a mechanism for referencing the values bound to the event's parameters, and if the rule language allows values to be passed from the condition to the action, then the action language probably includes a mechanism for referencing these values. Many active database rule languages allow a rule to specify a set of actions, usually with an ordering so that the multiple actions are executed sequentially.

1.3.4   Omitting the Event

As described in Section 1.2, an active database rule is triggered when its event occurs; the rule's condition is checked, and if the condition is true its action is executed. By contrast, AI rule languages and deductive databases normally use rules without events, and some active database rule languages support rules without events as well. When an active rule does not have an event, the meaning might be that the rule is triggered implicitly whenever a state is reached in which the rule's condition is true, or the meaning might be that the rule is triggered implicitly whenever data is modified so that new data satisfies the rule's condition.

There are a number of distinctions between Event-Condition-Action rules and Condition-Action rules. Including a triggering event as part of the rule language makes it possible to specify different actions when a given condition is satisfied, depending on which event occurred. For example, in a relational database one might wish to react to the violation of a referential integrity constraint differently, depending on whether the violation came about because a new tuple was inserted or because an old tuple was deleted. This kind of operation-specific behavior is not possible with Condition-Action rules, and is one reason active databases have generally adopted Event-Condition-Action rules. On the other hand, Condition-Action rules are generally considered more "declarative," and they can be easier to program since the burden of determining when to evaluate the condition lies with the system rather than the user.

1.3.5   Transition Values

Although the execution semantics of rules is not discussed until Section 1.4, to understand the concept of *transition values* in rule language design it is necessary to know that when a rule's condition is evaluated or its action is executed, it often occurs with respect to a database state change—a *transition*—which causes the rule to become triggered.

As will be explained in Section 1.4, transitions may consist of changes as small as the modification of a single tuple or object or as large as an entire database transaction. Regardless, in rule languages where conditions are evaluated and actions are executed with respect to transitions, the rule language usually includes a mechanism for referencing values associated with these transitions. One mechanism for referencing transition values already has been described, where a rule's triggering event is parameterized and these parameters can be referenced in the rule's condition and action. For example, a rule might be triggered by "*modified*(X)," where parameter X is bound to the data that is modified in the transition that triggers the rule, and X can be referenced in the rule's condition and action to access the modified data.

When event parameters are not used, the mechanisms for referencing transition values can either be *explicit* or *implicit*. Explicit transition value references take place through special keywords. For example, **inserted**, **deleted**, and **updated** might be reserved words that, when used in a rule condition or action, denote the data that was inserted, deleted, or modified in the triggering transition. In the case of a rule triggered by data modification, keyword **new** might be used to reference the new value of the modified data, while keyword **old** might be used to reference the old value.

Implicit transition value references vary from language to language, but the general principle is that when a rule is triggered by changes to some data item or data set D, then references to D in the rule's condition or action implicitly reference a transition value associated with D. For example, if a relational active database rule is triggered by insertions into a table T, then references to T in the rule's condition or action might implicitly reference only the tuples inserted into T, not the entire table.

1.3.6   Physical Versus Logical Events

As discussed in Section 1.3.1, the events that trigger rules usually are database operations, notifications from applications, or, in the case of temporal events, clock ticks. In all of these cases, the triggering event corresponds to physical execution of some activity. Sometimes it is more useful for rules to be triggered by the *effect* of activity, rather than by the actual operations performed. For example, suppose in a relational active database system that, before rules are processed, several tuples are inserted and then the same tuples are updated. The operations performed are insert and update, so rules specifying (physical) insert events and rules specifying (physical) update events are triggered. However, the net effect of inserting tuples and then updating the same tuples is equivalent to inserting the updated tuples. Hence, if the logical activity rather than the physical activity is considered, only rules specifying (logical) insert events are triggered.

Active database rule languages may support triggering events that are physical, logical, or both. In general, the more closely the triggering events correspond to physical activity, the lower the abstraction level of the rule language. A lower abstraction level allows more fine-grained control over how rules behave relative to triggering operations, while a higher abstraction level allow rules to be programmed in a more intuitive or "behavioral" way.

1.3.7   Other Features

In addition to the three main components of rules—events, conditions, and actions—and mechanisms for referencing transition values, several other useful features may be included in an active database rule language:

- **Rule commands.** The event, condition, and action for a rule usually are specified as part of a *create* command provided for rules. A corresponding *delete* command is necessary to remove rules. A *modify* command may be provided as well, so that components of a rule can be changed without deleting the rule and creating a new one. A pair of commands provided by some systems is *deactivate* (or *disable*) and *activate* (or *enable*); these commands allow certain rules to be "turned off" temporarily, so that the rules remain in the system but are not eligible to be triggered or executed.

- **Rule priorities.** The execution semantics for active database rules sometimes requires that one rule is selected from a set of eligible rules (see Section 1.4). For this reason, an active database rule language may include a mechanism for declaring rule *priorities*. Priorities might be specified by ordering the set of rules, by declaring relative priorities between pairs of rules, or by assigning a numeric priority value to each rule. Relative priorities are considered the most flexible, since they subsume the other two types of priority specification. Ordering the entire set of rules may not be necessary to achieve correct behavior (see Section 1.4), while numeric priorities can be difficult to use since they may need to be adjusted as the set of rules evolves.

- **Rule structuring.** The rule language might include features such as *rule sets* or *rule modules* for organizing or structuring the rules in the system. Rule sets or modules might be provided simply as a convenience, or they might affect rule execution.

Some active database systems, particularly object-oriented ones, treat rules as *first-class entities* within the database. There are a number of advantages to this approach: facilities already provided by the database system can be used directly for rule creation, deletion, and modification; for structuring the rules in the system (e.g., through classes, collections, and inheritance); for concurrency control and recovery (see Sections 1.6.2 and 1.6.3); and for authorization (see Section 1.6.4). However, in active database systems with a simple structured data model—such as relational systems—treating rules as first-class entities within the database usually is not possible.

1.4
Rule Execution Semantics

While the rule language prescribes what can be specified in each active database rule, the *rule execution semantics* prescribes how the active database system behaves once a set of rules has been defined. This behavior includes the semantics of rule processing itself, as well as the behavior of rule processing as it interacts with normal database query and transaction processing. Even factoring out the various alternatives in rule languages, there are a surprising number of alternatives for the semantics of rule execution. Furthermore, even for a small number of simple rules, rule execution behavior can be quite complex.

As a basis for discussion, a very simple model of rule execution is presented first. This simple model is followed by discussion of a number of directions in which the model can be completed, extended, and modified to obtain a full rule execution semantics.

Usually there are specific points at which rules may be processed during the execution of an active database system. As will be explained in Section 1.4.1, there are many choices for when these points occur. Regardless, once one of these points is reached, if one or more rules are triggered then a *rule*

```
while there are triggered rules do:
   1.  find a triggered rule R
   2.  evaluate R's condition
   3.  if R's condition is true then execute R's action
```

FIGURE 1.1
Simple rule processing algorithm.

processing algorithm is invoked. In its simplest form, the rule processing algorithm repeatedly finds a triggered rule, evaluates the rule's condition, and, if the condition is true, executes the rule's action. This algorithm is shown in Figure 1.1. Readers familiar with AI rule languages will notice the similarity of this algorithm to the basic *recognize-act cycle* of OPS5 [BFKM85].

1.4.1 Rule Processing Granularity

The *granularity* of rule processing specifies how often the points occur at which rules may be processed, i.e., how often the algorithm of Figure 1.1 is invoked. The finest granularity is "always"—rules may be processed at any point during the database system's execution, as soon as any rule's triggering event occurs. Observe, however, that this granularity makes sense only when rules may be triggered by the existence of database states or by temporal events; otherwise the execution of at least one database operation is required to generate a triggering event. In the next finest granularity, rules may be processed after each occurrence of the "smallest" database operation. For example, in a relational active database system, this granularity might correspond to the insertion, deletion, update, or fetch of a single tuple, while in an object-oriented active database system it might correspond to a single value modification or a method call.

In some database systems, data manipulation statements provide a granularity for rule processing that is coarser than database operations. For example, in a relational database system rules might be processed at the end of every SQL statement, where a statement inserts, deletes, updates, or fetches numerous tuples. During database processing, statements usually are grouped into transactions, so another useful granularity is transaction boundaries. It is unusual for rule processing granularity to be any coarser than transaction boundaries, although it is certainly possible. In some active database systems, the points at which rules may be processed are delineated by the user or application, although these systems usually provide a default granularity as well.

1.4.2   Instance-Oriented Versus Set-Oriented Execution

Active database rule execution is *instance-oriented* if a rule is executed once for each database "instance" triggering the rule or satisfying the rule's condition. For example, consider a relational active database rule R_1 that is triggered by deletions from a particular table. If rule execution is instance-oriented, then R_1's condition is evaluated and its action is executed once for each deleted tuple. (In AI terminology, each deleted tuple produces an *instantiation* of rule R_1.) Or, consider an object-oriented active database rule R_2 that has no triggering event, but that is triggered implicitly whenever objects in a particular class are inserted and satisfy the rule's condition. If rule execution is instance-oriented, then R_2's action is executed once for each inserted object satisfying the condition.

Active database rule execution is *set-oriented* if a rule is executed once for all database instances triggering the rule or satisfying the rule's condition. For example, in rule R_1 described above, if rule execution is set-oriented then R_1's condition is evaluated and its action is executed once for the entire set of deleted tuples. In rule R_2 described above, if rule execution is set-oriented then R_2's action is executed once for the entire set of inserted objects satisfying the condition.

The difference in actual effect between instance-oriented and set-oriented execution can be subtle. For example, consider a relational active database rule R that is triggered by insertions of employee records, and suppose R's action updates the value in attribute S of the inserted records to be 10 less than the average of the S values across all employee records. With set-oriented rule execution, since R executes once for all of the inserted employees, all employees are assigned the same value for attribute S. However, with instance-oriented execution, since R executes once for each inserted employee, different inserted employees may be assigned different values for S.

Note that the issue of instance-oriented versus set-oriented execution can be related to the issue of rule processing granularity. For example, suppose the rule processing granularity is as fine as possible, i.e., rule processing always occurs after a single operation on a single database instance. Then whenever a rule is triggered, it is triggered for at most one database instance; consequently, there is no difference between instance-oriented and set-oriented execution in this scenario.

For set-oriented rule execution, the behavior of the rule processing algorithm in Figure 1.1 is clear: steps 2 and 3 are executed for the entire set of instances relevant to the rule selected in step 1. However, for instance-oriented rule execution there is still a choice to be made. Either: (a) once a rule is selected in step 1, steps 2 and 3 are executed once for each instance relevant to the rule, or (b) once a rule is selected in step 1, steps 2 and 3 are executed for only one instance relevant to the rule; when the loop continues, the same or a different rule may be selected. In this choice too there can be subtle differences in effect. Choice (b) is the stated semantics of most AI rule languages, although some of these languages implement choice (a) as an optimization.

1.4.3   Iterative Versus Recursive Algorithms

The algorithm for rule processing in Figure 1.1 is iterative: it selects and processes one rule, then selects and processes another rule, and so on. However, consider a scenario in which the execution of a rule action may produce database changes that are larger than the rule processing granularity. For example, suppose in a relational active database system that rule processing occurs after changes to single tuples, but rule actions may execute SQL statements; or, suppose that rule processing occurs after SQL statements, but rule actions may execute multiple statements. In such cases rule processing may be invoked during the execution of a rule's action, i.e., rule processing may be invoked recursively. The behavior of recursive rule processing can be considerably different from the behavior of iterative rule processing.

1.4.4   Conflict Resolution

Step 1 in the rule processing algorithm of Figure 1.1 requires finding a single triggered rule. In most active database systems it is possible for many rules to be triggered at the same time. Rules triggered simultaneously may happen because:

- Several rules specify the same triggering event.

- The rule processing granularity is coarse enough that many triggering events occur before rules are processed.

- A rule is triggered but not selected in step 1, and the rule is still triggered the next time step 1 is reached.

Consequently, it may be necessary for one rule to be selected from a set of triggered rules. This process of rule selection sometimes is referred to as *conflict resolution* (adopted from the same concept in AI rule languages). There are numerous possibilities for conflict resolution; for example:

- A rule may be chosen arbitrarily.

- A rule may be chosen based on priorities specified in the definition of rules (recall Section 1.3.7).

- A rule may be chosen based on other static properties of rules, such as the time of rule creation or the data on which rules are defined.

- A rule may be chosen based on dynamic properties of rules, such as the recency of rule triggering.

1.4.5   Sequential Versus Concurrent Execution

The algorithm in Figure 1.1 performs rule processing in a sequential manner: one rule is executed at a time. Even in the case of recursive rule processing, at any given time only one rule actually is being executed. For this kind of sequential rule processing, a conflict resolution mechanism may be used to choose which rule to execute when multiple rules are triggered, as explained in Section 1.4.4. An alternative to executing one rule at a time is concurrent rule processing: if multiple rules are triggered, the rules' conditions are evaluated and their actions are executed concurrently. Concurrent rule processing avoids the issue of conflict resolution and, in the appropriate setting, can speed up rule processing. (However, usually some form of concurrency control is required so that concurrently executing rules do not interfere with each other.) Here again there can be subtle differences between the behavior of sequential and concurrent rule processing.

1.4.6   Coupling Modes

So far there has been little discussion of the relationship between rule processing and database transactions. The most straightforward approach is for a triggered rule's condition to be evaluated and its action executed within the same transaction as the triggering event, at the soonest rule processing point. However, for some applications it may be useful to delay the evaluation of a triggered rule's condition or the execution of its action until the end of the transaction; or, it may be useful to evaluate a triggered rule's condition or execute its action in a separate transaction. These possibilities yield the notion of *coupling modes*. One coupling mode can specify the transactional relationship between a rule's triggering event and the evaluation of its condition, while another coupling mode can specify the transactional relationship between a rule's condition evaluation and the execution of its action. Possible coupling modes are:

- **Immediate**: takes place immediately following, within the same transaction. For example, an immediate mode for the action with respect to the condition means that the action is executed as soon as the condition is evaluated (if the condition is true).

- **Deferred**: takes place at the commit point of the current transaction. For example, a deferred mode for the condition with respect to the event means that if the event occurs during transaction T, then the condition is evaluated at the end of transaction T. The deferred mode can be useful, e.g., for rules that enforce integrity constraints, since a transaction may execute several operations that violate a constraint (thus triggering the relevant rules), but the transaction may restore the constraint before it reaches its commit point.

- **Decoupled**: takes place in a separate transaction. This mode can further be subdivided into **dependent decoupled**, where the separate transaction isn't spawned unless the original transaction commits, and **independent decoupled**, where the separate transaction is spawned regardless of whether the original transaction commits. In addition, a *causality* between the transactions might be specified, such as requiring that the spawned transaction is later than the original transaction in the serialization ordering. The decoupled mode can be useful when a long series of rules are triggered, in order to decompose the resulting large transaction into a set of smaller ones.

Coupling modes are not entirely independent of other issues in rule processing. For example, a rule processing granularity of transaction boundaries implies that **immediate** mode between the event and condition may not be possible.

1.4.7   Termination

In almost all rule processing algorithms, regardless of whether the algorithm is iterative or recursive, sequential or concurrent, there is a danger of nontermination. For example, in the simple algorithm of Figure 1.1, the loop continues until there are no more triggered rules. If the execution of rule actions can produce events that trigger other rules—or trigger the same rule again—then it is possible for rules to trigger each other indefinitely. Analogous behavior is possible in recursive rule processing (where both the recursive calls and the processing loop have the potential to continue indefinitely) and in concurrent rule processing. There are several ways to handle termination:

- Nontermination is accepted as a possibility, and it is up to the rule designer to ensure that it will not occur. (This is similar to how nontermination is handled in programming languages.)

- There is a fixed upper limit—perhaps established as a system parameter—on how many rules can be executed during rule processing. If the limit is reached, rule processing terminates abnormally.

- Syntactic restrictions are enforced on the set of rules to ensure that rule processing always terminates. At the simplest level, restrictions could ensure that rules do not trigger each other at all. At a somewhat more sophisticated level, restrictions could ensure that rules may trigger each other, but not in a "cycle"; that is, a rule cannot directly or indirectly trigger itself. At an even more sophisticated level, cycles might be allowed as long as it can be guaranteed that along each cycle some rule's condition eventually will become false.

1.5
System Architecture

Although there are numerous possible architectures for active database systems, three broad categories are distinguished here: *layered*, *built-in*, and *compiled*.

1.5.1   Layered Architecture

In a layered architecture, all active database components reside in a module built "on top" of a conventional passive database system. This architecture sometimes is referred to as a *loosely coupled* approach, since rule management and processing is completely separated from the database system. In this approach, to monitor database events of interest, the active database module intercepts commands as they are submitted to the database system or intercepts data as it is returned from the database system to the user or application. (An alternative is to periodically poll the database, as described at the beginning of this chapter with respect to integrity constraints and triggers, but polling has the disadvantages pointed out earlier.) If application-defined events are allowed, these events are communicated directly from the application to the active database module. If temporal events are allowed, the active database module registers for appropriate notifications from the system clock. Once a triggering event occurs, the rule processor evaluates rule conditions and executes rule actions by calling application procedures or by submitting commands to the database system.

The advantages of a layered architecture are:

- A conventional passive database system can be converted into an active database system without modifying the passive database system at all.

- Several different conventional passive database systems can be converted into active database systems that provide the same interface. A uniform interface can be useful, for example, in applying active database technology to integrate heterogeneous database systems.

The disadvantages of a layered architecture are:

- There is potential for poor performance, since substantial communication overhead may be required between the active database module and the passive database system.

- Since the active database module implementation cannot interact with subsystems of the passive database system (such as the transaction manager, lock manager, authorization component, etc.), certain features that require access to these subsystems may not be supported (such as coupling modes, concurrency control for rules, authorization for rules, etc.).

1.5.2   Built-in Architecture

In a built-in architecture, all active database components become part of the database system itself. This architecture can be achieved by modifying an existing passive database system, by using a database system toolkit for conventional features while adding active database functionality, or by building an entire active database system from scratch. A built-in architecture sometimes is referred to as a *tightly coupled* approach, since rule management and processing are directly integrated into the database system. In this approach, the low-level data manager monitors the operations it performs on the data, notifying the active component when events of interest occur. Application-defined events are communicated from the application to the database system, and the database system registers with the system clock for notification of relevant temporal events. Once triggering events occur, the rule processor evaluates rule conditions and executes rule actions by calling application procedures or by performing operations directly on the database. For rule conditions or actions that are database operations, it usually is possible for the rule processor to exploit the database system's query evaluation facilities.

The advantages and disadvantages of a built-in architecture are exactly the converse of those for a layered architecture. The advantages are:

- Rule event monitoring, condition evaluation, and action execution can be performed efficiently since they occur directly within the database system.

- Access to database subsystems allows implementation of sophisticated features for rules and transactions, concurrency control, authorization, error recovery, etc.

The disadvantages are:

- The implementation effort can be substantial and may require modifying existing code.

- If different passive database systems are converted into active database systems, it is likely that differences in the passive database systems will carry over into the active components.

1.5.3   Compiled Architecture

In the compiled approach, no run-time activity is required at all. Rather, at the time application procedures or database operations are compiled, they are modified to include the effects of active database rules. This approach has the distinct advantage that event monitoring and rule processing are unnecessary, reducing the complexity of the implementation task and improving system performance. However, the compiled approach has the disadvantage that it is applicable only for restricted application languages, rule languages, and sets of rules:

- The application language (i.e., the interface between the user or application and the database system) must be amenable to modification so that operations can be added for evaluating rule conditions and conditionally executing rule actions.

- All triggering events must be detectable through the compiler; hence temporal events, complex composite events, and application events may not be possible.

- If rules can trigger each other or themselves, then the compiled approach may need to be applied recursively: if an application procedure or database operation is modified to include the effects of rules, these effects may need to be modified to include the effects of rules, and so on. Therefore, rules that create triggering cycles may need to be disallowed (even if they would terminate using a run-time approach), since otherwise the compilation phase may continue indefinitely.

1.6
Implementation Issues

While the previous section discussed the general architecture of active database systems, this section discusses several specific issues involved in implementing an active database system.

1.6.1 Rule Management

Every active database system must include a component for managing the set of rules in the system. This includes user-level facilities for performing operations on rules, such as *create*, *delete*, *modify*, *deactivate*, *activate*, etc. It also includes commands for manipulating rule sets or modules if these structuring facilities are provided. Once rules are defined, they must become a persistent part of the database system, which usually is achieved by storing rules in the database itself (similar to other meta-data such as schema information). Finally, a user-friendly active database system should provide facilities for querying or browsing the rules in the system.

1.6.2 Concurrency Control

Most conventional database systems allow multiple users or applications to access the system at the same time, with concurrency control mechanisms ensuring that database operations executed by different users or applications at the same time do not interfere with each other. Active database systems also must include concurrency control mechanisms to support multiple users. There are two facets to address:

(a) concurrency control for rule event monitoring, condition evaluation, and action execution

(b) concurrency control for operations on rules and rule sets

Part (a) usually can rely partially or entirely on conventional concurrency control features, especially if rule conditions are evaluated and actions are executed through the database query processor or by submitting database commands. Part (b) may require special concurrency control features, although if rules are treated as part of the schema or as first-class entities (recall Section 1.3.7), then existing concurrency control mechanisms may be applicable.

1.6.3   Crash Recovery

An important feature of conventional database systems is the ability to recover from system crashes, and this same feature should be present in active database systems. A conventional database system typically recovers from a system crash by using a system log to ensure that the database state after crash recovery includes the effect of all transactions that committed before the crash, but the database state after recovery does not include the effect of any transactions that did not commit before the crash. Active database systems can follow these same general principles, but there are additional considerations; for example:

- What happens if the system crashes while a rule is being processed in response to a non-database triggering event (such as a temporal or application-generated event)? If the rule's transaction has not committed, then the effect of the rule will not be reflected in the post-crash database state; however, the triggering event may not be regenerated during crash recovery.

- What happens if a rule's condition or action uses **decoupled** mode (recall Section 1.4.6), and at the time of the system crash the original transaction has committed but the spawned transaction has not? The spawned transaction may need to be restarted, depending on the execution semantics desired.

Both of these issues may require an active database system to augment the notion of correct crash recovery, and perhaps enhance the functionality of the system log. For example, an active database system may need to include in the log information about event occurrences or rule execution.

1.6.4   Authorization

The authorization component of a conventional passive database system controls which users (or applications) are allowed to perform which operations on data in the database. Typically, authorization is achieved by associating *privileges* with users and requiring certain privileges in order to perform certain operations. Usually only highly privileged users (such as database administrators) can modify the schema of a database. For each data item or set of items in the database, some users may have privileges to read and write the data, other users may have privileges only to read the data, and yet other users may not be permitted to access the data at all.

The notion of authorization privileges must be extended to accommodate the additional features in an active database system:

- Certain privileges may be required to create rules. Relatively high privileges probably are required, such as those of a database administrator.

- Certain privileges may be required to modify or delete rules, to deactivate or activate rules, or to manipulate rule sets or modules.

- If rule conditions and actions may execute database operations, then some user's privileges must be associated with the execution of these operations. These could be the privileges of the user creating the rule, or, in the case of rules triggered by database operations, these could be the privileges of the user executing the triggering operation.

- Certain privileges may be required to query or examine rules.

1.6.5   Error Handling

In most active database systems it is possible for errors to be generated during the processing of active database rules. There are various reasons why an error might be generated:

1. Data required by a rule for condition evaluation or action execution has been deleted.

2. Authorization privileges required for rule condition evaluation or action execution have been revoked.

3. A rule's condition or action uncovers an error condition.

4. The number of rules processed exceeds the system limit (recall Section 1.4.7 on termination).

5. Concurrently executing transactions create a deadlock.

6. A system-generated interrupt or error occurs.

Scenarios 1 and 2 can be avoided if the active database system tracks *dependencies*, such as the dependency of rules on the existence of data, or the dependency of rules on certain authorization privileges. However, in the absence of dependency tracking, a run-time error is possible. In Scenario 3, active database rules are used specifically to uncover error conditions. Scenario 4 is an error specific to rule processing, while Scenarios 5 and 6 are errors pertaining to the database system in general.

It is necessary for an active database system to trap errors during rule processing and respond appropriately. One possible response is to abort the current transaction, although in the case of **decoupled** rule execution, a more complex response might be appropriate (such as undoing the sequence of transactions that lead to the error). Other possible responses are to terminate execution of the rule generating the error and continue rule processing, to discontinue rule processing but continue transaction execution, or to return the error to the application for handling.

1.6.6   Rule Tracing

A facility for tracing and displaying rule behavior is an important implementation feature, both for application development and debugging, and for monitoring rule activity during on-line database execution. A tracing feature might include:

- the ability to trace rule triggering, condition evaluation, and action execution, either for all rules in the system or for a selected set of rules

- the ability to "single-step" through rule execution

- the ability to display, at any given time, the set of triggered rules

- the ability to find, for a given triggered rule, what event caused the rule to become triggered and what transition values, if any, are associated with the rule

1.6.7   Efficient Condition Evaluation

In many active database systems, the condition evaluation phase of rule processing incurs the largest performance overhead. By contrast, the event detection phase normally requires some system processing, but even in the case of complex events execution of time-consuming operations usually is not required. The action execution phase may involve executing large operations on the database or invoking expensive application procedures, but these operations or procedures are inherent in the behavior of the rules—otherwise, the rules would not perform their specified behavior. Like action execution, evaluating the conditions of triggered rules can involve executing large operations on the database, but in some cases these operations may be reduced or avoided.

Two methods for reducing the overhead in rule condition evaluation are *discrimination networks* and *incremental evaluation*. Discrimination networks originated in AI rule languages, where the condition of every rule is evaluated before one rule is selected for execution.[2] A discrimination network is a data structure derived from one or more rule conditions. The network takes as input database modifications and produces as output those rule conditions that are satisfied based on the modifications. Popular discrimination network algorithms for AI rule languages are *Rete* [SDLT86] and *TREAT* [Mir87]; these algorithms usually must be adapted for the active database setting. For further information on discrimination networks in active database systems see, e.g., [FRS93, WH92].

Discrimination networks can be regarded as one instance of a class of techniques known as incremental evaluation. In general, incremental evaluation techniques allow for the efficient evaluation of a database condition or query based on: (1) the results of a previous evaluation of the same condition or query, and (2) the database modifications since the previous evaluation. Since rule conditions may be evaluated multiple times, incremental evaluation techniques can be useful in optimizing the condition evaluation phase of rule processing. For further information on incremental evaluation in active database systems see, e.g., [QW91].

1.6.8   Rule Compilation

In conventional passive database systems, database operations submitted by a user or application usually are compiled (or *optimized*) to produce a *query execution plan*. During compilation, the query optimizer may take into account additional information, such as statistics that help predict the amount of data that will be accessed during query execution. A query plan

---

[2]There is a notable difference here between AI rule languages and most active database rule languages. In active database rule languages, usually it is sufficient to find one rule whose condition is true. One reason for this semantics is that in active database systems rule activation usually is based on triggering events rather than on true conditions; a second reason is to avoid the overhead involved in evaluating numerous, potentially expensive conditions.

produced by the query optimizer is expected to perform well as long as the additional information that was used by the query optimizer remains valid.

When rule conditions or actions in an active database system perform database operations, these operations also must be compiled into query execution plans. Hence, as with query compilation, the question arises as to when exactly rule conditions and actions should be compiled. If a rule's condition or action is compiled at the time the rule is defined, and if subsequently the additional information that was used in compilation becomes invalid, then the query execution plan for the condition or action may perform poorly. However, if a rule's condition is compiled each time it is evaluated, or if a rule's action is compiled each time it is executed, then significant overhead may occur during rule processing in the compilation alone.

1.6.9   Application Interaction

The rule language provided by an active database system may include features for interacting with database applications. For example, Section 1.3 explains how rules may be triggered by application-defined events, and how rules may invoke application procedures for condition evaluation or for action execution. Even when the rule language does not include features for application interaction (i.e., when triggering events are database or temporal events, and conditions are evaluated and actions are executed over the database only), some interface between rule processing and the application may be necessary. For example, if a rule action retrieves data from the database, then there must be some mechanism for passing this data to the application—in passive database systems, data is returned in response to explicit requests, while in active database systems data may be returned "spontaneously." More generally, applications may subscribe to or register for rule-generated events, and be notified synchronously or asynchronously when these events occur. When an error occurs during rule processing, it may be useful to notify the application of the error. In general, for tracking and debugging it may be useful for there to be a mechanism whereby certain applications can be aware, at some level, of which rules are triggered and executed during rule processing.

1.7
Application Development

It should be evident from Section 1.4 on the semantics of rule execution that rule processing in active database systems can be quite complex. Rules may react to a variety of events, both events external to the database system and events that occur as a result of the ad hoc data manipulation operations submitted by users and applications. Once rules are triggered, their execution may generate more events that trigger more rules, and so on. During rule processing, some triggered rules may be delayed if the conflict resolution strategy selects other rules, and if a nondeterministic conflict resolution strategy is used then the outcome of rule processing may depend on which rules are chosen. In general, predicting and understanding rule behavior can be very difficult, and it can be a significant task to develop a correct set of rules for a given application. Consequently, tools and techniques are needed to aid the process of developing rule applications in active database systems. Several such tools and techniques are discussed briefly in the following subsections.

1.7.1 Design Methodologies

There are well-established methodologies for database design based on application requirements (see, e.g., [BCN92]), but these techniques are applicable only to passive databases—the techniques are used to design an appropriate database schema and perhaps to design a set of queries or transactions. Considerable extensions to these techniques are required to develop a design methodology for active databases. In addition to supporting traditional database design tasks, an active database design methodology should aid the designer in determining how much behavior is to be encoded in active database rules (as opposed to in transactions or applications), and how rules should be specified to efficiently capture the desired behavior. Initial work on this topic is reported in [BS94, NTC92].

1.7.2 Structuring Mechanisms

Most active database rule languages provide few or no features for structuring the set of rules in the system. Some languages do provide a notion of rule sets or modules, but typically these mechanisms are provided primarily for convenience (such as for deactivating or activating multiple rules with one command, or for specifying orderings between sets of rules)—they do not provide structuring with respect to specifying or understanding rule behavior. Sometimes there may be structure inherent in the definition of rules. For example, in relational active database systems the set of rules triggered by operations on one table can be considered as a structural unit; similarly for object-oriented active database systems and the set of rules associated with objects in one class. However, if rule actions can perform arbitrary database operations, then still there may be unstructured and complex behavioral relationships between rules in different structural units.

Although it may simply be that the rule processing paradigm itself is inherently unstructured—indeed, there has been little progress in structuring mechanisms for AI rule languages—still it is useful to provide as much structuring as possible to aid the rule designer. Some initial work on modularizing active database rules is reported in [BCP94b], where structuring mechanisms are used to guarantee rule termination.

1.7.3   Rule Analysis

A challenging problem in designing a rule application is to predict how the rules will behave in all possible scenarios. This problem is exacerbated when a designer adds new rules to an existing application, since the new rules may interact with pre-existing rules in surprising ways. For some active database rule languages it is possible to perform automatic static analysis on sets of rules to predict certain aspects of rule behavior (see, e.g., [AWH92, BW94, KU94, vdVS93, ZH90]). For example, analysis techniques can be used to determine whether a set of rules is guaranteed to terminate, or whether a set of rules is guaranteed to behave deterministically. When useful properties are not guaranteed, rule analysis techniques may isolate the rules responsible for the problem.

There are, unfortunately, certain deficiencies with rule analysis:

- Most useful properties are undecidable in the general case, forcing rule analysis to be conservative. For example, analysis may determine when a set of rules is guaranteed to terminate or when the rules might not terminate; analysis may not be able to determine if a set of rules necessarily will not terminate.

- Since rule analysis techniques are applied statically, they do not take into account the database state actually present at run-time. Hence, analysis may determine that a certain property is not guaranteed, even though the run-time database state is such that the property is, in fact, always guaranteed.

- Rule analysis techniques are highly dependent on the constructs of the rule language. Individual rule events, conditions, and actions must be analyzed. When events correspond to a fixed set of operations, and when conditions and actions are specified using an algebraic database query language (such as SQL), then analysis of these components can be relatively straightforward. However, when events are arbitrarily complex or externally defined, or when conditions or actions are specified in an application programming language, then analysis of these components can be very difficult.

- Rule analysis techniques are highly dependent on the semantics of rule execution, which can vary considerably from system to system.

Despite these drawbacks, well-designed analysis techniques can be quite useful in supporting the rule designer: When an initial set of rules is defined, rule analysis aids the designer in predicting their behavior. When new rules are added to an existing application, rule analysis is used to predict and explain how the new rules will affect the overall behavior of the system.

1.7.4 Rule Derivation

For certain classes of active database applications it may be possible to derive automatically, from a specification of the application, active database rules that correctly implement the desired behavior. Consider as examples the *integrity constraint, authorization,* and *view* applications discussed at the beginning of this chapter. For each of these applications, it is natural to specify the application in a language that can be considered as "higher-level" than active database rule languages. (Higher-level here means more declarative, more structured, or more concise.) For example, integrity constraints can use a logical or algebraic language to describe the permitted database states, authorization can use a special-purpose declarative language to describe the access policies, and views can be described as queries or expressions in the database query language. Specifying applications in this way, rather than directly as active database rules, can relieve considerable burden from the application designer.

From a higher-level application specification, a special-purpose compiler is used to automatically derive rules that implement the application. For some applications it may not be possible to derive rules in a fully automatic way. For example, there may be several alternatives for how an active database rule action restores a particular constraint violation, or how a rule action enforces a particular authorization policy. However, even when fully automatic compilation is not possible, a semi-automatic rule derivation process still can be of help in supporting the rule designer. This approach to active database rule design may be appropriate for a number of applications in addition to those mentioned above; further discussion of this approach can be found in Chapter 10 and in [Cer92, Sto92].

1.7.5   Development Environments

Regardless of how a designer goes about creating the active database rules for an application, once rules are installed in the active database system it is useful if the development environment provides a set of tools for tracing and debugging rule execution. Rule tracing features were discussed in Section 1.6.6. In addition to tracing rule execution itself, it can be useful to provide what AI rule languages refer to as a post-execution *explain* feature. An explain feature is used at the end of rule processing to determine the sequence of rule firings that caused particular data values to be present in the final state. Further discussion of active database rule tracing and explaining can be found in [Sto92].

A debugging environment also must include facilities for querying the set of rules. In addition to simple queries, such as retrieving all rules associated with certain data, more complex queries may be useful, such as retrieving all rules with certain properties in their condition or action, or retrieving all rules with certain mutual interactions. Note that if the database system treats rules and rule components as first-class entities (recall Section 1.3.7), then ad hoc queries can be posed against rules using the standard query language of the database system.

Finally, since the execution of rules may have a significant direct affect on data in the database, for debugging purposes it is useful if an active database system provides a mechanism whereby rules can initially be defined and experimented with an on off-line version or subset of the database.

1.8
Research Projects

As a research field, the area of active database systems has indeed been very active. It is impossible to give a complete and "timeless" overview of all research projects in the field—new projects start, old projects end, the aims of projects change, and there may be projects of which we the authors are not aware. Consequently, included here are only a broad description and (possibly incomplete) enumeration of substantial active database research projects as of the early 1990s. For presentation, the projects are divided into those based on relational database technology and those based on object-oriented database technology. Within this subdivision, the projects are roughly grouped based on similarity. Seven of these projects—four of the relational systems and three of the object-oriented systems—are covered in detail in Chapters 2–8. These seven projects were chosen because they all are relatively large and mature, and they represent a broad spectrum of the field. The end of this section also briefly discusses some relevant active database research not associated with a particular project.

Collections of papers that describe in more detail many of the projects mentioned here appear in [Sel89] and [CL92]. The collection in [Sel89] emphasizes mostly relational active database systems, while the collection in [CL92] emphasizes mostly object-oriented active database systems. Papers presented at 1993 and 1994 workshops devoted to the topic of active database systems can be found in [PW93] and [WC94], respectively.

1.8.1 Relational Active Database Systems

Several relational active database projects support rule languages similar or identical to AI rule languages; the *DIPS, RPL, PARADISER*, and *DATEX* projects are described here.

The DIPS project, at the University of Maryland, supports OPS5. In DIPS, rules are stored in database relations in a form that is designed for efficient rule condition evaluation. DIPS also includes algorithms for parallelizing the condition evaluation phase of rule processing, and methods for concurrent rule execution with a guarantee of equivalence to the sequential execution semantics prescribed by OPS5. Details on DIPS can be found in [SLR88, SLR89].

The RPL project, at the University of Southwest Louisiana, implements a rule language with an execution semantics identical to OPS5 but with rule conditions and actions based on SQL. The RPL language is strictly more powerful than OPS5, and a prototype rule processor has been implemented and coupled with a commercial database system. Details on RPL can be found in [DE88, DE89, DWE89].

The PARADISER project, at Columbia University, introduces a new rule language called *PARULEL* that is similar to OPS5 but has a rule processing semantics based explicitly on parallel execution. The PARADISER system performs parallel rule execution in a distributed database environment, incorporating methods for rule fragmentation, incremental rule evaluation, and automatic load balancing. Details on PARADISER can be found in [DOS+92, DS94b, DS94a, ODSS94].

The goal of the DATEX project, at the University of Texas, is efficient processing of large OPS5 rule programs in an active database setting. Efficiency is achieved by introducing sophisticated data indexing techniques, where special indexes are constructed based on the set of rules in the system. Details on DATEX can be found in [BM93].

Since the DIPS, RPL, PARADISER, and DATEX projects all are focused on active database systems that efficiently support AI rule languages, these projects are ideally suited for data-intensive expert systems. An additional project falling into this class is described in [GP91], where the OPS5 language and the *Rete* discrimination network algorithm are extended to include set-oriented constructs, thereby adapting OPS5 for the relational database setting.

Three projects, the *Ariel* project at the University of Florida (formerly at the Wright Research and Development Center), the *POSTGRES* project at the University of California in Berkeley, and the *Starburst* project at the IBM Almaden Research Center, each include a new active database rule language and a complete implementation as an extension to a passive relational database system. The three rule languages have some similarities but many differences, and quite distinct approaches are taken by the three implementations. In broad terms, the focus of the Ariel project is on highly efficient rule condition evaluation, the focus of the POSTGRES project is on multiple classes of rules tailored for specific sets of applications, and the focus of the Starburst project is on a carefully specified language semantics and a fully integrated implementation. Ariel, POSTGRES, and Starburst are described in Chapters 3, 2, and 4, respectively.

The *A-RDL* project at INRIA originated as a project in which active rule technology was used as an implementation mechanism for a deductive database system. This implementation mechanism subsequently was extended and "elevated" to provide active database rules as a user-level feature of the database system. A-RDL is described in Chapter 5.

The *Alert* project, at the IBM Almaden Research Center, explores how an existing query language and a layered architecture can be used to transform a passive database system into an active database system with minimal effort. In Alert, an active database rule is expressed as an SQL *active query* over an append-only *active table*. Whenever tuples are appended to an active table, the associated active queries execute automatically. In effect, the **from** clause of an active query specifies a triggering event (an append to an active table), the **where** clause specifies a condition, and the **select** clause specifies an action. Details on Alert can be found in [SPAM91].

Some relational active database projects do not support a full rule language and rule processor, but rather focus on the efficient detection of complex triggering conditions. In these projects, triggering conditions may be *static* (based on single database states), *transitional* (based on pairs of database states), or *dynamic* (based on sequences of database states). These projects are related more to integrity constraint monitoring than to general active database systems, so they are not presented further here. Early examples of such projects are described in [BBC80, BC79, HS78]; more recent projects are described in [Cho92a, Coh89, GL93, SW92a, TC94, UO94].

The *Heraclitus* project, from the University of Southern California and University of Colorado, supports a database programming language tailored for programming active database behavior. Heraclitus introduces *delta relations* as first-class values, where a delta relation encapsulates a set of data modifications. (Delta relations are a form of transition value, as described in Section 1.3.5.) Various constructs for manipulating delta relations with respect to the underlying database allow Heraclitus to simulate several different active database rule processing semantics. Details on Heraclitus can be found in [GHJ92, GHJ+93, HJ91].

1.8.2   Object-Oriented Active Database Systems

There are a number of factors not present in relational database systems that complicate the extension of object-oriented database systems to include active behavior:

- There is no standard object-oriented data model. Hence, there are significant differences across the various conventional object-oriented database systems that are used as the basis for object-oriented active database projects.

- Because object-oriented models include complex user-defined types and type-specific methods, object-oriented database systems do not have the clear predetermined structure and operations of relational database systems.

- Since object-oriented databases incorporate behavior as well as data, it is less obvious in object-oriented systems how the behavioral aspects provided by an active database system should be integrated. In relational active database systems, all behavior is specified either by rules or by the application; in object-oriented active database systems, behavior can be specified by rules, by the application, or by methods.

Despite these factors, it is certain that object-oriented active database systems are important and useful, as evidenced by the blossoming of research projects in this area.

One of the earliest and largest object-oriented active database projects is *HiPAC*, from the Computer Corporation of America and later Xerox Advanced Information Technology. HiPAC provides a specification and several experimental implementations for an expressive active database rule language with a flexible execution semantics. The rule language includes various simple and composite triggering events, and it allows direct interaction with applications. The execution semantics uses a nested transaction model to support a full complement of coupling modes (recall Section 1.4.6). The HiPAC project is described in Chapter 7.

The *Sentinel* project, from the University of Florida, is a follow-on project to HiPAC. Issues being addressed in the context of Sentinel include an expressive event specification language (called *Snoop*), mechanisms for distributed event monitoring, integration of active database rules into a database programming language, and communication among applications using active rules. Details on Sentinel can be found in [AMC93, CHS92, CKAK94].

Like Sentinel, the *REACH* project, from the Technical University of Darmstadt, is a follow-on project to HiPAC. The goal of REACH is to develop an active object system that provides a mediation framework for heterogeneous data repositories. The active behavior of objects is specified using rules that include, in addition to triggering events, conditions, and actions, specification of time constraints on rule execution. In REACH, rules are used to implement internal access control, transaction management, and integrity control, as well as to enforce dependencies across heterogeneous data. The REACH system is implemented on top of Open OODB commercial object-oriented database system. Details on REACH can be found in [BBKZ93, BBKZ92].

The *Ode* project, from AT&T Bell Laboratories, extends the O++ object-oriented database programming language with facilities for expressing rules in the form of *constraints* and *triggers*. Constraint rules use a language and execution semantics well-suited for enforcing integrity constraints on objects, while trigger rules use a language and execution semantics well-suited for monitoring complex triggering events and invoking procedures when the events occur. The Ode project is described in Chapter 8.

Whereas Ode bases its active rules on the O++ programming language, the *Amos* project from the University of Linköping, described in [RS92], bases its active rules on the OSQL object-oriented query language. A focus of this project is on techniques for efficiently and incrementally evaluating rule conditions expressed in the OSQL-based language.

Four additional object-oriented active database projects centered in Europe are *ACOOD*, *ADAM/EXACT*, *NAOS*, and *SAMOS*. The *ACOOD* project [BL92], from the Universities of Exeter and Skövde, adds to the ONTOS commercial object-oriented database system a facility for active rule processing; rules are triggered before or after method invocations, rule conditions are expressed in the query language of ONTOS, and rule actions are method calls.

The *ADAM* project [DPG91], from the University of Aberdeen, is an object-oriented database system programmed in PROLOG that includes active rules as objects in the data model. Features of the ADAM system include complete integration of rules without additional mechanism or structures, and class-based indexing for efficient rule activation. The *EXACT* system, at University of Basque, is a follow-on project to ADAM. EXACT focuses on "extensibility," so that the rule programmer can select from a number of options regarding rule features and processing semantics and can group rules according to common behavior.

The *NAOS* project [CCS94], from the University of Grenoble, builds an active rule component into the O_2 commercial object-oriented database system. In NAOS, rule management is integrated into the core of the database system, allowing for efficient detection of events. Rules in NAOS are used for a number of applications, both internal and external to the database system.

Finally, the *SAMOS* project [GGD91, GD92, GD94], from the University of Zurich, includes as a central feature a rich language for expressing triggering events and an efficient Petri-net based mechanism for event detection.

Several ambitious database projects take an approach in which general rule processing facilities are provided to support a database system that is simultaneously object-oriented, deductive, and active. These projects include *LOGRES* at Politecnico di Milano [CCCR+90], *OSAM** at the University of Florida [ASL90, CHS92], *A DOOD RANCH* at Arizona State University [DUHK92], and the *Chimera* project at Politecnico di Milano [CM93]. Active rule processing is central to the Chimera system; Chimera is described in detail in Chapter 6.

1.8.3   Other Work

Some projects focus not on designing and building an object-oriented active database system, but rather on the formal foundations or on the applications of such a system. Work from the Hebrew University, reported in [BM91], presents a logical model for a powerful object-oriented active rule language. The *ATM* project, from the DEC Cambridge Research Laboratory, explores the use of object-oriented active database systems to support extended transaction models and workflow control [DHL90, DHL91]. The *DOM* project at GTE Laboratories [Buc91, BOH+92] also uses active rules for workflow management. The *ETM* project, from the University of Karlsruhe, explores the use of object-oriented active database systems to support semantic integrity and consistency control in CAD/CAM and other engineering systems [KDM88].

In [CJL91], performance tradeoffs associated with various coupling modes are studied (recall Section 1.4.6). Factors considered include workload, complexity of transactions and rules, number of rules triggered, and data contention. The results in [CJL91] indicate that the performance of an active database system can be very sensitive to the choice of coupling mode. In particular, if decoupled mode is used whenever possible—especially between rule conditions and actions—then the size of transactions is reduced and performance generally improves.

1.9
Commercialization

Several commercial relational database products, including *Allbase*, *Ingres*, *Informix*, *InterBase*, *Oracle*, *Rdb*, and *Sybase*, already support some form of active rule processing. The rule languages and rule execution paradigms provided by these products vary in their expressiveness and limitations, and most of them are considerably more restrictive than most of the research prototypes discussed. Still, even limited active database features can be used to specify quite powerful active behavior, and the fact that rules already are supported commercially indicates that more sophisticated rule processing is likely to emerge in products of the future.

Standards committees also recognize the importance of active rules. The *SQL3* standard, currently under development, includes rules as a significant component of the language. The rule language specified by SQL3 is likely to have many similarities to rule languages supported in current products.

Active database standards and commercial products are described in more detail in Chapter 9.

At the time of this writing, no commercially available object-oriented database products support active rule processing. However, active database features are under consideration or being developed for future versions of several commercial systems.

2

The POSTGRES Rule System

Spyros Potamianos and Michael Stonebraker

POSTGRES is a next generation extensible database management system. Among the main design goals of POSTGRES was to support active rules. The first implementation of an integrated rule system is described in [SHP88]. Since then, based on the initial experience with rules and user feedback [SHP89], a second version of the POSTGRES rule system was developed, sometimes referred to as PRS2. This chapter describes the PRS2 version of POSTGRES rules.

There are two alternate implementations of POSTGRES rules. The first implementation, the *Tuple Level System* (TLS), processes rules on a tuple by tuple basis. This system uses special markers called *rule locks*. When a rule is defined, these locks are stored in tuples that satisfy the rule's qualification (i.e., its condition part). When an appropriate event (e.g., retrieval of an attribute value, tuple modification, etc.) occurs in a tuple that has the appropriate rule locks, the corresponding rule actions are executed.

The second implementation, the *Query Rewrite System* (QRS), is based on a query rewrite mechanism similar to the view implementation mechanism presented in [Sto75]. Using this approach, a query is combined with all relevant rules, and a set of modified queries is generated. The execution of this new set of queries provides the desired result.

A distinguishing feature of POSTGRES rules is that they can provide both *forward chaining* and *backward chaining* functionality at the same time, as will be described shortly.

2.1
Syntax and Semantics of Rule Language

The query language of POSTGRES is called POSTQUEL; it is based on the INGRES query language QUEL, although some extensions and changes have been made to support the new features of POSTGRES [SHP88]. The syntax for defining a rule in POSTGRES is:

> define [tuple | rewrite] rule *rulename* is
> on *event* to *object*
> where *qualification*
> do [instead] *action*

The *event* can be any operation caused by a POSTQUEL command: retrieve, append, delete, or replace. The *object* can be either a relation (e.g., *EMP*), or a column of a relation (e.g., *EMP.salary*). The rule qualification is an ordinary POSTQUEL predicate and the *action* is a (possibly empty) collection of ordinary POSTQUEL commands or the special command *abort*. If the specified event occurs to the object and if the qualification is true, then the rule action is executed. If the special command *abort* is executed, the transaction is aborted. The optional keywords *tuple* or *rewrite* specify which rule implementation should be used, TLS or QRS respectively. If no keyword is present TLS is used.

If the optional keyword *instead* is not present, then both the rule action and the event that triggered the rule are executed. Otherwise, only the rule action is executed instead of the event. Not all combinations of *event*, *action*, and the *instead* keyword are allowed. The valid combinations are described in Section 2.1.1.

Both the qualification and the rule actions can contain the keywords *NEW* and *CURRENT*. *NEW* refers to the tuple being inserted if the event is an append command, or to the new value of an updated tuple if the event is a replace command. *CURRENT* refers to the tuple being retrieved if the event is a retrieve command, deleted if the event is a delete command, or to the old value of an updated tuple if the event is a replace command.

In POSTGRES rules, all rule actions are executed immediately as part of the command that caused their activation. The execution of a rule action can in turn trigger other rules, forming a cascading effect. Examples of such cases are discussed in Section 2.2. If a command triggers more than one rule, the order of rule activation is arbitrary.

2.1.1 Forward and Backward Chaining Rules

POSTGRES rules can be divided into two categories depending on their event and action: forward chaining rules and backward chaining rules.

If the rule action is a retrieve command then the event must be a retrieve and the rule is a *backward chaining* rule. Rules of this type can be used to implement derived data in a way very similar to Prolog or deductive databases. Backward chaining rules are subdivided into two further categories, depending on whether the object is a relation or a column.

If the object of a backward chaining rule is a relation, then the rule generates a set of tuples—the result of the retrieve command that appears in the rule action. These are called *view-type* backward chaining rules, because they can be used to implement semantics similar to ordinary *views*. If the keyword *instead* is present, the tuples stored in the retrieved relation are ignored, and only the tuples generated by the action of the rule are retrieved.

ACTION

EVENT	retrieve	append/delete/replace
retrieve relation	view-type backward chaining	forward chaining
retrieve column	column-type backward chaining	forward chaining
append/delete/ replace	not allowed	forward chaining

TABLE 2.1
Valid combinations of events and actions.

Otherwise both sets of tuples are retrieved.

If the object of a backward chaining rule is a column of a relation, then the rule will calculate values for this column. These are called *column-type* backward chaining rules. The semantics of these rules depends on the implementation used. If TLS is used then the keyword *instead* must be present, and the value that is physically stored in the tuple is replaced by the value returned by the *retrieve* statement of the rule's action. (If the statement returns more than one value then a value is randomly chosen; if no values are returned then the value stored in the tuple is used.) If the rule is implemented with QRS and *instead* is present, then for each value returned by the retrieve statement of the rule's action, a new tuple is generated that uses this value. If the rule is implemented with QRS and *instead* is not present, an extra tuple with the value physically stored in the tuple is also returned.

Retrieve commands are permitted in rule actions only for rules whose event is retrieve. If the rule action is not a retrieve command, then the rule is a *forward chaining* rule. These rules specify actions that must be executed when the specified event happens and the rule qualification is satisfied. If the keyword *instead* is used, then only the rule's action is executed, otherwise both the rule's action and the command that caused the rule activation are executed.

The valid combinations are presented in Table 2.1. In all of the valid combinations of this table the keyword *instead* may be present or absent and either TLS or QRS may be used, with one exception: *column-type backward chaining* rules without *instead* are implemented only in QRS.

2.2
Examples

The behavior of POSTGRES rules is now illustrated with a number of examples. The following rule:

> define rule an_instead_rule is
> on delete to EMP
> do instead append TEMP(username = user())

will append to relation *TEMP* the names of users who try to delete employee tuples. However, no tuples will actually be deleted from *EMP*. In contrast, the following rule:

> define rule not_an_instead_rule is
> on delete to EMP
> do append TEMP(username = user())

will append to *TEMP* the same information as the previous rule, but will not prevent the deletion of tuples from *EMP*.

The following rule shows how the keywords *CURRENT* and *NEW* can be used to specify transition constraints:

> define rule r1 is
> on replace to EMP.salary
> where NEW.salary > 1.1 * CURRENT.salary
> do abort

This rule is activated every time the salary of an employee is increased by more than 10%. The special command *abort* specifies that the current transaction should be aborted. If instead of aborting the transaction the update should simply be disallowed, then the rule can be rewritten as:

> define rule r2 is
> on replace to EMP.salary
> where NEW.salary > 1.1 * CURRENT.salary
> do instead

In this case there are no rule actions specified, and the keyword *instead* specifies that the event which activated the rule (the salary increase) should not be performed.

As mentioned earlier, a rule action might trigger other rules. For example, consider the following two rules:

```
define rule r3 is
on replace to EMP.salary
where CURRENT.name = 'John'
do replace E(salary = NEW.salary)
from E in EMP
where E.name = 'Fred'
```

```
define rule r4 is
on replace to EMP.salary
where CURRENT.name = 'Fred'
do replace E(salary = 3 * NEW.salary)
from E in EMP
where E.name = 'Mike'
```

An update on John's salary will trigger rule *r3* and Fred's salary will also be updated. This new update will trigger rule *r4*, which in turn will update Mike's salary. Rules like *r3* that specify additional actions to be taken when an update occurs, and that in turn may activate other similar rules, follow the forward chaining control flow paradigm.

Here is an example of a rule activated by a *retrieve* event:

```
define rule r5 is
on retrieve to EMP.salary
where CURRENT.name = 'Fred'
do instead retrieve (salary = E.salary)
from E in EMP
where E.name = 'John'
```

This rule will be activated every time a user attempts to retrieve Fred's salary. The action specifies that instead of retrieving whatever value is stored in the *salary* field of Fred's tuple, John's salary is retrieved. Any explicitly stored value for Fred's salary will be ignored, and a new value will be derived by the rule's action. The activation of such rules that derive values can trigger other similar rules. The result is a backward chaining control flow, similar to Prolog. For example, suppose the following rule is also defined:

```
define rule r6 is
on retrieve to EMP.salary
where CURRENT.name = 'Mike'
do instead retrieve (salary = 3*E.salary)
from E in EMP
where E.name = 'Fred'
```

and a user attempts to retrieve Mike's salary. Rule *r6* will be activated and will attempt to retrieve Fred's salary. As a result, rule *r5* will be activated and will retrieve John's salary. Therefore Mike will appear to have three times the salary of John. Rules *r5* and *r6* are *column-type backward chaining* rules (recall Section 2.1.1), and they have an effect similar to the forward chaining rules *r3* and *r4*.

The following rule is an example of a *view-type backward chaining* rule:

> define rule r7 is
> on retrieve to HIGH_SAL_EMP
> do instead retrieve(EMP.all)
> where EMP.salary > 10000

This rule states that whenever tuples are requested from the relation *HIGH_SAL_EMP*, employees that have a salary greater than 10,000 are retrieved from *EMP*. Because the keyword *instead* is used, the actual contents of relation *HIGH_SAL_EMP* (if any) are ignored.

As a final example, consider the following forward chaining rule:

> define rule r8 is
> on delete to DEPT
> do delete EMP
> where EMP.dept = CURRENT.dname

This rule is activated every time a department is deleted and causes the deletion of all employees working in it.

2.3
Rule System Architecture

Figure 2.1 illustrates the overall architecture of POSTGRES, including the rule system. The modules consist of:

The Parser:
> This module reads the user commands, performs syntax checking, and creates a *parse tree*—an internal structure describing the user command.

The Query Rewrite Rule System:
> This module handles the rules implemented with QRS. It combines the parse tree generated by the user query with the appropriate rules and generates a new set of parse trees.

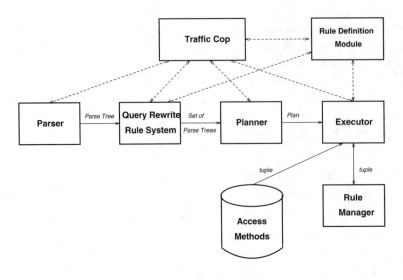

FIGURE 2.1
POSTGRES Architecture.

The Planner:
> This is the POSTGRES query optimizer. It takes as input a parse tree and creates a *plan*, which will be executed by the next module, the *executor*. The plan describes all the operations (relation scans, joins, etc.) that must be executed in order to generate the correct answer.

The Executor:
> This is the module responsible for the execution of the plans generated by the *planner*.

The Rule Manager:
> This is the module that handles the rules implemented with TLS. Whenever a TLS rule must be activated, the *executor* calls the *rule manager*. This module is responsible for testing the qualifications and executing the actions of TLS rules.

The Access Methods:
> These are low-level routines, responsible for all I/O operations required by the other modules: retrieving tuples from disk, creating new tuples, updating tuples and writing them back to disk, etc.

The Traffic Cop:

> This is the main module of the system. It calls and coordinates the execution of all other modules. It first calls the *parser*, and if the user command is an ordinary POSTGRES query it calls the *planner* and the the *executor*. If the command is a data definition command such as a relation creation or removal command, or a new rule definition, then it calls an appropriate library routine to perform the specified operation. One of these routines is the *rule definition* module.

The Rule Definition Module:

> This module is called whenever a new rule is defined. It stores the appropriate information in the system catalogs, and, if the rule is implemented with TLS, creates appropriate *rule locks* (described in the next section).

2.4
The Tuple Level Rule System Implementation

The *Tuple Level Rule System* (TLS) consists of a *rule definition module* and a *rule manager*, as described in the Section 2.3. The rule manager can further be subdivided into two parts. The first is the *view-rule manager*, which processes *view-type backward chaining* rules. The second is the *tuple-rule manager*, which processes *column-type backward chaining* rules as well as *forward chaining* rules.

When a new rule is defined, the *rule definition* module stores all the information needed in special system relations and adds appropriate *rule locks* to certain tuples. Ideally, only the tuples that satisfy the rule's qualification should get rule locks. However, in the current implementation a superset of these tuples is usually locked, so rule qualifications must always be checked. (A more detailed description of rule locking is presented in Section 2.4.1.)

When a plan for a POSTGRES command is processed by the *executor*, the execution can be divided into two phases. The first phase involves tuple retrievals only. Then, if the command is *append, delete,* or *replace,* there is a second phase involving tuple updates. Every time a retrieval or an update operation occurs on a tuple with a rule lock, the executor calls an appropriate rule manager. This calling procedure is now described in more detail.

During the first phase tuples are retrieved but not updated. Therefore only *on retrieve* rules (backward or forward chaining) need to be considered.

If one or more *view-type backward chaining* rules are defined on a relation, then when this relation is opened for reading and before the first tuple of the relation is retrieved, the *executor* calls the *view-rule* subsystem of the rule manager. This module executes the actions of all the view-type rules (which must be retrieve commands, recall Section 2.1.1), and returns all the generated tuples to the *executor*, which treats them as ordinary tuples. When all such view tuples have been retrieved, and if none of the *view* rules processed was an *instead* rule, then the *executor* continues by retrieving the tuples physically stored in the relation by calling the *access methods* module.

If at least one of the *view* rules was an *instead* rule, then the executor ignores the tuples physically stored in the relation. Otherwise, the executor continues by retrieving the tuples of the relation, one at a time. Each time a tuple with a rule lock is encountered, the tuple-rule manager is called. First, the tuple-rule manager processes backward chaining rules. If the qualification of a backward chaining rule is true, then its action is executed. This action will return zero or more values. These values may be used to alter the original tuple, as described in Section 2.1.1. (A simple mechanism is used to detect and resolve rule loops; see [Pot91] for a detailed description.) Then, the tuple-rule manager checks for forward chaining rules. When the qualification of such a rule is satisfied, the rule action is executed.

During the second phase, when a tuple is inserted, deleted, or updated, the *executor* again calls the tuple-rule manager for tuples with rule locks. Now there are only forward chaining rules to consider, since backward chaining rules with append, delete, or replace events are disallowed. The qualifications of the applicable rules are tested and the appropriate rule actions are executed.

The next two sections describe rule locks and stubs as implemented in POSTGRES. Some improvements have been designed and are described in Section 2.7.1.

2.4.1   Rule Locks

As mentioned earlier, when a rule is defined, special markers called *rule locks* are placed on a superset of the tuples that satisfy the rule qualification. Rule locks are permanent objects, stored along with the tuples on disk, and are distinct from the normal concurrency control locks. The presence of a rule lock in a tuple means that if an appropriate event happens to this tuple, then the rule lock is *broken*, and a rule might have to be activated. Rule locks contain the following information:

a) the name of (or a system generated unique identifier for) the corresponding rule
b) the type of the lock (explained below)
c) the attribute with which the lock is associated, when appropriate
d) a *rule plan* identifier

When a rule lock is broken, the qualification must be checked and, if true, the action of the corresponding rule must be executed. Information about rule qualifications and actions is stored in the system catalogs, and is uniquely identified by the *rule plan* identifier stored in the lock.

The reason a superset of satisfying tuples may be locked, rather than the exact set, is as follows. In the current implementation of TLS, locks are set based only the part of the rule qualification that involves columns of the locked relation and constants; any joins in the qualification are ignored. Furthermore, there actually are two different types of rule locks. *Tuple level* rule locks are stored in individual tuples (as described so far). *Relation level* locks are stored once in a system catalog and effectively lock all the tuples of the corresponding relation, i.e., the rule qualification is completely ignored. As a result, there are more "false alarms" with relation level locks than with tuple level locks, but as the rule lock is only stored once (in the system catalog), there can be a considerable amount of disk space saved.

As an example of rule locks, consider the rule:

```
define rule desk_rule is
on retrieve to EMP.desk
where CURRENT.salary > 50000
and CURRENT.dept = DEPT.dname
and DEPT.manager = 'Smith'
do instead retrieve(desk='wood')
```

If tuple level locks are used, then all *EMP* tuples that satisfy the subqualification:

```
salary > 50000
```

will be locked. The rest of the rule qualification is ignored. If a relation level lock is used, all the tuples of *EMP* are locked implicitly, and only one copy of the lock is actually stored on disk.

2.4.2   Rule Stubs

Suppose now that new tuples are appended to a relation specified in the event clause of a rule. If a new tuple satisfies the qualification of the rule, then it must (automatically) get some locks. In the case of relation level locks this is not a problem, because implicitly all tuples (even the new one) of the relation are locked. However, in the case of tuple level locks, every time a new tuple is added the system must check if the tuple satisfies the rule's qualification. For this, *rule stub records* are used.

Rule stub records are stored in the system catalogs; every relation has zero or more of them. Every stub record carries the following information:

  a) the rule name (or a unique identifier)
  b) a qualification
  c) a (tuple level) rule lock

Every time a new tuple is appended to a relation, its stub records are examined one by one. For every stub record, the system tests if the new tuple satisfies the qualification. If so, the specified rule lock is added to the new tuple.

2.5
The Query Rewrite Rule System Implementation

The *Query Rewrite Rule System* (QRS) consists of a module between the parser and the planner, as depicted in Figure 2.1. This module combines a user query with all applicable rules and generates a new set of queries that will have the desired effect. All rule handling is done by the QRS module, so the executor simply executes the new queries generated without considering any QRS rules. TLS and QRS coexist in POSTGRES.

As an example of QRS, consider the following rule:

    define rewrite rule qwr_1 is
    on retrieve to EMP.salary
    where CURRENT.name = 'Sam'
    do instead retrieve(salary = 3 * EMP.salary)
    where EMP.name = 'Bill'

If the following query is submitted for execution:

    retrieve (EMP.salary)
    where EMP.age > 30

the QRS module will rewrite it and replace it with the following two queries:

    retrieve (EMP.salary)
    where EMP.age > 30 and
    not(EMP.name = 'Sam')

```
retrieve (salary = 3 * E.salary)
from E in EMP
where EMP.age > 30
and EMP.name = 'Sam'
and E.name = 'Bill'
```

These two queries will then be optimized by the planner and executed by the executor. Their result will be combined and the desired answer will be generated.

To control the rewrite process, QRS uses a variant on rule locking. Every time a QRS rule is defined on a relation, an appropriate *QRS lock* is placed in the system catalog. When a POSTGRES query is issued, the QRS module finds all QRS locks for all relations referenced by the query. The locks identify the QRS rules that must be combined with the original query to generate the new set of queries. A detailed description of the algorithms used in QRS can be found in [Goh91, SJGP90].

Although there are some commonalities between QRS and TLS, these two systems are completely independent and very different in principle. As a result, in some cases they provide slightly different semantics. For instance, in the previous example, if there were more than one tuple for Bill in the *EMP* relation, rule *qwr_1* would generate an equal number of different salaries for Sam. The reason is that the second of the two generated queries:

```
retrieve (salary = 3 * E.salary)
from E in EMP
where EMP.age > 30
and EMP.name = 'Sam'
and E.name = 'Bill'
```

will create a cartesian product. Every tuple of *EMP* that satisfies the qualification:

```
EMP.age > 30 and EMP.name = 'Sam'
```

i.e., every tuple for Sam where the age is greater than 30 will be joined with every tuple of *E* (i.e., *EMP*) that satisfies:

```
E.name = 'Bill'
```

There is no way in POSTGRES or in any other relational system to select only one tuple (at random) out of the result of this join and discard the others.

Apart from the semantic differences between QRS and TLS, there are also some performance differences as well. In some situations QRS will be more efficient than TLS and vice versa. Intuitively, when the rule's qualification is satisfied by a small percentage of the tuples, TLS seems the best choice. For instance, rule *qwr_1* of the previous example may only apply to one tuple (Sam's tuple, if his age is greater than 30). If this rule is implemented with TLS, then an appropriate rule lock is placed in the one tuple, and the rule is activated only when the salary value of this tuple is retrieved. If a query retrieves the salaries of other employees, the lock will not be broken and no rule activation will occur. With the QRS implementation, however, there will be a significant overhead. Two queries will always be executed, and they will scan the *EMP* relation twice, although the second query will return very few tuples (one for each Bill, as explained above).

On the other hand, consider the following rule:

> on retrieve to EMP.manager
> do instead retrieve (DEPT.manager)
> where DEPT.dname = CURRENT.dept

and the user query:

> retrieve (EMP.name, EMP.manager)

QRS will rewrite the original query to:

> retrieve (EMP.name, DEPT.manager)
> where EMP.dept = DEPT.dname

This simple query is then appropriately optimized and executed. If TLS is used it will do a scan of the *EMP* relation, and for every tuple it will activate the rule. Each rule will do a scan of the *DEPT* relation in order to find the employee's manager. So there are as many rule activations and as many scans of the DEPT relation as the number of tuples in *EMP*. One can think of this approach as an *iterative substitution* (nested loop) execution of the equijoin of the query generated by QRS. However, in general this approach will be slower than the QRS one, especially if *EMP* is large: With QRS the planner can select a more efficient implementation of the join (e.g., merge-sort, hash-join, etc.). Furthermore, QRS avoids the initial overhead associated with every TLS rule activation.

2.6
Applications

One of the goals of the POSTGRES rule system was to provide a simple framework that would facilitate the implementation of other database services, such as view support and versions. In conventional systems these services require special purpose code. However, in POSTGRES they could be implemented with a minimal effort on top of the rule system. This section describes the implementation of views and versions.

2.6.1   Implementing Views Using POSTGRES Rules

View-type backward chaining rules (recall Section 2.1.1) can be used to implement virtual views. For example, the following rule implements a view containing employees and the floors they work on:

> define rule emp_floor_rule is
> on retrieve to EMP_FLOOR
> do instead retrieve (EMP.name, EMP.dept, DEPT.floor)
> where EMP.dept = DEPT.dname

This rule is activated whenever an attempt is made to retrieve the tuples of relation *EMP_FLOOR*. Because the keyword *instead* is used, the tuples (if any) of *EMP_FLOOR* are ignored. In their place the system substitutes the tuples that are returned by execution of the rule's action.

One problem with conventional implementations of views is that in some cases view updates are ambiguous. Because the updates happen to virtual tuples, the system must have a way to map these updates to updates on real tuples. Unambiguous mappings are not always possible. For example, updates to the *EMP_FLOOR* view may have ambiguous semantics, so conventional systems will disallow the updates. In POSTGRES it is possible to use rules to resolve ambiguous view updates. The user could define the following rule:

> define rule delete_emp_floor_rule is
> on delete to EMP_FLOOR
> do instead delete EMP
> where EMP.name = CURRENT.name

Then, when there is an attempt to delete Mike's tuple (say) from *EMP_FLOOR*, the system will know to delete Mike's tuple from *EMP* (rather than, e.g., delete Mike's department).

It is also possible to use POSTGRES rules to specify partially materialized views. For example, one might want to have a view of the employees working in the toy and shoe departments. Suppose the tuples of the toy department employees are very often read but almost never updated, while the tuples of the shoe department employees are seldom read but often updated. Then it would be most efficient to materialize the toy department part of the view, while calculating the shoe department part of the view on demand. This complex goal can be achieved with a simple set of POSTGRES commands and rules:

> retrieve into TOY_SHOE_EMP(EMP.all)
> where EMP.dept = 'toy'

This command materializes the currently existing tuples of employees working in the toy department.

> define rule toy_shoe is
> on retrieve to TOY_SHOE_EMP
> do retrieve (EMP.all)
> where EMP.dept = 'shoe'

This rule takes care of the "calculated on demand" tuples of the shoe department employees, adding them to the current materialized view. Finally, some rules must be added to correctly maintain the materialized part of the view when updates occur to EMP. For example, a rule is needed that appends tuples to TOY_SHOE_EMP whenever a new toy department employee is appended:

> define rule toy_shoe_append is
> on append to EMP
> where NEW.dept = 'toy'
> do append to TOY_SHOE_EMP(NEW.name, NEW.salary ....)

Similar rules are used to handle deletions and updates.

2.6.2   Implementing Versions using POSTGRES Rules

POSTGRES also includes a version mechanism implemented using rules. As an example, suppose there is a relation *EMP* and one wishes to create a version of it called *EMP1*. First the system will create two relations. One relation, called *EMP1_added*, has the same attributes as the base relation *EMP*. It is used to store the tuples that are added to the version, or tuples that exist in the base relation but are updated in the version. The second relation is:

> EMP1_deleted(del_oid=OID)

Relation *EMP1_deleted* stores the object identifiers of all tuples that were either deleted or updated in the version. (Each tuple in POSTGRES has a unique object identifier.)

When retrieving the tuples of the version, all tuples are retrieved that exist in the union of *EMP* and *EMP1_added* if their object identifiers do not appear in *EMP1_deleted*. The following rule provides the appropriate semantics:

> define rule EMP1_retrieve is
> on retrieve to EMP1
> do instead
> retrieve (EMP1_added union EMP).all
> where EMP.oid not_in EMP1_deleted.del_oid

Whenever a tuple is deleted from the version and that tuple exists in the base relation, then its object identifier is appended to the *EMP1_deleted* relation. If the deleted tuple exists in the *EMP1_added* relation, then it is deleted from *EMP1_added*. Note that a tuple might exist both in *EMP* and *EMP1_added* if it was a base tuple updated in the version. The following rule provides the appropriate semantics:

> define rule EMP1_delete is
> on delete to EMP1
> do instead
> {
>   append EMP1_deleted(del_oid = EMP.oid)
>   where CURRENT.oid = EMP.oid
>
>   delete EMP1_added
>   where CURRENT.oid = EMP1_added.oid
> }

Similar rules are used to handle version insertions and updates. For a more complete discussion of implementing versions using POSTGRES rules, see [Ong91].

2.7
Future Directions

2.7.1 Improved rule locks and stubs

The current TLS implementation of POSTGRES rules supports rule locks and stubs as described in this chapter. In order to improve efficiency, more sophisticated varieties of rule locks and stubs have been designed, although not yet implemented.

One problem with stub records is that every new tuple is tested against all the existing stub records. In the presence of a large number of rules this could be very expensive. A more efficient approach is to use *index stub records*. Index stub records are similar to relation stub records, except they are placed in index records. Whenever a tuple is added to a relation, appropriate index records must also be added to all of the relation's indices. During these insertions of index records, all the related index stubs are examined and locks are added to the tuple appropriately.

A second deficiency is that the rule locks and stubs described in this chapter cannot efficiently handle rules with qualifications that involve joins. For example, consider the following rule:

> define rule first_floor is
> on retrieve to EMP.desk
> where CURRENT.dept = DEPT.dname and DEPT.floor = 1
> then do instead retrieve(desk = 'wood')

Ideally, rule locks should be placed in the tuples of all employees who work on a first floor department. However, updates in the relation *DEPT* might cause some rule locks to need to be inserted or deleted. (For example, if the floor of a department is changed from *2* to *1*, then new rule locks must be added to all the employees of this department. Similarly, when the floor of a department is changed from *1* to *2* some rule locks must be deleted.) To provide the needed functionality, *propagation locks* can be used. Propagation locks are similar to rule locks, except when they are broken, instead of triggering a rule's action, they propagate insertions and deletions of rule locks to other relations.

For further details on index stub records and propagation locks, see [Pot91].

2.7.2   Deferred rules

Another potential for future work is to implement rule systems with different semantics on top of the current POSTGRES rules. For example, in the current implementation, all rule actions are executed immediately as part of the command that caused their activation. As a result, rules cannot see the updates of other rules or the effect of the command itself. There are some applications where it would be beneficial to defer rule execution until the command that activated the rule has finished, or until the end of the current transaction. Although in the current implementation this option is not supported, [Pot91] discusses how such a *deferred rule system* could be built on top of POSTGRES rules. Each deferred rule is compiled to a

POSTGRES rule that, when activated, appends appropriate information to special a system catalog. At the end of the command or transaction, this catalog is checked and the appropriate rule actions are executed.

3

The Ariel Project

Eric N. Hanson

A modified version of this chapter will appear in a forthcoming
issue of *IEEE Transactions on Knowledge and Data Engineering*
as a paper entitled "The Design and Implementation of the Ariel
Active Database Rule System."

The Ariel system is an implementation of a relational DBMS with a built-in rule system. The Ariel rule system is based on the production system model [BFKM85]. The approach taken in the design of Ariel has been to adopt as much as possible from previous work on main-memory production systems such as OPS5, but make changes where necessary to improve the functionality and performance of a production system in a database environment. These changes include a rule language extension to POSTQUEL [SRH90] with a query-language-like syntax, a discrimination network for rule condition testing tailored to the database environment, and measures to integrate rule processing with set-oriented database update commands and transactions. Ariel is a complete implementation of a relational DBMS with a rule system that is tightly coupled with the query processor. Ariel's rule condition testing mechanism, called A-TREAT, is a variation of the TREAT algorithm [Mir87] enhanced with features to speed up testing of selection predicates in rule conditions, reduce the amount of state information kept in the network, and handle event, transition, and pattern-based conditions in a uniform way.

3.1
The Ariel Query and Rule Languages

3.1.1   Query Language

Ariel is based on the relational data model and provides a subset of the POSTQUEL query language of POSTGRES for specifying data definition commands, queries, and updates [SRH90]. POSTQUEL commands **retrieve**, **append**, **delete**, and **replace** are supported, along with other commands for creating and destroying relations and indexes, and performing utility functions such as loading relations, gathering statistics on data in relations, and so forth. The syntax of POSTQUEL data manipulation commands is shown below. Square brackets indicate optional clauses.

> **retrieve** (*target-list*)
> [**from** *from-list*]
> [**where** *qualification*]

> **append** [**to**] *target-relation* (*target-list*)
> [**from** *from-list*]
> [**where** *qualification*]

delete *tuple-variable*
[**from** *from-list*]
[**where** *qualification*]

replace [**to**] *tuple-variable* (*target-list*)
[**from** *from-list*]
[**where** *qualification*]

In POSTQUEL, the *target-list* is used to specify fields to be retrieved or updated, the *from-list* is used to specify tuple variable bindings, and the *qualification* is used to specify a predicate that the data affected by the command must match. In addition, a relation name can be used as a tuple variable name by default, avoiding the need to use a **from** clause in most cases.

3.1.2   Rule Language

The Ariel rule language is a production rule language with enhancements for defining rules with conditions that can contain relational selections and joins, as well as specifications of events and transitions. The Ariel rule syntax is based on the syntax of the query language. Hence, the syntax of a rule condition is nearly identical to that of the **where** clause of a query. The general form of an Ariel rule is the following:

define rule *rule-name* [**in** *ruleset-name*]
[**priority** *priority-val*]
[**on** *event*]
[**if** *condition*]
then *action*

A unique *rule-name* is required for each rule so the rule can be referred to later by the user. The user can optionally specify a *ruleset-name* to place the rule in a ruleset. Rulesets are merely a convenient way of grouping rules so they can be activated and deactivated simultaneously, displayed together, etc. If no ruleset name is specified when a rule is defined, the rule is placed in the system-defined ruleset *default_rules*.[1]

The optional **priority** clause allows specification of a numeric priority to control the order of rule execution. The priority can be a floating-point number in the range -1000 to 1000. If the priority clause is not present, priority

---

[1] Ariel's ruleset facility is a simplified version of the one used in Postgres [SHP89].

defaults to 0. Priorities are used to help the system order the execution of rules when multiple rules are eligible to run.

The **on** clause allows specification of an event that will trigger the rule. The following types of events can be specified after an **on** clause:

- **append** [**to**] *relation-name*

- **delete** [**from**] *relation-name*

- **replace** [**to**] *relation-name* [(*attribute-list*)]

Event specifications are provided since, in a database environment, it may be important to trigger a rule based on operations performed, not just data values in a new or updated tuple.

The *condition* after the **if** clause has the following form:

qualification [**from** *from-list*]

The *qualification* part of a rule's **if** condition has the same form as the qualification of a **where** clause in a query, with some exceptions. A rule's qualification clause can contain only selection and join conditions. Aggregates and the relational projection operation are not allowed. This design was chosen to simplify rule condition testing. The **from** clause is for specifying bindings of tuple variables to relations. Relation names can be used as default tuple variables.

To allow *transition conditions* to be specified in Ariel, a special keyword **previous** lets a condition refer to the previous value of an attribute. The value that a tuple attribute had at the beginning of a transition can be accessed using the following notation:

previous *tuple-variable.attribute*

There will be cases where a rule must be triggered when any tuple value exists in a relation. To allow any tuple in a relation to be matched, the following conditional expression is provided:

any (*tuple-variable*)

Any can be thought of as a way to specify a rule condition element (tuple variable) with no selection condition and no joins to any other condition element.

The **then** part of the rule contains the action to be performed when the rule fires. The action can be a single data manipulation command, or a *compound command* which is a **do** ... **end** block surrounding a list of commands.

The binding between the condition and the action of a rule is specified by using the same tuple variable(s) in both. This means a tuple variable appearing in both the rule condition and action ranges in the action only over the data that has matched the rule condition since the last execution of the rule.

3.1.3 Semantics of Rule Execution

The Ariel rule system uses a production system model. Execution of rules is governed by a *recognize-act cycle* similar to that used in OPS5 [BFKM85]. Ariel rule instantiations are *set-oriented*, which means that when a rule fires, all combinations of tokens that have matched the rule condition since the last time the rule fired are processed at once.

Transitions

Ariel rules are processed after each database *transition*. A transition in Ariel is defined to be the changes in the database induced by either a single command, or a **do** ... **end** block containing a list of simple commands. Blocks may not be nested. The programmer designing a database transaction thus has control over where transitions occur. If desired, the programmer can put a **do** ... **end** block around all the commands in the transaction so the entire transaction is a single transition. Each command in a transaction will be considered a transition by itself unless it is enclosed in a block. Blocks are provided to allow programmers to safely update the database with multiple commands when data integrity or consistency might be temporarily violated during the update. Programmers are encouraged to only put a block around groups of commands which might violate integrity or consistency, since use of blocks does incur some performance overhead.

Ariel treats transitions as a set of logical events (insertions, modifications, and deletions). These logical events are derived by composing the physical events as they occur. Consider the following sequence of changes to the database, where S_i is a database state, E_i is the net effect of a transition T_i, and T_0 is a user-issued transition. In addition, F_i is the i'th firing of a rule action. $T_i[F_i]$ is the transition induced by rule action firing F_i.

$$S0 \xrightarrow[\;T0\;]{\;E0\;} S1 \xrightarrow[\;T1[F1]\;]{\;E1\;} S2 \xrightarrow[\;T2[F2]\;]{\;E2\;} S3 \;...\; \xrightarrow[\;Tn\text{-}1[Fn\text{-}1]\;]{\;En\text{-}1\;} Sn$$

The net effect of the transition from state S_l to state S_k is the composition of E_l through E_{k-1}.

The net effects of the changes to the database are logically updated after each user-issued command or **do ... end** block, and the changes continue to accumulate until rules terminate. After rules terminate, the changes are discarded. The old value of each old/new tuple pair accumulated is always the value that the tuple had at the *beginning* of the transition (state S_0).

Logical vs. Physical Events

In Ariel, triggering of event-based rules is based on *logical* events rather than physical events. A logical event is the net effect of one or more physical events. Logical events are defined as follows. The life of an individual tuple t updated by a single transition always falls in one of the following four categories, where i, m and d represent insertion, modification, and deletion respectively. Superscripts $*$ and $+$ indicate a sequence of zero or more and one or more individual updates, respectively.

update type	description	net effect
im^*	insertion of t followed by zero or more modifications	insert
im^*d	insertion of t followed by zero or more modifications and then deletion.	nothing
m^+	t existed at the beginning of the transition and was modified one or more times.	modify
m^*d	t existed at the beginning of the transition, was modified zero or more times, and then deleted.	delete

The table above shows how the net effect of a sequence of updates to one tuple can be summarized as a single insert, delete, or modify operation, or no operation.

The Rule Execution Cycle

Rules in Ariel are processed using a control strategy called the *recognize-act cycle*, shown in Figure 3.1, which is commonly used in production systems [BFKM85]. The *match* step finds the set of rules that are eligible to run. The *conflict resolution* step selects a single rule for execution from the set of eligible rules. Finally, the *act* step executes the statements in the rule action. The cycle repeats until no rules are eligible to run.

initial match
while (*rules left to run*) {
    conflict resolution
    act
    match
}

FIGURE 3.1
The recognize-act cycle.

The conflict resolution strategy for Ariel is motivated by the LEX strategy used in OPS5 [BFKM85]. The idea is to let the rule whose condition was most recently matched go first. However, Ariel's conflict resolution scheme is not the same as LEX because Ariel uses set-oriented instantiations and OPS5 uses instance-oriented ones. Ariel picks a rule to execute during the conflict resolution phase using the following criteria (after each of the steps shown below, if there is only one rule still being considered, that rule is scheduled for execution, otherwise the set of rules still under consideration is passed to the next step):

- *Select the rule(s) with the highest priority.*

- *Select the rule(s) most recently awakened.* If two or more different rules with the highest priority had their conditions satisfied by the same database transition, then those rules would be tied at this point. If two or more different rules with the highest priority had their conditions satisfied by different transitions, then only the ones that had their conditions satisfied by the *latest* transition would still be considered after this point.

- *Select the rule(s) whose condition is the most selective.* The selectivity is estimated by the query optimizer at the time the rule is compiled. This is possible because the rule condition has the same form as the **where** clause of a query.

- *If more than one rule remains, select one arbitrarily.*

Because Ariel uses set-oriented instantiations, there are situations where a rule that has been on the agenda for a long time and has a lot of data bound to its condition can be "promoted" to the head of the agenda by a small update that causes one new data item to match its condition. This is because how recently a rule was awakened is determined by the last time *any* data matched the rule's condition. This sort of behavior is inherent in the use of set-oriented instantiations.

3.2
Examples

Examples are now presented using the following relations:

emp(name, age, salary, dno, jno)
dept(dno, name, building)
job(jno, title, paygrade, description)

The first rule illustrates condition-action binding based on common tuple variables in the rule condition and action:

> **define rule** FritzRule
> **if** emp.name = "Fritz"
> **then delete** emp **where** emp.sal > 30000

This rule deletes people named "Fritz" from the emp relation if they earn more than $30,000 a year. It does *not* delete everyone earning more then $30,000 a year if there is someone named "Fritz." The rule will be triggered if an updated emp tuple has name field "Fritz."

A rule that will fire if there is any tuple in R1 and there is a tuple in R2 with attribute "a" greater than 7 can be created as follows:

> **define rule** AnyRule
> **if** any(R1) and R2.a > 7
> **then** ...

Ariel's use of logical rather than physical events is illustrated by the following rule:

> **define rule** NoBobs
> **on append** emp
> **if** emp.name = "Bob"
> **then delete** emp

The effect of this rule is to never let anyone named "Bob" be appended to the emp relation. Consider the following block of update commands:

> **do**
>> **append** emp(name="", age=27, sal=55000, dno = 12)
>> **replace** emp (name="Bob") **where** emp.name = ""
>
> **end**

The first command creates a new emp tuple with the empty string as name field and the second one sets the name to "Bob." If events are interpreted as physical operations, then this sequence of commands will not trigger rule NoBobs. However, NoBobs will be triggered if the block is treated as the following single logical event:

> **append** emp(name="Bob", age=27, sal=55000, dno = 12)

An alternative to the NoBobs rule that is not event based is the following:

> **define rule** NoBobs2
> **if** emp.name = "Bob"
> **then delete** emp

This rule deletes all emp records with name "Bob" whether they are created by an **append** or a **replace** command.

The next rule illustrates use of a transition condition:

> **define rule** raiseLimit
> **if** emp.sal > 1.1 * **previous** emp.sal
> **then append to** salaryError(emp.name, **previous** emp.sal, emp.sal)

The effect of this rule is to place the name and new/old salary pair of every employee that received a raise of greater than ten percent in a relation salary-Error. Other rules could be defined to trigger on appends to salaryError to take an appropriate action, such as reversing the update, or notifying a person to verify the correctness of the update.

As an example of how ordinary conditions and transition conditions can be combined, suppose one wished to make the raiseLimit rule specific to just the Toy department. This can be done using a selection condition to select the Toy department, and joining the resulting tuples to the emp tuple variable in the normal fashion. A rule that does this is the following:

> **define rule** toyRaiseLimit
> **if** emp.sal > 1.1 * **previous** emp.sal
> **and** emp.dno = dept.dno
> **and** dept.name = "Toy"
> **then append to** toySalaryError(emp.name, **previous** emp.sal, emp.sal)

Event, transition, and normal select and join conditions can all be combined. Consider this example of a rule that uses all three types of conditions to log "demotion" of an employee in the demotions relation:

> **define rule** findDemotions
> **on replace** emp(jno)
> **if** newjob.jno = emp.jno
> **and** oldjob.jno = **previous** emp.jno
> **and** newjob.paygrade < oldjob.paygrade
> **from** oldjob **in** job, newjob **in** job
> **then append to** demotions
>   (name=emp.name, dno=emp.dno, oldjno=oldjob.jno,
>   newjno=newjob.jno)

3.3
System Architecture

The architecture of Ariel, shown in Figure 3.2, is similar to that of System R [ABC$^+$76] with additional components attached for rule processing. Ariel is implemented in the E programming language, an extension of C++ that is part of EXODUS [CDF$^+$86, RCS89]. E extends C++ with persistent objects and object collections. The current version of Ariel consists of about 31,000 lines of E code. Ariel has a front end consisting of a lexer, parser, semantic analyzer, and query optimizer. The back end of Ariel consists of a query plan executor, and is built on top of E language persistent collections. These collections in turn are built on top of the EXODUS storage manager.

In addition to the standard front end and back end components, Ariel has a *rule catalog* for maintaining the definitions of rules, a *discrimination network* for testing rule conditions, a *rule execution monitor* for managing rule execution, and a *rule action planner* for binding the data matching a rule condition with the rule action and producing an execution plan for that action. Ariel rule conditions are matched against the data in relations. Hence, relations in Ariel play the role of "working memory" in OPS5 terminology.

The rule catalog is composed of a persistent collection of rule objects. Each rule object contains the rule name, ruleset name, status of the rule (active or inactive), and persistent syntax tree for the rule. The persistent rule syntax tree is obtained by making a persistent copy of the syntax tree output by the parser at the time the rule is defined. The rule catalog maintains the definitions of all rules in the system, and is used whenever a rule is accessed,

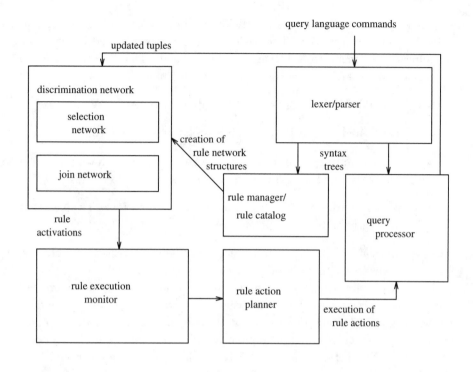

FIGURE 3.2
Diagram of the Ariel system architecture.

including the time when a rule is defined, destroyed, activated, deactivated, or triggered.

3.4
The Discrimination Network

An efficient strategy for incrementally testing rule conditions as small changes in the database occur is very important for fast rule processing. Rete [For82] and TREAT [Mir87] are data structures called *discrimination networks* that are used in main memory implementations of production systems. A simulation study comparing Rete and TREAT in a database rule system environment determined that TREAT usually outperforms Rete [WH92]. Therefore, a variation of TREAT, called A-TREAT, is used in Ariel. The A-TREAT network in Ariel is a persistent data structure subject to database concurrency control and recovery, unlike the volatile discrimination networks used for typical OPS5 implementations. The basic TREAT structures used by Ariel are introduced first, then the A-TREAT modifications to TREAT are explained.

Logically, a TREAT network consists of the following:

- a **root** node that accepts tokens describing changes to the database,

- a set of **select** nodes[2] that test single-relation selection conditions,

- a set of α-**memory** nodes, one per select node, that contain the tuples matching the condition in the associated select node, and

- a set of **P-nodes** that contain tuples or combinations of tuples that have recently matched rule conditions.

The α-memory nodes are connected by join edges labeled with join predicates. For each transaction there is one P-node for each rule. All types of nodes except P-nodes are persistent. P-nodes are volatile objects that are created on a per-transaction basis for a rule whenever a transaction first causes data to match that rule. The P-nodes created for a transaction are destroyed at the end of the transaction. It is possible that the same rule could be active in two or more transactions simultaneously. Each such transaction would have its own local P-node for that rule.

Changes to the database are packaged as "+" tokens and "−" tokens, representing inserts and deletes, respectively. Modifications of existing records are modeled as deletes followed by inserts. Condition matching is performed by propagating tokens through the TREAT network. When a tuple is inserted into the database, a + token t is created containing the tuple value and passed to the root node. The root broadcasts it to all the select nodes. If a token matches the condition of a select node it is inserted into the associated α-memory node. Next, join processing is performed. A set called a temporary result (TR) is formed, and initialized to contain only the token t. Then the following algorithm is executed:

```
while(there are more α-memory nodes yet to be joined to TR
        and TR is not empty)
{
        Let A be any α-memory that has a join edge
        to another α-memory that has already been processed
```

---

[2]In the production systems literature, select nodes are called t-const nodes, but the more self-explanatory term borrowed from relational algebra is used here.

and is thus already accounted for in TR.
      Let TR = join(TR,A)
}

Once this loop completes, if TR is empty, processing stops. Otherwise, the contents of TR are passed to the P-node (if a P-node does not exist for the rule who's condition was just matched, then a P-node will be created). If the rule is not yet on the *rule agenda*, a rule instantiation is created and placed on the agenda for later execution (see Section 3.5 for details of the rule agenda). The instantiation contains the rule identifier, and the data in TR. Since Ariel's instantiations are set-oriented, they contain the entire set of tuples or compound tuples that have recently matched the rule condition. If the rule is already on the agenda when TR is passed to the P-node, the data in TR is added to the data already in the rule instantiation. For a given rule, there will never be more than one active instantiation in a transaction.

Ariel uses a standard optimization to the TREAT join processing algorithm, which is to check immediately after a token is inserted into an α-memory node to see if any other α-memory nodes for the same rule have zero tokens in them. If so, processing stops immediately since no matching can occur.

If a tuple in the database is deleted, a $-$ token for the tuple is created and broadcast from the root. Processing is similar to that for a $+$ token, except that when a token arrives at an α-memory node it is deleted from the node, but no joins are performed. Instead, the P-node is scanned to see if any compound tokens in the P-node contain the deleted token as a component. If so, those compound tokens are removed from the P-node. This may cause one or more rule instantiations to be taken off the agenda.

As an example, consider the rule in Figure 3.3. The TREAT network for this rule is shown in Figure 3.4. For each tuple variable in the rule, there is a selection condition. The portion of the network above the α-memory nodes alpha1, alpha2, and alpha3 shows the root node and the select nodes. As an example, suppose the following record was inserted into emp:

(name= "Hilda",age=34,salary=50000,dno=22,jno=17)

After this insert, the TREAT algorithm would create a $+$ token t containing this tuple value. To see if any rule conditions had their conditions matched due to insertion of the tuple, t would be propagated from the root node in Figure 3.4 to all nodes connected to the root. It would match only the condition above alpha2, sal>30000. It would then be inserted into alpha2.

define rule SalesClerkRule
if emp.sal > 30000
and emp.dno = dept.dno
and dept.name = "Sales"
and emp.jno = job.jno
and job.title ="Clerk"
then *action*

FIGURE 3.3
Example rule.

Then, if alpha1 and alpha3 were not empty, t would be joined to either alpha1 or alpha3. The α-memory to join to first would be chosen arbitrarily. Then, if the TR formed was not empty, it would be joined to the remaining α node, creating the new, final value of TR. Finally, the contents of TR would be passed to the P-node and the rule agenda would be updated accordingly.

A-TREAT is designed to both speed up rule processing in a database environment and reduce storage requirements compared with standard TREAT. An important performance optimization in A-TREAT is the use of a special selection predicate index for testing selection conditions of rules. In addition, A-TREAT introduces a technique for reducing the amount of state information stored in the network, whereby α-memory nodes are replaced in some cases by *virtual* α-memory nodes which contain only the predicate associated with the node, not the tuples matching the predicate. In addition to these performance enhancement techniques, some extensions to the standard TREAT network have been developed in order to effectively test both transition and event-based conditions with a minimum of restrictions on how such conditions can be used. Each of these modifications is now discussed in more detail.

3.4.1   The Selection Predicate Index

Ariel builds a special *selection predicate index* for testing the single-relation selection predicates appearing in rules. Searching the index with a tuple t quickly returns a list of all the predicates that match t. An appropriate index for this is one that can efficiently support *stabbing queries* where, given

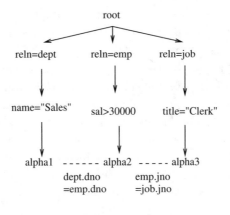

P(SalesClerkRule)

FIGURE 3.4
TREAT network for rule SalesClerkRule.

a point, the index can be searched to find all intervals that overlap the point. The index also needs to be efficiently updatable on-line, so predicates can be rapidly inserted or deleted, and it should be relatively simple to implement for different key data types.

In the design of Ariel, two such indexes have been developed, the *interval binary search tree* (IBS-tree) and the *interval skip list* (IS-list). Both the IS-list and the IBS-tree support the execution of stabbing queries. Currently, the IBS-tree is used in the Ariel implementation. However, the IS-list is somewhat easier to implement and would be preferred for a future implementation. For a complete discussion of the IBS-tree and IS-list, see [HC90, HCKW90] and [HJ92], respectively.

3.4.2   Saving Storage Using Virtual α-memories

The A-TREAT variation of TREAT is tuned particularly to minimize storage use. In the standard TREAT algorithm, there is an α-memory node for every selection condition on every tuple-variable present in a rule condition. If the selection conditions are highly selective, this is not a problem since the α-memories will be small. However, if selection conditions have low selectivity, then a large fraction of the tuples in the database will qualify, and α-memories will contain a large amount of data that is already stored in base tables. Storing large amounts of duplicate data is not acceptable in a database environment since the data tables themselves can be huge.

In order to avoid this problem, for memory nodes that would contain a large amount of data, a *virtual* memory node can be used which contains a predicate describing the contents of the node rather than the qualifying data itself. This virtual node is like a database view. When the virtual node is accessed, the predicate stored in the node is processed to derive the value of the node. Before processing, the predicate can also be modified by substituting constants from a token in place of variables in the predicate to make the predicate more selective, reducing processing time.

The algorithm for processing a single insertion token t in an A-TREAT network containing a mixture of stored and virtual α-memory nodes is as follows. A stored α-memory node contains a collection of the tuples matching the associated selection predicate. A virtual α-memory node contains a selection predicate P and the identifier of the relation R on which P is defined. In addition, each transaction maintains a data structure *ProcessedMemories* containing a set of the identifiers of the virtual α-memory nodes into which token t has been inserted. ProcessedMemories is initially empty and is emptied before processing of each token.

Suppose a single tuple X is to be inserted in R. *Before* actually inserting X in R, a token t is created from X and t is propagated through the selection network. When t filters through the network to an α-memory node A, if A is virtual, the identifier of A is placed in ProcessedMemories. Next, t is joined to any α-memories connected to A by a join condition. When joining the token t just placed in A to a memory node A', if A' is a normal α-memory, the system checks to see if t joins to anything in A', just as in the standard TREAT algorithm. If A' is virtual, then the system finds the tuples in the relation from which A' is derived that match the predicate P' of A', and also match the join condition between t and A'. In addition, if ProcessedMemories contains A', then t belongs to A'. Hence, the system checks whether the copy of t just placed in A and the copy of t in A' together match the join condition between A and A'. All the compound tokens created by joining t to A' are placed in a temporary collection, and the system processes each of those compound tokens in a manner similar to the way t was processed. After t is completely processed, ProcessedMemories is emptied and the tuple X is inserted into relation R. An analogous procedure is used for processing a deletion token. This algorithm has the same effect as the normal TREAT strategy because at every step, a virtual α-memory node implicitly contains exactly the same set of tokens as a stored α-memory node.

In the current Ariel prototype, an α-memory is made virtual only if there is no selection predicate. Further details on Ariel's virtual α-memory nodes can be found in [Han92].

3.4.3   Testing Transition, Event, and Normal Conditions Together

Unlike standard production systems, Ariel allows rules with transition and event-based conditions in addition to normal selection and join conditions. To integrate all these types of conditions into a coherent framework, the notions of both tokens and α-memory nodes were generalized.

To accommodate transitions, in addition to standard $+$ and $-$ tokens used in traditional TREAT, Ariel uses $\Delta+$ and $\Delta-$ tokens which contain an old/new pair for a tuple with the value it had before and after being updated. A $\Delta+$ token inserts a new transition event into the discrimination network, and a $\Delta-$ token removes a transition event from the network.

To accommodate events, all tokens have an event specifier of one of the following forms to indicate the type of event that created the token:

- **append**

- **delete**

- **replace**(*target-list*)

The target-list included with the **replace** event specifier indicates which fields of the tuple contained in the token were updated. **On**-conditions in the selection predicate index are the only conditions that examine the event specifier on a token.

Both transition and event-based conditions have the property that the data matching them is relevant only during the transition in which the matching occurred. Afterwards, the binding between the matching data and the condition should be broken. This is accomplished in Ariel using α-memory nodes that are *dynamic*, i.e., they only retain their contents during the current transition.

To support uniform testing of ordinary conditions as well as transition and event conditions, a total of seven kinds of α-memory nodes have been introduced. They are:

stored-α: a standard memory node holding a collection of tuples matching the associated selection predicate.

virtual-α: a virtual memory node holding the predicate but not a collection of matching tuples.

dynamic-ON-α: a dynamic memory node for an **on**-condition which has a temporary tuple collection that is flushed after each database transition.

dynamic-TRANS-α: a dynamic memory node for a transition condition which is also flushed after each transition.

simple-α: an alpha memory for a rule with an ordinary condition containing only one tuple variable. "Simple" memories are only used when the rule has just one tuple variable in its condition. They never contain a persistent collection of data matching the condition associated with them, since matching data is passed directly to the associated P-node.

simple-TRANS-α: a simple memory node for a transition condition.

simple-ON-α: a simple memory node for an event-based **on**-condition.

If a rule condition has more than one tuple variable, then only stored-α, virtual-α, dynamic-ON-α, and dynamic-TRANS-α nodes will be used for the rule.

A different action needs to be taken when each type of token arrives at each type of memory node. The actions for each of the possible combinations are shown in the table in Figure 3.5. In the table, "$\pi_{new}t$" represents projection of just the new part of the new/old pair contained in t. A "discard t" entry indicates that the memory node should ignore the token since the combination is not defined.

3.5
The Rule Execution Monitor

The rule execution monitor maintains the rule agenda, firing rules as required. The rule agenda is a priority queue with one entry, called a *priority group*, for each group of rules with equal priority. Within a priority group, rules are ordered such that the one whose condition was most recently matched is first.

The interface to the rule execution monitor includes the following operations:

α-memory type	type of token t			
	$+$	$-$	$\Delta+$	$\Delta-$
stored-α	insert t	delete t	insert $\pi_{new}t$	delete $\pi_{new}t$
virtual-α	insert t	delete t	insert $\pi_{new}t$	delete $\pi_{new}t$
dynamic-ON-α	insert t	delete t	insert $\pi_{new}t$	delete $\pi_{new}t$
dynamic-TRANS-α	discard t	discard t	insert t	delete t
simple-α	insert t in P-node	delete t from P-node	insert $\pi_{new}t$ in P-node	delete $\pi_{new}t$ from P-node
simple-TRANS-α	discard t	discard t	insert t in P-node	delete t from P-node
simple-ON-α	insert t in P-node	delete t from P-node	insert $\pi_{new}t$ in P-node	delete $\pi_{new}t$ from P-node

FIGURE 3.5

Table showing actions taken by each α-memory type for each token type

- **addRule,** called by the discrimination network when a new tuple or combination of tuples matching a rule condition is found. If the rule is not already on the agenda, an activation for the rule is created, and placed at the head of the list for the appropriate priority group.

- **removeRule,** called by the discrimination network when a tuple or combination of tuples that used to match the rule condition no longer matches. This tuple or combination of tuples is removed from the P-node for the rule. If the P-node becomes empty, then the rule is removed from the agenda.

- **runRules,** called by the query executor at the end of processing a database transition. This method transfers control to the rule execution monitor, which dispatches the most recently triggered rule from the highest priority group for execution by calling the rule action planner.

The operations described above are sufficient to allow the rule execution monitor to maintain a current list of rules eligible to run, and to assume control and run those rules at the appropriate time.

3.6
Optimization and Execution of Rule Actions

At the time an Ariel rule is scheduled for execution, the data matching the rule condition is stored in the P-node for the rule. Binding between the condition and action of an Ariel rule is indicated by using the same tuple variable in both. These tuple variables are called *shared*. To run the action of the rule, a query execution plan for each command in the action is generated by the query optimizer. Shared tuple variables implicitly range over the P-node. When a command in the rule action is executed, actual tuples are bound to the shared tuple variables by including a scan of the P-node in the execution plan for the command.

When an Ariel rule is first defined, its definition, represented as a syntax tree, is placed in the rule catalog. At the time the rule is *activated*, the discrimination network for the rule is constructed,[3] and the binding between the condition and the action of the rule is made explicit through a process of query modification, after which the modified definition of the rule is stored in the rule catalog. During query modification, references to tuple variables shared between the rule condition and the rule action are transformed into explicit references to the P-node. Specifically, for a tuple variable V found in both the condition and action, every occurrence of an expression of the form $V.attribute$ is replaced by $P.V.attribute$. In addition, if V is the target relation of a **replace** or **delete** command, then it is replaced by $P.V$, and the command is modified to be **replace'** or **delete'** as appropriate. The commands **replace'** and **delete'** behave similarly to the standard **replace** and **delete** commands, except that the tuples to be modified or deleted are located by using tuple identifiers that are part of tuples in the P-node, rather than by performing a scan of the relation to be updated.

Further details on the optimization and execution of Ariel rule actions can be found in [Han92].

---

[3]Actually, the discrimination network components (memory nodes, selection nodes, etc.) for the rule are built and added to the existing discrimination network. This is different from the approach used by systems like OPS5 where the entire network is built at once, and portions of the network cannot be added or deleted incrementally.

3.7
Performance Results

Performance figures have been obtained for installing and activating Ariel rules, for testing tokens using the discrimination network, and for executing rule actions. Performance was measured on a Sun SPARCstation 1 computer, running at approximately 12 MIPS. Three types of rules were defined such that type 1, 2, and 3 rules have 1, 2, and 3 tuple variables, respectively. Rules with different numbers of tuple variables were considered in order to assess the cost of testing join conditions of rules. Each rule type has a single-relation predicate on a table R of the form $C_1 < R.A$ and $R.A \leq C_2$. For each rule type, a set of unique rules was created by starting with one rule as the base rule (rule 0) and generating rule i by adding i times 1,000 to C_1 and C_2, for $i = 1$ to the total number of rules.

The three relations used for the tests contain only a small number of tuples (25, 7, and 5 respectively). It would have been preferable to use larger relations, but Ariel does not support indexes on relations, and without indexes the cost of processing rules would be dominated by sequential scans of relations and α-memory nodes. Hence, the results would not reflect the potential performance of the discrimination network in the presence of indexes. Performance depends on the structure of the discrimination network, not just the size of the database, so the results with small relations are still somewhat meaningful. With large tables and appropriate indexes defined on those tables, performance results similar to the ones reported here are expected. The Ariel architecture is designed to make use of indexes for installing and activating rules and testing tokens through the discrimination network. B-trees for Ariel will be developed using a new EXODUS B-tree facility.

Figures 3.6 and 3.7 show the total time required to install and activate 25 to 200 type 1 and 2 rules, as well as the time to test a token generated by a single insert into a relation. Figure 3.8 shows the same information for 25 to 200 type 3 rules. Rule installation involves storing a persistent copy of the rule syntax tree in the rule catalog, and rule activation involves running one one-variable query for each tuple variable in the rule condition to "prime" the α-memory nodes, plus running a query equivalent to the entire rule condition to load the P-node. These figures show quite reasonable performance for rule installation, which takes a fraction of a second, and rule activation, which takes just under a second. Token testing time takes 2 to 3 milliseconds in the tests performed. This speed should scale to much larger numbers of rules (given rules of similar structure) because of Ariel's selection predicate index.

no. of rules	installation	activation	token test
25	3.29	11.84	0.0021
50	7.18	24.50	0.0024
100	16.29	79.89	0.0025
200	32.50	97.26	0.0026

FIGURE 3.6

Times for one-tuple variable rules in seconds.

no. of rules	installation	activation	token test
25	4.08	21.80	0.0021
50	8.78	44.45	0.0025
100	18.71	90.47	0.0026
200	41.44	196.82	0.0028

FIGURE 3.7

Times for two-tuple variable rules in seconds.

no. of rules	installation	activation	token test
25	4.48	27.80	0.0025
50	10.49	58.38	0.0026
100	20.03	112.59	0.0027
200	44.56	228.03	0.0028

FIGURE 3.8

Times for three-tuple variable rules in seconds.

Not shown in the figures is that it takes approximately 0.06 seconds to run the action of a type 1, 2, or 3 rule in all cases.

3.8
Conclusions

Ariel is a DBMS with an active rule system that:

- is based on the production system model,

- is set-oriented,

- is tightly integrated with the DBMS,

- provides condition-action binding based on shared tuple variables,

- supports event, transition, and ordinary conditions in a uniform way, and

- is implemented in an efficient fashion using a specially designed discrimination network, and a rule-action planner that takes advantage of the existing query optimizer.

Ariel uses a selection-predicate index that can efficiently test point, interval, and range predicates of rules on any attribute of a relation, regardless of whether indexes to support searching (e.g., B+-trees) exist on the attribute. The virtual α-memory nodes introduced in Ariel save a considerable amount of storage, yet still allow efficient testing of rules with joins in their conditions. Ariel introduces generalized tokens and memory nodes to support transition, event, and ordinary conditions uniformly. Ariel demonstrates that the semantic features of an active database rule language can be made more powerful than OPS5, yet a discrimination network can still be used to make rule condition testing efficient.

For the future, there are a number of research areas being investigated to enhance Ariel. One involves optimization of the discrimination network structure to provide good performance given the database update pattern, size of relations and memory nodes, join relationships in the rule condition, etc. [Han93]. Another considers support for streamlined development of reliable, recoverable applications that can receive data from rules asynchronously [HDR93]. Potential applications of this proposed active database/application communication mechanism are safety and integrity alert monitors, financial trading analysis programs, and command and control systems. Finally, a long-term goal for Ariel is to support fast rule condition testing and execution in a DBMS using large-scale parallel processors.

4

The Starburst Rule System

Jennifer Widom

The *Starburst* system is a prototype extensible relational DBMS developed at the IBM Almaden Research Center [HCL+90]. Starburst's extensibility allows the database system to be customized for advanced and non-traditional database applications. One of Starburst's extensions is an integrated active database rule processing facility called the *Starburst Rule System*.

There were two primary goals in the development of the Starburst Rule System. The first goal was designing a rule definition language with a clearly defined and flexible execution semantics. This was achieved by basing the rule language on arbitrary database state transitions rather than tuple- or statement-level changes. The second goal was rapidly implementing the rule system as a fully integrated component of the Starburst database system (including query and transaction processing, concurrency control, authorization, etc.). This was achieved by exploiting the extensibility features of Starburst.

4.1
Syntax of Rule Language

The language for defining and manipulating rules in the Starburst Rule System consists of five commands: **create rule**, **alter rule**, **deactivate rule**, **activate rule**, and **drop rule**. Rules may be grouped into *rule sets*, which are defined and manipulated by the commands **create ruleset**, **alter ruleset**, and **drop ruleset**. Details of these eight commands are described below. The Starburst Rule System also includes commands for querying and displaying rules, which are not described in this chapter, and commands for user or application initiation of rule processing, which are described in Section 4.2.3.

4.1.1   Rule Creation

The **create rule** command is used to define a new rule. The syntax of the command is:

> **create rule** *name* **on** *table*
> **when** *triggering-operations*
> [**if** *condition*]
> **then** *action-list*
> [**precedes** *rule-list*]
> [**follows** *rule-list*]

The *name* names the rule, and each rule is defined on a *table*. Square brackets indicate clauses that are optional.

The **when** clause specifies one or more events, any of which will trigger the rule. The possible triggering events correspond to the three standard relational data modification operations: **inserted**, **deleted**, and **updated**. The **updated** triggering event may specify a list of columns, so that the rule is triggered only when one of those columns is updated; specifying **updated** without a column list indicates that the rule is triggered by updates to any column.

The **if** clause specifies the rule's condition, which can be any SQL **select** statement. The condition is true if the **select** statement produces one or more tuples. The **if** clause may be omitted, in which case the rule's condition is always true.

The **then** clause specifies the rule's actions. Each action may be any database operation, including SQL data manipulation commands (**select, insert, delete, update**), data definition commands (e.g., **create table, drop rule**), and **rollback**. The actions are specified as a list to be executed in order.

The optional **precedes** and **follows** clauses are used to specify priority orderings between rules. When a rule R_1 specifies a rule R_2 in its **precedes** list, this indicates that if both rules are triggered, R_1 will be considered first, i.e., R_1 precedes R_2. If R_1 specifies R_2 in its **follows** list, this indicates that if both rules are triggered, R_2 will be considered first. Cycles in priority ordering are not permitted.

Rule conditions and actions may refer to arbitrary database tables; they also may refer to special *transition tables*. There are four transition tables: **inserted**, **deleted**, **new-updated**, and **old-updated**. If a rule on table T specifies **inserted** as a triggering operation, then transition table **inserted** is a logical table containing the tuples that were inserted into T causing the rule to be triggered; similarly for **deleted**. Transition table **new-updated** contains the current values of updated tuples; **old-updated** contains the original values of those tuples.[1] A transition table may be referenced in a rule only if it corresponds to one of the rule's triggering operations.

4.1.2   Other Rule Commands

The **alter rule** command is used to change components of a rule after it has been defined. The syntax of this command is:

---

[1] If a rule is triggered by **updated** on any column, then transition tables **new-updated** and **old-updated** contain tuples for which any column was updated. If a rule is triggered by **updated** on particular columns, then transition tables **new-updated** and **old-updated** contain the entire tuples for which at least one of the specified columns was updated.

> **alter rule** *name* **on** *table*
> [**if** *condition*]
> [**then** *action-list*]
> [**precedes** *rule-list*]
> [**follows** *rule-list*]
> [**nopriority** *rule-list*]

The **if**, **then**, **precedes**, and **follows** clauses use the same syntax as the corresponding clauses in the **create rule** command. The **if** clause specifies a new rule condition that replaces the existing one. Similarly, the **then** clause specifies a new list of actions that replaces the existing list. The **precedes** and **follows** clauses specify rules to be added to the existing **precedes** and **follows** lists, while the **nopriority** clause is used to remove priority orderings. Notice that the **when** clause of a rule may not be altered; to change triggering operations, a rule must be dropped and then re-created (due to implementation details).

To delete an existing rule, the **drop rule** command is issued:

> **drop rule** *name* **on** *table*

Sometimes it is useful to temporarily *deactivate* rules. When a rule is deactivated, it will not be triggered and its actions will not be executed, even if its triggering operations occur. A deactivated rule behaves as if the rule were dropped, except it remains in the system and can easily be reactivated. A rule is deactivated by issuing the command:

> **deactivate rule** *name* **on** *table*

To reactivate a rule that has been deactivated, the following command is issued:

> **activate rule** *name* **on** *table*

4.1.3   Rule Sets

Rule sets can be used for structuring rule applications in conjunction with the command "**process ruleset** *S*" described in Section 4.2.3. Rule sets are defined using the **create ruleset** command:

> **create ruleset** *name*

Rules are added to and deleted from rule sets using the **alter ruleset** command:

alter ruleset *name*
[**addrules** *rule-list*]
[**delrules** *rule-list*]

Each rule may be in any number of rule sets (including none), and each set may contain any number of rules. Rule sets are deleted by issuing the command:

drop ruleset *name*

4.2
Semantics of Rule Execution

This section explains the semantics of rule execution in Starburst, including the relationship of rule processing to query and transaction processing. Further details on this subject can be found in [WF90, Wid92]. For the descriptions of rule behavior in this section, assume that some number of rules have already been created, and that these rules are not altered, deactivated, activated, or dropped. (The subtle interactions between transactions in which rules are changed and other concurrently executing transactions are discussed in Section 4.5.3.)

In Starburst, rules are processed automatically at the end of each transaction that triggers one or more rules. In addition, rules may be processed within a transaction in response to special user commands. The semantics of rule execution is closely tied to the notion of database state transitions. Hence, transitions are described first, then end-of-transaction rule processing, then rule processing in response to user commands.

4.2.1   Transitions

The determination of whether a rule is triggered, and the value of the rule's transition tables, is based on a precise notion of database state *transition*. A transition is the transformation from one database state to another that results from the execution of a sequence of SQL data manipulation operations. Since rule processing always occurs within a transaction and considers only the operations performed in that transaction, issues such as concurrent transactions and failures need not be considered in defining rule semantics. Furthermore, since rules are triggered by data modification only, and not by data retrieval, execution of SQL **select** statements may be ignored.

Suppose a sequence of SQL data modification operations (**insert**, **delete**, and/or **update**) is executed, transforming the database from a state S_0 to a state S_1. The resulting transition τ is depicted as follows:

$$S_0 \xrightarrow{\quad \tau \quad} S_1$$

Rules consider the *net effect* of transitions, rather than the individual operations creating a transition. The net effect of a transition consists of a set of inserted tuples, a set of deleted tuples, and a set of updated tuples. Considering transition τ above, associated with each inserted tuple is its value in state S_1, associated with each deleted tuple is its value in state S_0, and associated with each updated tuple is its (old) value in S_0 and its (new) value in S_1.

If a tuple is modified more than once during a transition, it still appears in at most one set in the net effect of the transition. Specifically:

- If a tuple is inserted and then updated, this is considered as an insertion of the updated tuple.

- If a tuple is updated and then deleted, this is considered as a deletion of the original tuple.

- If a tuple is updated more than once, this is considered as an update from the original value to the newest value.

- If a tuple is inserted and then deleted, it does not appear in the net effect at all.

For clarity, transitions resulting from user- or application-generated data manipulation operations are denoted by dashed arrows, while transitions resulting from rule-generated operations are denoted by solid arrows. For example, the following depicts a user-generated transition followed by three rule-generated transitions:

$$S_0 \dashrightarrow_{\tau_1} S_1 \xrightarrow{\tau_2} S_2 \xrightarrow{\tau_3} S_3 \xrightarrow{\tau_4} S_4$$

Rules often consider *composite* transitions. For example, a rule might be triggered by transition τ, which is the net effect of transitions τ_1, τ_2, and τ_3:

$$S_0 \dashrightarrow_{\tau_1} S_1 \xrightarrow{\tau_2} S_2 \xrightarrow{\tau_3} S_3$$

4.2.2   End-of-Transaction Rule Processing

If the net effect of the data modification operations in a transaction includes any operations that trigger rules, then rule processing is invoked automatically at the end of that transaction. The transaction itself creates the initial triggering transition; as rules are executed, they create additional transitions that may trigger additional rules or trigger the same rules again. If a rule action executes **rollback**, then the entire transaction aborts. Otherwise, the entire transaction commits when rule processing terminates.

Rule processing is an iterative algorithm in which:

1. A triggered rule R is selected for *consideration* such that no other triggered rule has priority over R (rule selection is described further in Section 4.2.4)

2. R's condition is evaluated

3. If R's condition is true, R's actions are executed

For step 1, a rule is triggered if one or more of its triggering operations occurred in the composite transition since the last time the rule was considered, or since the start of the transaction if the rule has not yet been considered.

As illustration, suppose a user transaction creates transition τ_1. Rule R is triggered by transition τ_1, R is selected for consideration, its condition is true, and its actions are executed. Execution of R's actions creates a second transition τ_2 (the notation $\tau_2 (R)$ is used to denote that transition τ_2 is caused by rule R):

$$S_0 \xrightarrow{\tau_1} S_1 \xrightarrow[\tau_2 (R)]{\tau} S_2$$

At this point, any rule that was not considered in state S_1 is triggered if one or more of its triggering operations occurred in the composite transition τ; R is triggered (again) if one or more of its triggering operations occurred in transition τ_2.

The effect of this semantics is that every rule considers every change exactly once. This is illustrated by the following example, showing the (composite) transitions considered by rule R during several steps of rule processing. Here R' is used to denote any rule other than rule R.

$$S_0 \xrightarrow{\tau_1} S_1 \xrightarrow{\tau_2 (R')} S_2 \xrightarrow{\tau_3 (R)} S_3 \xrightarrow{\tau_4 (R)} S_4 \xrightarrow{\tau_5 (R')} S_5 \xrightarrow{\tau_6 (R')} S_6$$

Finally, note that during condition evaluation and action execution, the contents of a rule's transition tables always reflect the rule's triggering transition.

4.2.3   Rule Processing Commands

While end-of-transaction rule processing is sufficient for many applications, sometimes it is useful for rules to be processed within a transaction. For this, Starburst provides three commands:

> **process rules**
> **process ruleset** *set-name*
> **process rule** *rule-name*

Execution of the **process rules** command invokes rule processing with all rules eligible to be considered and executed. The behavior of rule processing in response to a **process rules** command is identical to end-of-transaction rule processing. In particular, recall from the previous section that a rule is triggered if one or more of its triggering operations occurred in the composite transition since the last time the rule was considered, or since the start of the transaction if the rule has not yet been considered. This behavior is valid even if rules are processed multiple times within a transaction as well as at the end of the transaction, and this behavior retains the semantic property that every rule considers every change exactly once.

Execution of the **process ruleset** command invokes rule processing with only those rules in the specified set eligible to be considered and executed. Again, the behavior of rule processing is identical to end-of-transaction rule processing, except in this case any rules that are not in the specified set will not be considered for execution during rule processing, even if they are triggered. (Such rules eventually will be considered for execution, however, at end-of-transaction rule processing if not sooner.)

Execution of the **process rule** command invokes rule processing with only the specified rule eligible to be considered and executed. Once again, the behavior of rule processing is identical to end-of-transaction rule processing, except in this case any rules other than the specified rule will not be considered for execution. Note that although only one rule is eligible to be considered and executed, rule processing still may involve several rule executions if the rule triggers itself.

Since **process rules**, **process ruleset**, and **process rule** are executable Starburst commands, these commands may be used in rule actions. Execution of such rule actions results in "nested" invocations of rule processing. This behavior is acceptable and well-defined, and it may be useful in certain scenarios; however, it can be difficult to understand and frequently results in infinite rule triggering.

4.2.4 Rule Selection

The **precedes** and **follows** clauses in rules allow them to be ordered in any way, as long as a cycle is not produced. During rule processing, these user-specified priorities influence which rule is selected for consideration when more than one rule is triggered (step 1 in Section 4.2.2). Since the user-specified ordering on rules may be only a partial ordering (indeed, no ordering is required), it still may be necessary for the system to choose between multiple triggered rules. This selection is performed deterministically by using an algorithm that induces a total ordering on all rules. The total ordering is consistent with the user-specified partial ordering, and consequently also is consistent with any ordering transitively implied by the user-specified ordering. (I.e., if rule R_1 is specified to precede rule R_2 and rule R_2 is specified to precede rule R_3, then R_1 will precede R_3.) As a "tie-breaker," rules that have no user-specified or transitively implied ordering are ordered based on rule creation time (i.e., R_1 is ordered before R_2 if and only if R_1 was created before R_2), unless this ordering is not possible given the user-specified and transitively implied orderings. Further details on this deterministic rule ordering strategy are described in [ACL91].

4.3
Examples

Examples are now given to illustrate the syntax of rule creation and the semantics of rule execution. Consider the following generic relational database schema:

emp(emp-no, name, salary, dept-no)
dept(dept-no, mgr-no)

The first example implements a variation on the *cascaded delete* method of enforcing referential integrity constraints. The rule is triggered whenever managers are deleted; its actions delete all employees in departments managed by deleted employees, then delete the departments themselves. Assume a hierarchical structure of employees and departments, and assume that employee numbers are not immediately reused—that is, a single transaction will not delete an employee and then insert a new employee with the same employee number.

```
create rule cascade on emp
when deleted
then delete from emp
     where dept-no in
        (select dept-no from dept
          where mgr-no in (select emp-no from deleted));
     delete from dept
     where mgr-no in (select emp-no from deleted)
```

Notice in particular that this rule has no condition (i.e., its condition is always true), it has two actions to be executed in order, and it references transition table **deleted**. As will be shown below, the self-triggering property of this rule under the semantics specified in Section 4.2 correctly reflects the rule's recursive nature.

As a second example, consider a salary control rule: Whenever employees are inserted or salaries are updated, check the average salary. If the average salary exceeds 50, then delete all inserted or updated employees whose salary exceeds 80.

```
create rule sal-control on emp
when inserted, updated(salary)
if (select avg(salary) from emp) > 50
then delete from emp
     where emp-no in (select emp-no from inserted
                          union select emp-no from new-updated)
     and salary > 80
precedes cascade
```

Notice in particular that this rule has two triggering operations (either of which will trigger the rule), it has a condition, it references transition tables **inserted** and **new-updated**, and it is specified to have priority over rule *cascade*.

Now consider rule processing when both of these rules are defined. Let the initial state of the database include six employees, Jane, Mary, Jim, Bill, Sam, and Sue, with the following management structure:

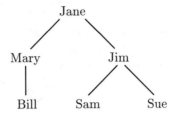

Suppose a transaction deletes employee Jane, and the same transaction updates Mary's salary to exceed 80 so that the average salary exceeds 50. Both rules *cascade* and *sal-control* are triggered; note that *cascade* is triggered with respect to set {Jane} of deleted employees. Since *sal-control* has priority over *cascade*, *sal-control* is chosen for consideration. Its condition is true so it executes its action, deleting employee Mary; it is not triggered again. Now rule *cascade* is triggered by the composite transition since the initial state, so its set of deleted employees is {Jane, Mary}. The rule executes its actions, deleting all employees and departments whose manager is either Jane or Mary. Employees Bill and Jim are deleted by this transition, and rule *cascade* is triggered a second time. Now the rule considers only the most recent transition, so the set of deleted employees is {Bill, Jim}. The rule's actions delete all employees and departments managed by either Bill or Jim—employees Sam and Sue are deleted. Finally, *cascade* executes a third time with deleted employees {Sam, Sue}, but no additional employees are deleted.

4.4
System Architecture

The Starburst rule language as described in Sections 4.1 and 4.2 is fully implemented, with all aspects of rule definition and execution integrated into normal database processing. The implementation took about one woman-year to complete; it consists of about 28,000 lines of C and C++ code including comments and blank lines (about 10,000 semicolons). Along with the core capabilities of rule management and rule processing, the implementation includes considerable infrastructure for program tracing, debugging, and user interaction.

The implementation relies heavily on three extensibility features of the Starburst database system: *attachments*, *table functions*, and *event queues*. Brief descriptions of these features are given here; details can be found in [HCL+90].

- The *attachment* feature is designed for extensions that require procedures to be called after each tuple-level database operation. A new *attachment type* is created by registering a set of procedures: a procedure to be invoked when an *attachment instance* is created on a table, a procedure to be invoked when an instance is dropped, a procedure to be invoked when an instance is altered, and procedures to be invoked after each tuple-level insert, delete, or update operation on a table with one or more attachment instances. Once an attachment type is established by registering these procedures, instances of that type may be created, dropped, and altered on any table. When an attachment instance is created on table T, the procedure registered for creation may build an *attachment descriptor*. This data structure is stored by the system and provided to the extension whenever subsequent attachment procedures are invoked for T.

- A *table function* is a virtual table whose contents are generated at run time by a host language procedure, rather than stored in the database. A new table function is created by registering a name along with the procedure for producing the tuples of the table. The procedure may perform any computations as long as it generates tuples of the appropriate schema. Any table listed in the **from** clause of a Starburst **select** operation may be a table function. When a query referencing a table function is processed, the table function's registered procedure is called to produce the contents of the table.

- The *event queue* feature is designed for deferred execution of procedures. Once an event queue is declared, arbitrary procedures can be placed on the queue to be executed when the queue is invoked. The rule system uses two built-in event queues: one for procedures to be executed during the *prepare-to-commit* phase of each transaction, and one for procedures to be executed in the case of *rollback*.

Figure 4.1 illustrates the general architecture of the rule system, showing most of the execution modules and data structures, how they fit together, and how they interact with Starburst. In the diagram, Starburst, its query processor, and its data repository appear on the left. The ovals in the center column indicate execution modules of the rule system. The rectangles on the right represent memory-resident data structures maintained by the rule system. An arrow from an execution module to data indicates that the execution module creates the data, while the reverse arrow indicates that the execution

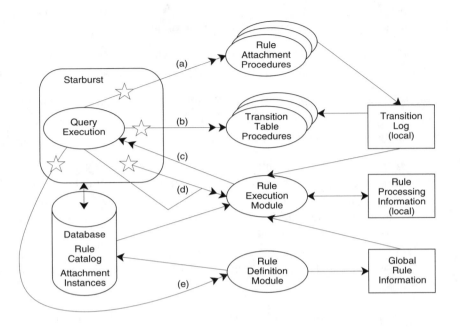

FIGURE 4.1
Architecture of the Starburst Rule System.

module uses the data. A double-headed arrow from one execution module to another indicates that the first module calls the second. When these arrows pass through or originate from a star, this indicates that the call is made through an extensibility feature of Starburst. The arrows are labeled by the event causing a call to occur:

(a) Tuple-level insert, delete, or update on a table with one or more rules

(b) Reference to a transition table (transition tables are implemented as table functions)

(c) Evaluation of a rule condition or execution of a rule action

(d) Prepare-to-commit (event queue) or execution of a **process rules, process ruleset**, or **process rule** command

(e) Execution of a rule definition command (**create rule, alter rule, drop rule**, etc.)

The data maintained by the rule system can be divided into:

- *Rule Catalog*: The Rule Catalog resides in the database; it stores all information about the currently defined rules and rule sets.

- *Global Rule Information*: For efficiency, some information regarding rules and rule sets also is stored in main memory. This information is shared by all user processes.

- *Transition Log*: This is a highly structured log of those operations occurring within a transaction that are relevant to currently defined rules. It is stored in main memory and is called a *transition* log since, during rule processing, information about triggering transitions is extracted from the log. The log also is used to produce transition tables. This data structure is *local*, i.e., one Transition Log is maintained for each user process. Further details on the Transition Log are given in Section 4.5.1.

- *Rule Processing Information*: This also is local. It includes all information pertinent to executing rules within a given transaction, including which rules have been considered and when, and which rules are potentially triggered at a given point in time.

In addition, an attachment type *Rule* has been registered in Starburst. A table has one instance of this attachment type if and only if at least one rule is defined on the table. The attachment descriptor for an instance contains an indicator of what information needs to be written to the Transition Log when operations occur on the table (see Section 4.5.1).

The execution modules depicted in Figure 4.1 are:

- *Rule Definition Module*: This component processes all eight rule definition commands described in Section 4.1. (*Rule definition* is used generically to mean any command for manipulating rules or rule sets.) The Rule Definition Module is responsible for maintaining the Rule Catalog and updating the Global Rule Information. It also creates, deletes, and modifies rule attachment instances and descriptors as appropriate.

- *Rule Attachment Procedures*: This set of procedures writes to the Transition Log whenever relevant table modifications occur. A rule attachment procedure is called automatically whenever an insert, delete, or update operation occurs on a table with at least one rule.

- *Transition Table Procedures*: This set of procedures produces transition tables that are referenced in rule conditions and actions. Transition tables are implemented as table functions, so procedures for **inserted**, **deleted**, **new-updated**, and **old-updated** are registered with Starburst as described above. At run time, these procedures produce transition tables by extracting appropriate tuples from the Transition Log.

- *Rule Execution Module*: This component is responsible for selecting and executing triggered rules. It is invoked automatically at the commit point of every transaction for which a rule may have been triggered; it also is invoked whenever the query processor encounters a **process rules**, **process ruleset**, or **process rule** command. To determine which rules are triggered, the Transition Log, the Global Rule Information, and the local Rule Processing Information are examined to see which operations have occurred and which rules are triggered by these operations. In the case of **process ruleset** and **process rule** commands, the Rule Execution Module considers only the specified subset of rules. Rule conditions are checked and actions are executed by calling the Starburst query processor. Further details on rule execution are given in Section 4.5.2.

The rule system also contains several components not illustrated in Figure 4.1:

- *System Start-Up*: When Starburst is started or restarted, the rule system initializes the Global Rule Information from the Rule Catalog. Rule attachments are initialized automatically by Starburst.

- *Process Start-Up* and *Transaction Clean-Up*: At process start-up, the rule system allocates its local data structures—the Transition Log and the Rule Processing Information. Initially, these structures are empty. They are used during the course of each transaction, then reset after end-of-transaction rule processing.

- *Rollback Handler*: The rule system must be prepared for a partial or complete rollback at any time. The Rule Catalog and attachment information is rolled back automatically by Starburst. However, the rule system must ensure that all memory-resident data structures are modified to undo any changes made during the portion of the transaction being rolled back. This is achieved by having each modification place an appropriate undo operation on the *rollback* event queue.

4.5
Implementation Features

While the previous section described the overall architecture of the Starburst Rule System, this section addresses five specific and important features of the implementation: transition information management, rule execution, concurrency control, authorization, and error handling. Efficient transition information management and rule execution are crucial for system performance, while concurrency control, authorization, and error handling are necessary for full integration with database processing. Further details on these features, along with details on features described in the previous section, can be found in [WCL91].

4.5.1   Transition Information

The attachment procedures that write to the Transition Log save information during query processing so that the Rule Execution Module can determine which rules are triggered and so the transition table references in rule conditions and actions can be evaluated. Since the effect of rule action execution also is considered by rules, the Transition Log must be maintained during rule processing as well; this happens automatically since rule actions are executed by the query processor (recall Figure 4.1).

The semantics of rule execution dictates that, at any given time, different rules may need to be considered with respect to different transitions. To do this, entries in the Transition Log include a (logical) time stamp, and the Rule Processing Information includes the most recent time at which each rule has been considered. The transition for a given rule is then computed based on entries in the Transition Log occurring after that time.

The triggering operations and transition table references in rules determine which operations and what information must be written to the Transition Log. As an example, suppose a rule R is triggered by **inserted** on a table T, but does not reference the **inserted** transition table. It is necessary to log the times at which insertions occur on T; it also is necessary to log the times at which deletions occur for tuples in T that were previously inserted, since the net effect of an insert followed by a delete is empty. Now suppose R does reference the **inserted** transition table. In this case, the values of the inserted tuples must be logged. In addition, the new values of updated tuples must be logged for those tuples that were previously inserted, since the **inserted** transition table must contain current values for its tuples. Finally, suppose R also is triggered by **updated**, and suppose it references transition table

new_updated but not **old_updated**. Now, the new values of all updated tuples must be logged; the old values need not be logged since transition table **old_updated** is not referenced. Clearly there are many cases to consider, and their enumeration is omitted here. From the set of rules on each table, the composite set of triggering operations and transition table references is computed. Based on this set, an *information code* is stored in the table's rule attachment descriptor. When attachment procedures are invoked, they use this code to determine what information should be written to the Transition Log. This approach guarantees that all and only the necessary information is saved in the Transition Log.

4.5.2   Rule Execution

The Rule Execution Module is invoked by the query processor whenever a **process rules**, **process ruleset**, or **process rule** command is encountered. The Rule Execution Module also must be invoked at the commit point of every transaction for which rules may have been triggered. For end-of-transaction rule processing, the first time a rule attachment procedure is called during a transaction—indicating that a relevant operation has occurred—the attachment procedure places the Rule Execution Module on the *prepare-to-commit* event queue. Then, when the transaction is ready to commit, rule execution is invoked automatically. This design ensures that no overhead is incurred by transactions for which no rules are triggered.

During rule processing, a local data structure references those rules potentially triggered at each point in time. These rules are only "potentially" triggered because they are a conservative estimate—every triggered rule is referenced, but there may be rules referenced that actually are not triggered: At the end of each transition, all rules triggered by operations that occurred during the transition are added without considering the net effect of the transition. In practice, it is rare for operations in a transition to be "undone" in the net effect, so this approach usually is not overly conservative. However, before processing a rule, the net effect must be computed to verify that the rule is indeed triggered. Note that by maintaining the potentially triggered rules, rather than the actually triggered rules, a net effect must be computed for only one rule in each "cycle" of rule execution, rather than for all triggered rules.

When a triggered rule is selected for consideration, it must be chosen such that no rules with higher priority also are triggered. This is achieved by maintaining the potentially triggered rules as a sort structure based on rule ordering.

4.5.3   Concurrency Control

Since Starburst is a multi-user database system, the rule system must behave correctly in the presence of concurrently executing transactions. For most transactions, including those with triggered rules, concurrency control is handled automatically by the database system since rule conditions and actions are executed through the Starburst query processor. However, since rules themselves may be manipulated on-line (using the eight rule definition commands described in Section 4.1), the rule system must enforce concurrency control for transactions that include rule definition.

As examples of consistency issues involving rule definition, consider the following scenarios:

- Suppose a transaction X modifies table T while a concurrent transaction deactivates rule R on T. Should R be triggered by X?

- Suppose a transaction X triggers rules R_1 and R_2 while a concurrent transaction alters the relative priority of R_1 and R_2. Which ordering should be used by X?

- Suppose a transaction X executes "**process ruleset** S" while a concurrent transaction adds rule R to set S. Should R be triggered by X?

The Starburst Rule System addresses these issues by ensuring that transactions are serializable not only with respect to data but also with respect to rules (including rule triggering and rule sets). Furthermore, the equivalent serial transaction schedule with respect to rules is the same as the equivalent serial schedule with respect to data.

For serializability with respect to rule definition and rule triggering, rule definition on a table is treated as a "read" operation: a transaction X performing rule definition on a table T must obtain a table-level shared lock on T. This forces X to wait until all transactions currently modifying T (and therefore potentially triggering rules on T) have committed, and it disallows future modifications to T by other transactions until X commits.

For serializability with respect to rule set modification and **process ruleset** commands, Starburst uses locking on rule sets: Before modifying (creating, altering, or dropping) rule set S, a transaction must obtain an exclusive lock on S. Before processing rule set S, a transaction must obtain a shared lock on S.

For serializability with respect to rule ordering, Starburst uses locking on rules. When a rule R is added to the data structure of potentially triggered rules (recall Section 4.5.2), a shared lock is obtained on R. When a rule definition command that affects rule ordering is executed (**create rule**, **alter rule**, or **drop rule**), an exclusive lock is obtained on every rule whose ordering relative to other rules is affected by the command.

Lastly, it is necessary to ensure that two transactions modifying the same rules or rule sets do not conflict. This is enforced automatically, since rule and rule set modifications are reflected in the Rule Catalog, and the Rule Catalog is subject to Starburst's concurrency control mechanisms for data.

Complete details of the consistency specifications and concurrency control protocols used by the Starburst Rule System are given in [Coc92], along with proofs of their correctness.

4.5.4 Authorization

The Starburst Rule System authorization component addresses a number of distinct issues, including authorization to create rules on a given table, authorization to create rules with given conditions and actions, authorization to alter or drop given rules, authorization for rule sets, and authorization at rule execution time. In Starburst, lattices of *privilege types* can be defined for arbitrary database objects, with higher types subsuming the privileges of lower types. For example, for database tables the highest privilege is *control*; below this are privileges *write*, *alter*, and *attach*; below *write* are privileges *update*, *delete*, and *insert*; below *update* and *delete* is privilege *read*. When a table is created, its creator automatically obtains *control* privilege on the table, which includes the ability to grant and revoke privileges on it.

The lattice of privilege types for rules is linear: The highest privilege is *control*, below this is *alter*, and privilege *deactivate/activate* is lowest. As with tables, a rule's creator obtains *control* privilege on the rule and may grant and revoke privileges on it. To create a rule R on table T, R's creator must have both *attach* and *read* privileges on T. During rule creation, R's condition and actions are checked using the creator's privileges. If the condition or actions contain commands the creator is not authorized to execute, then the **create rule** command is rejected. To drop a rule R on table T, the requirement is either *control* privilege on T or *attach* privilege on T with *control* privilege on R. To alter a rule, privilege *alter* is required; to deactivate or activate a rule, privilege *deactivate/activate* is required. During rule processing, each rule's condition and actions are executed using the privileges of the rule's creator.

There are two privilege types for rule sets, *control* and *alter*, with *control* subsuming *alter*. A rule set's creator obtains *control* privilege on the rule set and may grant and revoke privileges on it. Privilege *control* is needed to drop a rule set; privilege *alter* is needed to add or delete rules from a rule set. No privileges on rules are needed to add or delete them from rule sets, and no privileges are needed to execute **process rules**, **process ruleset**, or **process rule** statements.

4.5.5   Error Handling

If an error occurs during the execution of a rule definition command (due to, e.g., the creation of cyclic priorities, the inclusion of an action the creator is not authorized to execute, or a syntactic flaw), then the rule definition command is rejected. During rule processing, two types of errors can occur: an error may be generated during the evaluation of a rule's condition or execution of a rule's action, or rules may trigger each other or themselves indefinitely. In the first case, if an error is generated by the query processor when it executes a rule condition or action, then the rule system terminates rule processing and aborts the current transaction. For the second case, the rule system includes a timeout mechanism: Once more than some number n of triggered rules have been considered, rule processing terminates and the transaction is aborted; limit n is established by a system administrator.

4.6
Applications

The Starburst Rule System provides a rule definition language through which users can create and modify rules to build one or more database rule applications. Starburst rules also can be used as a "compiler target language": for some rule applications, rules can be generated automatically from application specifications. In the context of the Starburst Rule System, compilers have been designed for three common database rule applications: integrity constraints, materialized views, and deductive data.

4.6.1   Integrity Constraints

Users specify integrity constraints as SQL predicates over the database. From these specifications, the compiler generates rules that monitor and enforce the constraints. For each constraint, any database modification that may violate the constraint triggers a rule, the rule's condition checks whether the constraint actually is violated and, if so, the rule's actions restore the constraint or roll back the transaction. If constraints need only be valid at the end of each transaction, then automatic end-of-transaction rule processing is sufficient. If validity of a constraint C is required within a transaction, then the rules associated with C are placed in a rule set S_C, and "**process ruleset** S_C" is executed whenever validity is required. The description of a semi-automatic constraint compiler is given in [CW90]; it is extended to a fully automatic compiler in [CFPT94].

4.6.2   Materialized Views

Users specify views as SQL **select** statements. Each view is computed once and stored as a database table (i.e., the view is materialized). From the view definition, the compiler automatically generates a set of rules that ensure that the materialized view remains correct through subsequent modifications to the base tables comprising the view. The generated rules are triggered by modifications to the base tables; their actions incrementally modify the materialized view according to the base table modifications. A description of the compiler is given in [CW91].

4.6.3   Deductive Data

Users specify derived relations using Datalog with recursion, built-in predicates, and stratified negation [Ull89]. From a Datalog program, a set of rules can be generated to maintain materializations of the derived relations, or a set of rules can be generated for on-demand computation of non-materialized derived relations. For materialized derived relations, whenever base table modifications affect the value of a derived relation, rules are triggered whose actions modify the derived relation accordingly. (Recursion is achieved through self-triggering rules.) For non-materialized derived relations, rules perform the iterative *semi-naive* evaluation often used for deductive databases [Ull89]. A description of the compiler is given in [CW94].

4.7
Summary and Future Directions

The Starburst Rule System is a fully functional extension to the Starburst relational DBMS at the IBM Almaden Research Center. The Starburst rule language is flexible and general, with a well-defined semantics based on arbitrary database state transitions. A rule set facility is available for application structuring, and commands are provided for rule processing within transactions in addition to automatic rule processing at the end of each transaction.

Rule processing is fully integrated with database query and transaction processing, including concurrency control, authorization, rollback recovery, and error handling. A number of applications have been developed using the Starburst Rule System.

While the Starburst Rule System is considered complete, there are several directions in which it may be extended:

- Only initial cursory performance results have been obtained. These can and should be elaborated, which requires developing a mechanism for accurate measurement and a sufficient suite of test applications.

- The rule language can be extended to allow rules triggered by operations on multiple tables. (The restriction that rules are defined on a single table simplifies the implementation and does not affect the semantics; this restriction can be eliminated with some additional implementation effort.)

- The rule language can be extended to allow arbitrary host language procedures in rule actions.

- Rule conditions are evaluated over the database as "brute force" queries. It may be possible to adapt incremental condition monitoring methods (such as those used in Ariel and OPS5) to optimize rule condition evaluation. Other run time optimizations may also be possible.

- The rule system includes only primitive facilities for rule execution tracing and for interaction with application programs; these issues offer considerable opportunity for useful extensions.

- Statement-level rule processing is achieved in the Starburst Rule System by issuing a **process rules** command after each statement; it would be useful to provide a more convenient mechanism for this. For example, a system-defined rule set *Statement* could be created, users could add rules to this set, and the system could execute "**process ruleset** *Statement*" automatically after each statement. A similar mechanism could be provided for tuple-level rule processing.

Finally, the Starburst Rule System has been used as a platform for investigating a number of issues in active databases:

- *Rule analysis*: Methods have been developed for statically analyzing sets of Starburst rules to determine (conservatively) whether they are guaranteed to always terminate, to always produce a unique final state, and to always produce a unique stream of observable actions (such as **select** and **rollback**). This work is reported in [AWH92].

- *Distributed and parallel environments*: Mechanisms for adapting the Starburst Rule System to distributed and parallel environments are investigated in [CW92]. The focus is on providing *transparency*, i.e., ensuring that distributed or parallel rule processing is equivalent to rule processing in the corresponding centralized environment.

- *Secure active databases*: Extensions to the Starburst Rule System necessary for incorporating it into a multilevel secure data model are investigated in [Smi94, SW92b]. Syntactic, semantic, and implementation issues are addressed.

- *Dynamic constraints*: In addition to monitoring traditional static integrity constraints (Section 4.6.1), Starburst rules can be used to monitor *dynamic* and *real-time* constraints—constraints on sequences of database states occurring over time. Methods for using the Starburst Rule System to efficiently monitor dynamic and real-time constraints (without saving database histories) are described in [Cho92a, Cho92b].

- *Managing semantic heterogeneity*: While Starburst rules alone are not sufficient for maintaining consistency across loosely coupled, semantically heterogeneous databases, consistency can be maintained by rules together with a *persistent queue* mechanism. In [CW93], a method is given for compiling consistency specifications into Starburst rules that monitor the databases and, in the case of consistency violations, restore consistency using persistent queues.

5

The A-RDL System

Eric Simon and Jerry Kiernan

The A-RDL research project is a continuation of the RDL1 project, whose goal was to develop a production rule language for databases [dMS88b, dMS88a, SdM88, KdMS89, KdMS90]. The RDL1 language is a powerful high level language for specifying queries, views, and transactions. The challenge successfully taken by the A-RDL project is to demonstrate that RDL1 can be easily extended towards an active database rule language [SKdM92].

The design of the A-RDL language rests on three basic ideas. The first idea is to introduce "delta relations" that record, within a transaction, the net effect of data modification events on extensional relations. The use of delta relations in the condition of a rule enables the user to express arbitrary conditions over the cumulative effect of data modification events that occurred between the beginning of the transaction and the point where the rule is executed. The second idea is to organize rules into modules, which are of two kinds. Virtual definition modules define intensional relations, called virtual relations, from other intensional relations and extensional relations. A virtual relation can be queried by the user as any extensional relation. Base definition modules specify how extensional relations must be changed depending on conditions over extensional, virtual, or delta relations. These modules may also have rules whose only action is to execute procedural code. The last idea is to generalize the execution semantics of RDL1 to encompass both active and deductive rule behavior, as will be described below.

The A-RDL language has the following features. First, it combines modules of rules that derive data from other data and modules of active rules that react to data modification events. Second, the events capable of triggering active rules need not be explicitly provided by the user. They can be automatically generated by the system. Third, the semantics of the language is formally defined using fixpoint operators, thereby capitalizing on deductive database languages and forward-chaining production rule languages. This formalization facilitates the use of optimization techniques descended from deductive databases (e.g., rewriting techniques [Ull89, CGT90]) and forward chaining rule systems (e.g., incremental evaluation algorithms [FRS93]).

5.1
Syntax of the Rule Language

This section presents the syntax of the A-RDL rule language. Rules are encapsulated into basic units called rule modules. For the sake of clarity, the syntax of rules is first presented, followed by the presentation of rule modules.

5.1.1   Different Kinds of Relations

A rule can reference three kinds of relations: extensional, intensional, and delta relations. *Extensional* relations correspond to the physically stored relations. *Intensional* relations are not physically stored but are actually defined by means of rules. Intensional relations are themselves subdivided into virtual and local relations. *Virtual* relations are accessible to the user (i.e., they can be queried) whereas *local* relations can only be used within rules. *Delta relations* are system-defined relations that record the net effect of the changes performed on extensional relations during the execution of a transaction. Three delta relations are associated with every extensional relation.

DEFINITION   *Delta Relations.*

If $T(A_1, \ldots, A_n)$ is a schema of an extensional relation, then the delta relations associated with T have the following schemas:

inserted_T $(A_1, \ldots, A_n)$,

deleted_T $(A_1, \ldots, A_n)$,

updated_T $(oldA_1, \ldots, oldA_n, A_1, \ldots, A_n)$

Intuitively, for some given transaction, relation *inserted_T* $(A_1, \ldots, A_n)$ contains at a point in time all tuples that are inserted into T as a result of the net effect of the transaction up to that point. Similarly, *deleted_T* $(A_1, \ldots, A_n)$ contains all tuples that are deleted from T, and *updated_T* $(oldA_1, \ldots, oldA_n, A_1, \ldots, A_n)$ contains all tuples of T that are updated together with their old values.

5.1.2   Syntax of a Rule

The general syntax for rule definitions is given in Table 5.1. A BNF-like notation is used to describe the language statements. Within this grammar, non-terminal symbols are enclosed in angle brackets <>; terminal symbols that are keywords of the language are in boldface; alternative productions are introduced with |; [a] means that a is optional; and {a} ... means that a is repeated one or more times.

Each rule has a name and consists of an **if-then** statement. The coupling modes can be defined once for all rules after the keyword **rules** or separately for every rule after the **is** keyword. Intuitively, the coupling mode **immediate** specifies that a rule must be evaluated just after a data modification event occurs, and the mode **deferred** specifies that the rule must be evaluated just before processing a checkpoint or a commit event issued by a transaction.

TABLE 5.1

Syntax for rule definitions

<rule_definition>	:	**rules** [<coupling_mode>] <rule> [{,<rule>} ...]
<rule>	:	rule_name **is** [{ c_code }] [<coupling_mode>]
		if <condition-part>
		<then_mode> <action-part> { c_code };
<then_mode>	:	**then** | **thenonce**
<coupling_mode>	:	**immediate** | **deferred**

A C code section can appear between the name of the rule and the if-part of the rule. The C variables occuring in this code section have to be declared either in the main C program of the application program that will trigger the rule, or in the variable declaration part of the module to which the rule belongs. This C code is executed just before evaluating the query associated with the condition of the rule. Similarly, a C code section can be defined after the then-part of the rule. This code is executed just after the rule is fired by the rule system. These C code sections are useful to trace the execution of rule programs, to enable interaction with the user, or to assign values to variables.

The if-part of a rule, also called the condition, is a tuple relational calculus expression. Its general syntax is given in Table 5.2. The range of *tuple variables* is defined by means of *range predicates*. Extensional, intensional, and delta relations can be used as relation names in range predicates but delta relation names only occur in positive range predicates. The condition that the variables must satisfy is written in a conjunctive normal form. Comparison predicates are written following the ISO SQL syntax. *Module variables*, which are declared in a specific section of a rule module (described in Section 5.1.3), are used like constants in comparison predicates. Nested quantified expressions are allowed. The "**exists** var **in** <rel_name>" statement is used to test the emptiness of a relation. A rule condition is required to obey the *range restricted property*, which says that every free tuple variable (i.e., not quantified by a quantifier **exists** or **forall**) must be defined in a positive range predicate.

The then-part of a rule, also called the action, is a set of elementary actions, each being either a database update, a rollback statement, a variable assignment, or a procedure call. (Procedures do not update the database.) Variable assignments assign specific values to module variables only. If a rule

TABLE 5.2
Syntax for rule conditions

<condition_part>	:	<range_condition> [(<sub_formula>)]
<range_condition>	:	<pos_range_predicate>
		| **not** <neg_range_predicate>
		| <range_condition> **and** <range_condition>
<pos_range_predicate>	:	<rel_name> (<var>)
<neg_range_predicate>	:	extensional_relation_name (<var>)
		| intensional_relation_name (<var>)
<sub_formula>	:	<expression>
		| **not** <expression>
		| <sub_formula> **and** <sub_formula>
<expression>	:	<quant_formula>
		| SQL comparison predicate
<quant_formula>	:	**exists** <var> **in** <rel_name>
		| <quant><var> **in** <rel_name>
		(<sub_formula>)
<quant>	:	**exists** | **forall**
<var>	:	string
<rel_name>	:	extensional_relation_name
		| intensional_relation_name
		| delta_relation_name

issues a **rollback** action then the transaction in which the rule executes is rolled back. The keyword **then** is the usual one that precedes the then-part of the rule. When the keyword **thenonce** is used instead (see Table 5.1), it means that the rule can only be fired once and will never become firable again during rule processing. Only extensional and intensional relations can be referenced in the then-part of a rule. Each rule action obeys the range-restricted property, i.e., every tuple variable occurring in the then-part of the rule must be defined in a positive range predicate in the if-part of the rule. The syntax for rule actions is given in Table 5.3.

5.1.3   Syntax of a Rule Module

Rules are encapsulated into rule modules, which provide structure to a rule program. A rule module is a compilation unit for the A-RDL system. It is also associated with an access right mechanism that protects rules from

TABLE 5.3

Syntax of a rule action

\<action_part>	:	\<action> [{\<action>}, ...]
\<action>	:	\<insertion> | \<deletion> | \<update>
		| \<var_assignment> | \<side_effect>
		| **rollback**
\<insertion>	:	+ \<rel_name> (\<project_list>)
\<deletion>	:	− \<rel_name> (\<project_list>)
\<update>	:	− + \<rel_name> (\<t_var> ; \<project_list>)
\<rel_name>	:	extensional_relation_name
		| intensional_relation_name
\<project_list>	:	\<project> [{\<project>}, ...]
		| \<t_var>
\<project>	:	\<attribute name> = \<value_term> ;
\<var_assignment>	:	\<m_var> = proc_name ([{\<value_term>,} ...])
		| \<m_var> = \<value_term>
\<value_term>	:	\<t_var>.\<attribute name>
		| \<m_var>
		| value
\<side_effect>	:	proc_name ([{\<value_term>, } ...]);
\<t_var>	:	tuple variable name
\<m_var>	:	module variable name

other users. Finally, a specific execution strategy can be assigned to a rule module using a control language that will be presented later. The notion of module is very similar to the popular notion of *rule set* in rule-based expert system shells. The general syntax of a rule module is given in Table 5.4.

There are two kinds of modules. The first kind, called *virtual definition* module, defines some virtual relations from a set of extensional or intensional relations. The second kind, called *base definition* module, specifies changes to extensional relations depending on conditions expressed over extensional, delta, or intensional relations.

A module is composed of several declaration sections. The first one is the relation declaration section which declares relations as base, input, output, or local relations. The *output* declaration section declares a set of intensional relations as virtual. These relations are computed by the rules of the module and can be queried by end users similarly to the extensional relations.

TABLE 5.4

Syntax of a rule module

<module_definition>	:	**create module** <module_name>;
		<rel_declaration>
		[<var_declaration>]
		<rule_definition>
		[<control_declaration>]
		[<init_section>]
		[<wrapup_section>]
		end module
<rel_declaration>	:	<relV_declaration> | <relB_declaration>
<relV_declaration>	:	[**base** <ext_rel> ; [{<ext_rel> ;} ...]]
		[**input** <virt_rel> ; [{<virt_rel> ;} ...]]
		[**local** <int_rel> ; [{<int_rel> ;} ...]]
		output <int_rel> ; [{<int_rel> ;} ...]
<relB_declaration>	:	**base** <ext_rel> ; [{<ext_rel> ;} ...]
		[**input** <virt_rel> ; [{<virt_rel> ;} ...]]
		[**local** <int_rel> ; [{<int_rel> ;} ...]]
<ext_rel>	:	extensional relation schema
<virt_rel>	:	virtual relation schema
<int_rel>	:	intensional relation schema
		| **like** relation name
<var_declaration>	:	**var** <name> : <domain>
		[{, <name> : <domain> } ...];
<control_declaration>	:	**control** <control_string>;
<init_section>	:	**init** <c_code>;
<wrapup_section>	:	**wrapup** <c_code>;

The relations declared in the *base* declaration section are all the extensional relations occuring in the rules of the module. The relations declared in the *input* section are virtual relations that are passed as arguments to the module and computed by other rule modules. Finally, intensional relations that are computed by the rules of the module, but which are not declared in the output section, must be declared in the *local* declaration section. These relations are used as intermediate results by the rules of the module. Unlike output relations, local relations are not accessible to end users and they cannot be passed as arguments to another module. Also, local relations do not persist after the time a module is executed.

Following the relation declaration section is the module variable declaration section. The type of any variable must be a type supported by the underlying DBMS. The scope of a variable is local to a rule module but its value can be assigned within an application program and passed to a rule module. However, this requires the use of a specific recognizable command in the application program (e.g., **sql_let** <var> = value) that enables the assignment of values to module variables. These variables can appear in both the condition and action parts of rules. They play various useful roles such as passing values between rules, implementing control between rules, and assuring communication between rules and application programs.

The rule declaration section lists all the rules of the module according to the syntax given in Table 5.1. All rules in a virtual definition module must be declared as immediate rules. For the sake of clarity, the procedural control declaration section will be described after having introduced the semantics of the A-RDL language.

The two last declaration sections of a module are the **init** and the **wrapup** sections. They both define C code that is executed respectively before and after the execution of the rules declared in the module.

5.1.4 Well-Formed Rule Modules

Several syntactic restrictions are imposed on rule modules. First, a preliminary definition:

DEFINITION *Relationships Between Relations.*

Let r be a rule, T a relation occuring in the condition of a rule r in a module $\mathcal{M}$, and T' a relation occuring in the action of r, then it is said that T *defines* T', noted $T \overset{d}{\to} T'$. If $T \overset{d}{\to} T'$ then $T \overset{d*}{\to} T'$. If there exists T' such that $T \overset{d}{\to} T'$ and $T' \overset{d*}{\to} T''$ then $T \overset{d*}{\to} T''$.

The above definition is used in the next definition, which specifies when virtual definition modules are well formed.

DEFINITION *Well-Formed Virtual Definition Modules.*

A virtual definition module $\mathcal{M}$ is said to be well formed if for any relation T, and T' occuring in the relation declaration section of $\mathcal{M}$:

1. if T is declared as output then T cannot be declared as deduced or output in another module,

2. if T is declared as input then T can only occur in the conditions of rules in $\mathcal{M}$,

3. extensional relations can only occur in the conditions of rules in $\mathcal{M}$,

4. no delta relation occurs in some rule of $\mathcal{M}$, and

5. if T is declared as input and T' is declared as output in $\mathcal{M}$, then there is no relation T'' and no virtual definition module $\mathcal{M}'$ such that T'' is declared as input in $\mathcal{M}'$, T is declared as output in $\mathcal{M}'$, and $T' \stackrel{d*}{\rightarrow} T''$.

Item 4 of the definition enforces the fact that the instance of a virtual relation is defined independently of any data modification event, which means independently of any delta relation. It is important to remark that the definition also imposes that a virtual relation is defined as output of a single module, and virtual definition modules must form a hierarchy without cycles (see last item of the definition).

DEFINITION   *Well-Formed Base Definition Modules.*

A base definition module $\mathcal{M}$ is said to be well formed if for any relation T occuring in the relation declaration section of $\mathcal{M}$:

if T is declared as input then T can only occur in the conditions of rules in $\mathcal{M}$.

In a base definition module, rules specify how instances of base relations must be changed using conditions over base, delta, virtual, or local relations.

In the remainder of the chapter all modules are considered to be well formed.

5.2
Basics for Semantics

The events treated by the A-RDL system are specified first. Then the semantics of delta relations is presented, followed by a description of how delta relations are constructed from database modification events. Finally, the interaction between external event processing and rule processing is presented.

5.2.1 Events

The A-RDL system makes a distinction between transactional events and data manipulation events.

Transactional events correspond to the SQL transactional commands, that is, SQL commit, rollback, and checkpoint. The checkpoint command, which is not actually part of the SQL standard, enables the user to set assertion points within a transaction (see [ISO94]).

Data manipulation events consist of database access events and database modification events. The SQL select command that retrieves data from the database generates database access events. The evaluation of rule conditions requires access to data and therefore generates data access events too. The SQL insert, SQL delete, and SQL update commands, as well as the execution of rule actions, generate data modification events. In the following, it is assumed that SQL select commands can query both extensional and intensional relations, but SQL data modification commands can modify extensional relations only.

Events that are generated by commands issued either by interactive transactions or by transactions that are part of application programs connecting the database system are called *external events*. Events that are generated by rule execution are called *internal events*. In the following, any transaction $\mathcal{T}$ is viewed, from the A-RDL system viewpoint, as a sequence of external events, noted $(e_1, e_2, \ldots, e_n)$.

A specific notation is introduced to represent database modification events extensionally. If e is an event that inserts tuples $t_1, \ldots, t_p$ into a relation T then e is represented as the set $\{+T(t_1), \ldots, +T(t_p)\}$. Similarly, a deletion event is represented as the set $\{-T(t_1), \ldots, -T(t_p)\}$, and an update event that replaces tuples t_i, $1 \leq i \leq p$, by tuples t_i' is represented as the set $\{-+T(t_1, t_1'), \ldots, -+T(t_p, t_p')\}$.

5.2.2   Delta Relations

Let I_0 be some initial database state and I_k be the current database state reached by a transaction. The goal of delta relations is to record the *net* change on extensional relations between I_0 and I_k. More precisely, for every extensional relation T, the following equalities are satisfied:

$$I_k[T] - I_0[T] = inserted\_T \cup \Pi_{A_1, \ldots, A_n} (updated\_T)$$

$$I_0[T] - I_k[T] = deleted\_T \cup \Pi_{oldA_1, \ldots, oldA_n} (updated\_T)$$

From what precedes, it is possible to define the *current* instance of any extensional relation in terms of its initial instance, using the following equation:

$$
\begin{aligned}
I_k[T] = I_0[T] \quad &- \quad [deleted\_T \cup \Pi_{oldA_1, \ldots, oldA_n}(updated\_T)] \\
&\cup \quad [inserted\_T \cup \Pi_{A_1, \ldots, A_n}(updated\_T)]
\end{aligned}
$$

Conversely, the initial instance of an extensional relation can be defined in terms of its current instance:

$$I_0[T] = I_k[T] \quad \cup \quad [deleted\_T \cup \Pi_{oldA_1,...,oldA_n}(updated\_T)]$$
$$- \quad [inserted\_T \cup \Pi_{A_1,...,A_n}(updated\_T)]$$

The decision to store the current state of a relation or to derive it from the initial state is an implementation decision. In the A-RDL system, the current state is stored and the initial state is calculated.

In order to guarantee the validity of the above equalities, delta relations have to obey to six axioms that are enforced by the A-RDL system.

DEFINITION   *Axioms for Delta Relations.*

For any database state I reached by a transaction, the delta relations associated with a relation T obey the following axioms:

1. $inserted\_T \cap deleted\_T = \emptyset$

2. $deleted\_T \cap \Pi_{oldA_1,...,oldA_n}(updated\_T) = \emptyset$

3. $deleted\_T \cap \Pi_{A_1,...,A_n}(updated\_T) = \emptyset$

4. $inserted\_T \cap \Pi_{A_1,...,A_n}(updated\_T) = \emptyset$

5. $inserted\_T \cap \Pi_{oldA_1,...,oldA_n}(updated\_T) = \emptyset$

6. $\Pi_{oldA_1,...,oldA_n}(updated\_T) \cap \Pi_{A_1,...,A_n}(updated\_T) = \emptyset$

5.2.3   Construction of Delta Relations

There may be various ways to enforce the previous axioms. Table 5.5 gives an example of how they are enforced by the A-RDL system. In this table, an extensional employee relation with schema (name, salary), called *EMP*, is used. The first column describes different sequences of database modification events. Each event is intended to have a net effect on the database. The second column describes how these events are captured by the delta relations *inserted_EMP*, *deleted_EMP*, and *updated_EMP*.

This process is now formalized. For the sake of conciseness, delta relations *inserted_T*, *deleted_T*, and *updated_T* are respectively denoted ΔT^+, ΔT^- and ΔT^{-+}. The construction of delta relations is successively described for insertions, deletions, and updates.

TABLE 5.5
Database modification events and their effect on delta relations.

Database modification events	Effects on delta relations
Bob is inserted into *EMP*	Bob is in *inserted_EMP*
Bob is deleted from *EMP*	Bob is not in *inserted_EMP*
(Bob,10K) is inserted into *EMP*	(Bob,10K) is in *inserted_EMP*
Bob's salary is updated to 20K	(Bob,10K) is not in *inserted_EMP*
	(Bob,20K) is in *inserted_EMP*
Bob is in *EMP* and Bob's salary is updated from 10K to 20K	(Bob,10K,Bob,20K) is in *updated_EMP*
Bob's salary is updated to 30K	(Bob,10K,Bob,20K) is not in *updated_EMP*
	(Bob,10K,Bob,30K) is in *updated_EMP*
(Bob, 30K) is deleted	(Bob,10K,Bob,30K) is not in *updated_EMP*
	(Bob,10K) is in *deleted_EMP*

DEFINITION   *Application of an Event to Delta Relations.*

Let e be a data modification and I_k a state. The function *apply* maps I_k into a new state $I_{k+1} = apply(e, I_k)$ as follows.

Insertions: if $e = \{+T(t_1), \ldots, +T(t_p)\}$ then for every delta relation associated with T, I_{k+1} consists of the facts:

- $\Delta T^+(t)$ if $\Delta T^+(t) \in I_k$
- $\Delta T^+(t)$ if $+T(t) \in e$, $\Delta T^-(t) \notin I_k$, $\Delta T^{-+}(t, t') \notin I_k$, and $T(t) \notin I_k$
- $\Delta T^+(t')$ if $\Delta T^{-+}(t, t') \in I_k$ and $+T(t) \in e$
- $\Delta T^-(t)$ if $\Delta T^-(t) \in I_k$ and $+T(t) \notin e$
- $\Delta T^{-+}(t, t')$ if $\Delta T^{-+}(t, t') \in I_k$ and $+T(t) \notin e$

Deletions: if $e = \{-T(t_1), \ldots, -T(t_p)\}$ then for every delta relation associated with T, I_{k+1} consists of the facts:

- $\Delta T^-(t)$ if $\Delta T^-(t) \in I_k$
- $\Delta T^-(t)$ if $-T(t) \in e$, $\Delta T^+(t) \notin I_k$, $\Delta T^{-+}(t', t) \notin I_k$, and $T(t) \in I_k$
- $\Delta T^-(t')$ if $\Delta T^{-+}(t, t') \in I_k$ and $-T(t') \in e$
- $\Delta T^+(t)$ if $\Delta T^+(t) \in I_k$ and $-T(t) \notin e$
- $\Delta T^{-+}(t, t')$ if $\Delta T^{-+}(t, t') \in I_k$ and $-T(t') \notin e$

Updates: if $e = \{- + T(t_1, t_1'), \ldots, - + T(t_p, t_p')\}$ then for every delta relation associated with T, I_{k+1} consists of the facts:

- $\Delta T^+(t)$ if $\Delta T^+(t) \in I_k$ and $- + T(t, t') \notin e$

- $\Delta T^+(t')$ if $\Delta T^+(t) \in I_k$ and $- + T(t, t') \in e$

- $\Delta T^-(t')$ if $\Delta T^-(t') \in I_k$ and $- + T(t, t') \notin e$

- $\Delta T^-(t)$ if $\Delta T^-(t') \in I_k$ and $- + T(t, t') \in e$

- $\Delta T^{-+}(t, t')$ if $\Delta T^{-+}(t, t') \in I_k$ and $- + T(t', t'') \notin e$

- $\Delta T^{-+}(t, t'')$ if $\Delta T^{-+}(t, t') \in I_k$ and $- + T(t', t'') \in e$

- $\Delta T^{-+}(t, t')$ if $T(t) \in I_k$, $T(t') \notin I_k$, and $- + T(t, t') \in e$

5.2.4 Synchronizing External Events and Rule Execution

Rule processing takes place at specific points during the execution of a transaction and these points are determined by external events. The processing of a set of rules at a specific point is called a *rule processing phase*. When a set of rules executes, the processing of internal events is governed by the rule language semantics.

The synchronization between rule processing and external event processing is achieved in two ways. Immediate rules are processed immediately after the processing of each external data modification event, and deferred rules are processed just before the processing of a checkpoint or a commit event.

In the initial database state, called I_0, before the transaction executes, the instances of delta and virtual relations are empty. The first external event of the transaction, e_1, is processed. If it is a data modification event then the set of tuples that are either inserted, deleted, or updated is computed and the delta relations are constructed according to the semantics given earlier. Calling the resulting state I_1, $I_1 = apply(e_1, I_0)$. All the immediate rules of base definition modules are processed from state I_1 until no more rules are applicable.[1] As will be explained later, the processing of base definition modules may cause the execution of virtual definition modules. The resulting state is noted $fix(Imm, I_1) = I_2$ and represents the fixpoint of the set of immediate rules, called *Imm*, on state I_1. Indeed, this is a partial fixpoint because neither the termination of the execution nor the uniqueness of the result can be guaranteed for general rule programs (see e.g., [AS91]).

---

[1]This notion will be formalized in the next section.

If e_1 is a database access event then the database state I_0 remains unchanged, thus $I_1 = I_0$. All rules of virtual definition modules, noted *Virt*, are processed yielding a new state $I_2 = fix(Virt, I_1)$, and e_1 is processed on I_2.

This process continues until a transactional event e_{p+1} is encountered. If e_{p+1} is a rollback statement then the transaction is aborted. Because rule processing is a part of the execution of this transaction and because of the atomicity property of transactions, none of the updates performed by both the external and internal data modification events will be integrated into the database.

If e_{p+1} is a commit or a checkpoint event, all deferred rules of base definition modules, called *Def*, are processed on state $fix(Imm, I_{2p-1}) = I_{2p}$ and a new state $fix(Def, I_{2p}) = I_{2p+1}$ is obtained. As before, the processing of *Def* rules may cause the processing of *Virt* rules. Then the commit or the checkpoint event is normally processed by the database system. Now, if e_{p+1} is a commit event then I_{2p+1} is the final state reached by the transaction and $I_{2(p+1)} = I_{2p+1}$. Otherwise, the next event e_{p+2} is processed just as e_1 before.

To summarize, for a transaction $\mathcal{T} = (e_1, e_2, \ldots, e_{p+1}, \ldots)$, the evaluation process can be depicted using a graphical notation as shown below. According to the type of the event e_1, either the event is processed first and *Imm* rules are executed or *Virt* rules are executed and then event e_1 is processed. Deferred rules are executed when a checkpoint or commit event occurs.

$$I_0 \xrightarrow{e_1} I_1 \xrightarrow{fix(Imm, I_1)} I_2 \longrightarrow \ldots$$

$$I_{2p} \xrightarrow{fix(Def, I_{2p})} I_{2p+1} \xrightarrow{e_{p+1}} I_{2(p+1)} \ldots$$

$$I_0 \xrightarrow{fix(Virt, I_1)} I_1 \xrightarrow{e_1} I_2 \longrightarrow \ldots$$

5.3
Examples of Rules and Rule Modules

Several examples of rules are presented, illustrating their syntax and semantics. Then, examples of rule modules are given. Using the examples, the notion of triggering event is informally introduced.

5.3.1   Examples of Rules

In the following examples, two extensional relations are used: an employee relation, called EMP, with schema (name, emp_no, dept_no, sal); and a department relation, called $DEPT$, with schema (mgr_no, dept_no).

The first rule specifies that when the salary of an employee named Bob (tuple variable e_1 in the rule) is updated then the employee named Alice (tuple variable e_2 in the rule) must receive the same salary as Bob. In the rule, EMP represents the current value of the employee relation. According to the definition of Section 5.2.2, this means that either Alice was in the initial database state (i.e., before the transaction started) or Alice was inserted during the transaction as a result of external events or as a result of the execution of other rules before r_1 (i.e., internal events).

```
r1 is deferred
if updated_EMP(e1) and EMP(e2) (e1.name = "Bob" and e2.name =
    "Alice" and e1.oldsal <> e1.sal and e1.sal <> e2.sal)
then -+ EMP(e2; sal = e1.sal);
```

Note that if r_1 fires then *updated_EMP* is necessarily not empty. Hence, it is said that "update to EMP" is a *triggering event* for rule r_1.

Table 5.6 describes in the first column a sequence of database modification events followed by a checkpoint or a commit event, which results in the execution of rule r_1. The second column describes how these events, as well as the firing of r_1, are transforming delta relations.

If Bob is inserted instead of being updated then rule r_1 will never fire. The next rule expresses that Alice's salary should always be the same as Bob's salary. Regardless of the event that concerns Bob, rule r_2 always maintains the same salary for Bob and Alice.

```
r2 is deferred
if EMP(e1) and EMP(e2) (e1.name = "Bob" and e2.name = "Alice"
    and e1.sal <> e2.sal)
then -+ EMP(e2; sal = e1.sal);
```

TABLE 5.6
Database modification events and their effect on delta relations.

Database modification events	Effects on delta relations
(Alice,20K) is inserted into EMP	(Alice,20K) is in *inserted_EMP*
Bob's salary is updated from 20K to 30K	(Bob,20K,Bob,30K) is in *updated_EMP*
commit or checkpoint event	
rule r_1 fires	(Alice,20K) is not in *inserted_EMP*
	(Alice,30K) is in *inserted_EMP*

In rule r_2, both variables e_1 and e_2 range over the current value of relation EMP. If there is no event that either inserts tuples into EMP or updates tuples in EMP then rule r_2 will not fire. Thus, "insertions to EMP" and "updates to EMP" are two triggering events for rule r_2. In particular, if a transaction inserts (Bob,20K) into EMP and updates Alice's salary from 25K to 30K then rule r_2 fires and sets Alice's salary to 20K. Note that "deletions to EMP" is not a triggering event for the rule.

Now, suppose one wants to express that whenever Bob is inserted or his salary changes then Alice gets the same salary as Bob, and when Alice is inserted or her salary is updated then Bob gets the same salary as Alice. Rule r_2 does not fulfill this requirement when, for instance, Alice's salary changes. However, this can be expressed by the two following rules, r_{21} and r_{22}.

```
/* if Bob changes then Alice gets the same salary as Bob */
r21 is deferred
if EMP(e1) and EMP(e2) (e1.name = "Bob" and e2.name = "Alice"
    and e1.sal <> e2.sal
    and (exists e3 in inserted_EMP (e1.emp_no = e3.emp_no)
       or exists e4 in updated_EMP (e1.emp_no = e4.emp_no)))
then -+ EMP(e2; sal = e1.sal);
```

```
/* if Alice changes then Bob gets the same salary as Alice */
r22 is deferred
if EMP(e1) and EMP(e2) (e1.name = "Bob" and e2.name = "Alice"
    and e1.sal <> e2.sal
    and (exists e3 in inserted_EMP (e2.emp_no = e3.emp_no)
       or exists e4 in updated_EMP (e2.emp_no = e4.emp_no)))
then -+ EMP(e1; sal = e2.sal);
```

If Bob is inserted, Alice was in the database, and her salary has not been updated, then rule r_{22} is not firable and only rule r_{21} can be firable. Now, if Bob and Alice are inserted, both rules r_{21} and r_{22} can be firable thereby causing a non-deterministic effect on Bob's and Alice's salaries. If a deterministic effect is desired (for instance, giving Bob the same salary as Alice) one must specify that r_{22} has priority over r_{21}. If the two rules belong to the same module then this priority is easily expressed using the procedural control language presented in the next section.

Now suppose that the original schema of the EMP relation is augmented with an attribute *email* that specifies the electronic mail address of every employee. The next rule specifies that if the salary of an employee (variable e_1 in the rule) is updated so that this employee earns more than his manager (variable e_2 in the rule) then the manager is alerted using an electronic message that contains the name and the new salary of the employee.

```
r3 is deferred
if updated_EMP(e1) and EMP(e2) and DEPT(d)
    (e1.oldsal <> e1.sal
    and e1.dept_no = d.dept_no and e2.emp_no = d.mgr_no
    and e1.sal > e2.sal)
thenonce alert(e2.email, e1.name, e1.sal);
```

In the action part, *alert* is a procedure name and the procedure is invoked for every instantiation of variables e_1, e_2, and d that satisfy the condition part of the rule. The use of the **thenonce** keyword prevents the rule from being fired more than once within the same "rule processing phase" (see definition of a rule processing phase in Section 5.2.4).

The semantics implemented by the A-RDL system guarantees that rule r_3 will only be executed when no other deferred rule is capable of modifying the instances of the EMP and $DEPT$ relations. Thus, when r_3 executes, the instances of EMP and $DEPT$ are definitely computed. This implicit ordering between rules, called *chain ordering*, will be formally explained later.

Rules can also be used to disambiguate user's updates. Suppose that a new extensional relation, called $MANAGES$, with schema (mgr_no, emp_no), is defined. Suppose that the database indicates that Bob works in department 1, Alice and Tom work in department 2, and Bob and Tom are the respective managers of these two departments. Suppose that relation $MANAGES$ is updated by the user so that Tom now supervises Alice. This can be interpreted as the fact that either Tom becomes manager of department 1, or Alice is assigned to department 2. Rule r_4 fixes the correct interpretation of an update to attribute mgr_no in $MANAGES$ by saying that if an employee gets a new manager then he should work in the department of his new manager.

```
r4 is immediate
if updated_MANAGES(e1) and EMP(e2) and EMP(e3)
    (e1.oldmgr_no <>
    e1.mgr_no and e1.mgr_no = e2.emp_no and
    e1.emp_no = e3.emp_no)
then -+ EMP(e3; dept_no = e2.dept_no)
```

The next rule defines the instance of an intensional relation, called S_EMP (standing for Suspect EMPloyees), containing all employees who earn more than their manager. This relation is defined from the EMP and $DEPT$ relations and has the same schema as EMP.

If the user can access relation S_EMP (i.e., S_EMP is a virtual relation) then r_5 must be defined as an immediate rule. Otherwise, if S_EMP is a relation local to a module and it is only used by deferred rules, then rule r_4 may be defined as a deferred rule too.

Since S_EMP is an intensional relation, its instance has only to be computed when it is needed. This means that S_EMP is needed either by the condition of a rule (internal access event), or by a data manipulation command issued by the transaction (an external access event). Thus, "access to S_EMP" is the only triggering event for rule r_5.

```
r5 is immediate
if EMP(e1) and EMP(e2) and DEPT(d)
    (e1.dept_no = e2.dept_no and
    d.mgr_no = e1.emp_no and
    e1.sal < e2.sal)
then + S_EMP(e2)
```

The last rule shows how the procedural code sections that appear before the if-part and after the then-part of a rule can be used to trace the execution of rules. When rule r_6 is evaluated, the string "r6 is evaluated" is printed. If the rule is fired, the string "r6 has been fired" is printed.

```
r6 is deferred
{puts("r6 is evaluated");}
if ...then ...
{puts("r6 has been fired");}
```

5.3.2   Examples of Rule Modules

The first module implements an integrity constraint over two relations EMP and $DEPT$ saying that: "an employee cannot earn more than his manager". This is a base definition module. The only action taken by the rule is to rollback the transaction when the constraint is violated. Insertions and updates to EMP and $DEPT$ are the triggering events for rule r in the module.

```
create module control_salary;
base EMP (name string, emp_no integer, dept_no integer, sal float);
    DEPT (mgr_no integer, dept_no integer);
rules
r is deferred
if EMP(e1) and EMP(e2) and DEPT(d) (e1.dept_no = e2.dept_no
    and d.mgr_no = e1.emp_no and e1.sal < e2.sal)
then rollback;
end module
```

The next module implements a rule to promote manager salaries. If the salary of an employee is increased, then one rule checks that this employee does not receive a salary higher than his manager. If the employee's salary is higher, then the manager's salary is set to 20% more than the salary of the best paid employee in the department.

```
create module promote_managers;
base EMP (name string, emp_no integer, dept_no integer, sal float);
    DEPT (mgr_no integer, dept_no integer);
local PROMOTED like EMP;
    BESTPAID (dept_no integer, sal float);

rules deferred
r1 is
if updated_EMP(e1) and EMP(e2) and DEPT(d) (e1.sal > e1.oldsal
    and e1.dept_no = e2.dept_no and e2.emp_no = d.mgr_no
    and e1.sal > e2.sal)
then + PROMOTED(e2);

r2 is
if EMP(e1) (foreach e2 in EMP (e1.dept_no <> e2.dept_no
    or e1.sal < e2.sal))
then + BESTPAID (dept_no = e1.dept_no, sal = e1.sal);

r3 is
if PROMOTED(e1) and EMP(e2) and BESTPAID(b) (e1.dept_no = b.dept_no
    and e1.emp_no = e2.emp_no)
then - PROMOTED(e1)
    -+ EMP(e2; sal = b.sal * 1.2);

control seq(r1,r2)
end module
```

Again, this is a base definition module. The extensional relations used by the module are the EMP and $DEPT$ relations. In addition, the module uses two intensional relations, called $PROMOTED$ and $BESTPAID$, that are purely local to the module. This means that the existence of these two relations is hidden from the users and from the other rule modules. It also means that the instances of these relations are destroyed as soon as the execution of the module terminates. These two relations are declared as local relations in the module.

The first rule records into relation $PROMOTED$ all managers whose salary must be augmented. Rule r_2 calculates the highest salary for every department and records the result into relation $BESTPAID$. Finally, the last rule takes all managers of EMP (tuple variable e_2) that are also in $PROMOTED$ and computes their new salary. At the same time, relation $PROMOTED$ is cleaned up by removing all managers that have been augmented.

The "control string" seq(r1,r2) expresses that r_1 and r_2 must be executed sequentially (i.e., r_1 precedes r_2) in the module. If r_1 is not firable, the A-RDL system automatically stops the execution of the module. Indeed, the system knows that $PROMOTED$ is empty and thus r_3 is not firable. Since r_2 is only useful for r_3, there is no need to execute r_2.

The triggering events associated with this module are now explained. Globally, this module maps a database state I_k into a new state I_{k+1} which only differs from I_k on the instance of $updated\_EMP$ and EMP. Now, if $updated\_EMP$ is empty in I_k, no new instance can be generated by the module, whatever other events occur for EMP and $DEPT$. Thus, "updates to EMP" is said to be a triggering event for the module. Since there is no other event that has the same property, this is the only triggering event.

Suppose that Tom is the manager of department 1 in which Alice and Bob work. Tom earns 35K, and Alice and Bob earn 30K. The first column of Table 5.7 below describes a sequence of database modification events followed by a checkpoint or a commit event which causes the evaluation of the module. Then, the sequence of rule firings is given. The second column describes how delta and local relations are transformed.

The next example rule module demonstrates the use of module variables and procedural code sections. The first rule has a Boolean condition that tests if any inserted or updated employee has a salary greater than 100. If true, a global variable, named *change*, is set to 1. If the variable has been set to 1, the second rule sets the salaries of all inserted employees to 50. Both the rules r_1 and r_2 are executed once during the same rule processing phase because

TABLE 5.7

Database modification events and their effect on delta relations.

Database modification events	Effects on delta relations
Alice's salary is updated from 30K to 40K	(Alice,30K,Alice,40K) is in *updated_EMP*
Bob's salary is updated from 30K to 38K	(Bob,20K,Bob,30K) is in *updated_EMP*
commit or checkpoint event	
rule r_1 fires	Tom is in *PROMOTED*
rule r_2 fires	(1,40K) is in *BESTPAID*
rule r_3 fires	(Tom,35K,Tom,48K) is in *updated_EMP*
	Tom is not in *PROMOTED*

of the use of the keyword **thenonce**. If variable *change* is set to 1, the third rule recursively reduces each existing employee's salary by 10% if it is greater than 100. Existing employees include the inserted and the updated ones. The control string seq(r_1, r_2, r_3) indicates that r_1, r_2, and r_3 are executed sequentially in their specified order.

```
module insert_update_control;
base EMP (name string, emp_no integer, dept_no integer, sal float);
var integer change;
rules deferred
r1 is
if (exists e1 in inserted_EMP (e1.sal > 100)) or (exists e2 in
    updated_EMP (e2.  sal > 100))
thenonce change = 1;

r2 is
if inserted_EMP (e) (change = 1)
thenonce -+ EMP (e; sal = 50);

r3 is
if EMP (e) (change = 1 and e.sal > 100)
then -+ EMP (e; sal = .9 * e.sal);

control seq (r1, r2, r3)
init {change = 0;}
end module
```

The last module illustrates how virtual relations can be used in base definition modules. In some sense, the example shows a combination of deductive and active rules.

Suppose there exists a virtual definition module, called *shortest_path*, that computes the shortest path between two intersections in a network of roads. The module uses three base relations: a relation containing all segments of roads; a relation containing all congested or closed roads (i.e., roads to be avoided); and a relation, called *GOAL*, with schema (dep_id, arr_id), containing pairs of intersections, a departure one and an arrival one. There is a single output (i.e., virtual) relation, called *SH_PATH*, with schema (dep_id, arr_id, road_id, dist), that describes for every tuple in *GOAL* the set of segments of roads that constitute the shortest path between intersections dep_id and arr_id. Attribute *dist* indicates the length of each segment of road. It is assumed that before starting any transaction, relation *GOAL* is always empty.

Suppose also that there are two extensional relations, called *TRAVEL*, with schema (emp_no, mis_id, from, to), and *ITINERARY*, with schema (mis_id, road_id, dist). The first one describes business travels to be done by employees. Attribute *mis_id* identifies a mission for an employee, and attributes *from* and *to* indicate the departure and arrival intersections. The second relation describes the best itineraries for these travels.

Suppose a policy is to automatically compute the best itineraries as soon as plans for travels are entered into the database. This policy is implemented by the following base definition module, called *best_itinerary*. The module has three base relations and one input relation.

```
create module best_itinerary;
base TRAVEL (emp_no integer, mis_id integer, from integer,
             to integer);
    ITINERARY (mis_id integer, road_id integer, dist real);
    GOAL (dep_id integer, arr_id integer);
input SH_PATH (dep_id integer, arr_id integer, road_id integer,
             dist real);
rules deferred
r1 is
if inserted_TRAVEL(t) thenonce + GOAL(dep_id = t.from,
                                      arr_id = t.to);
```

```
r2 is
if inserted_TRAVEL(t) and SH_PATH(p)
   (t.from = p.dep_id and t.to = p.arr_id)
then + ITINERARY(mis_id = t.mis_id, road_id = p.road_id,
                 dist = p.dist);


r3 is
if inserted_TRAVEL(t) and GOAL(g)
   (t.from = g.dep_id and t.to = g.arr_id)
then - GOAL(g);


control r2 \ r3
end module
```

Suppose that a transaction inserts a new travel into $TRAVEL$ and then issues a commit event. Module *best_itinerary* executes. Rule r_1 takes the inserted travel and generates a new tuple into $GOAL$. Remember that, by hypothesis, relation $GOAL$ was empty. Then rule r_2 is processed. This rule references relation SH_PATH, an input relation, thereby causing the execution of module *shortest_path*. Rule r_2 can now be executed and returns the best itinerary into $ITINERARY$. Finally, rule r_3 removes the tuples inserted by the modules into $GOAL$. Note that since $GOAL$ is now empty, rule r_1 could be executed again. This is why the **thenonce** keyword is used in rule r_1. Finally, the control string specifies that rule r_2 must be evaluated before rule r_1.

As shown by this example, the virtual definition module that defines the virtual relation SH_PATH plays the role of a procedure or service that can be invoked by other modules. Thus, virtual relations are not only useful to present data to the users, but also to help structure the rules into modular and reusable blocks. Generic rules that perform a specific computation can be grouped into a virtual definition module. In fact, in the above example the two modules "interact." The base definition module writes into a base relation, $GOAL$, consumed by the virtual definition module, which in turn produces a result, relation SH_PATH, consumed by the base definition module.

5.4
Semantics of Rule Execution

Preliminary definitions are introduced first. Then, the semantics of a set of rules are defined by means of a nested partial fixpoint operator. Finally, the notion of procedural control over a set of rules is presented and the control language is specified.

5.4.1   Preliminaries

In the following, a database instance consists of a set of facts over a database schema plus a set of instances of module variables. Given a module variable v, an instance of v is noted $\theta(v)$. This slight generalization enables taking into account the state of the module variables used in rules. Formally, this is not a problem since a module variable can be viewed as a relation having one attribute and one tuple (see [KdMS90]).

There is an implicit partial ordering between rules built from two kinds of ordering called *chain ordering* and *action ordering*. The chain ordering expresses that a rule precedes another one if the result of the first rule is needed by the second rule. This ordering is reflexive, anti-symmetric, and transitive.

DEFINITION   *Chain Ordering.*

Let r_1 and r_2 be two rules in a module. Then r_1 is said to precede r_2 in a chain ordering, noted $r_1 \leq_c r_2$, iff there exists a relation T_1 in r_1 and T_2 in r_2 such that $T_1 \overset{d*}{\to} T_2$, and there is no relation T_1' in r_1 and T_2' in r_2 such that $T_2' \overset{d*}{\to} T_1'$.

The action ordering expresses that a rule precedes another rule if the first rule inserts tuples into a given relation and the second one deletes tuples from the same relation.

DEFINITION   *Action Ordering.*

Let r_1 and r_2 be two rules in a module. Then r_1 is said to precede r_2 in an action ordering, noted $r_1 \leq_a r_2$, iff there exists a relation T_1 such that $+T_1(t)$ occurs in the action part of r_1 and $-T_1(t)$ occurs in the action part of r_2, and there is no relation T_2 such that $+T_2(t)$ occurs in the action part of r_2 and $-T_2(t)$ occurs in the action part of r_1.

The general definition of an implicit ordering between rules can now be given. This ordering is also reflexive, anti-symmetric, and transitive.

DEFINITION   *Implicit Ordering.*

Let r_1 and r_2 be two rules in a module. Then r_1 is said to precede r_2, noted $r_1 \leq r_2$, iff either

1. $r_1 \leq_a r_2$ and $r_1 \not\leq_c r_2$, or

2. $r_1 \leq_c r_2$, and $r_1 \not\leq_a r_2$

This definition, as discussed in [dMS88a], can be viewed as a generalization of the ordering of rules based on the notion of stratification, which is commonly used in deductive databases.

Given a set of rules $\mathcal{R}$ in a module, $(\mathcal{R}, \leq)$ denotes the set of rules provided with its implicit ordering. There is also an implicit ordering between virtual definition modules. As stated by the definition of Section 5.1.4, modules form a hierarchy with respect to their input/output clauses.

DEFINITION   *Ordering of Modules.*

Let $\mathcal{M}$ and $\mathcal{M}'$ be two modules. $\mathcal{M}$ precedes $\mathcal{M}'$, noted $\mathcal{M} \prec \mathcal{M}'$, in the module hierarchy iff there exists a relation T declared as output in $\mathcal{M}$ and as input in $\mathcal{M}'$.

Note that for well-formed virtual definition modules, if $\mathcal{M} \prec \mathcal{M}'$ then it is impossible to have $\mathcal{M}' \prec \mathcal{M}$.

Let r be a rule "if condition then action," henceforth noted $C \rightarrow A$. The *pure portion* of A, noted *pure_A*, is defined to be the restriction of A to insertion, deletion, update, and variable assignment actions. Thus, rollback, and side effect actions are omitted from *pure_A*.

5.4.2   Virtual Definition Modules

The semantics of virtual definition modules is defined using a partial fixpoint operator. Before presenting the semantics, a few auxiliary definitions are useful.

DEFINITION   *Effect of a Rule.*

Let $r: C \rightarrow A$ be a rule and I a database instance. Let r' be an instantiation of r such that (i) each (tuple) variable is valuated to some fact in I, and (ii) condition C evaluates to true. Then r' is said to be a *satisfying instantiation* of r in I. The set of all satisfying instantiations of r in I is noted $satisf_r(I)$, and the set of actions in *pure_A* of all the satisfying instantiations of r in I is called the *effect* of r, noted $effect_r(I)$.

Intuitively, the effect of rule r on I is the global effect obtained by considering the actions of all the satisfying instantiations of r in I. There is a simple way of constructing $effect_r(I)$. Suppose that the condition of r has q free variables ranging over relations $T_1, \ldots, T_q$ (not necessarily pairwise distinct). The set of all tuples in the product $T_1 \times T_2 \times \ldots \times Tq$ that satisfy the condition part of r returns the set of all satisfying instantiations of r. Each tuple in this set yields an instantiation of the variables used in the pure portion of the action part of r, and hence a set of instantiated actions. The union of these sets for each tuple in $satisf_r(I)$ yields $effect_r(I)$.

DEFINITION   *Consistent Effect of a Rule.*

The effect of a rule r in I, $effect_r(I)$, is said to be *consistent* if

1. For any relation T occuring in the action of r there are no tuples t, t', and t'' such that either:

    - $+T(t)$ and $-T(t) \in effect_r(I)$, or
    - $+T(t)$ and $-+T(t,t') \in effect_r(I)$, or
    - $-T(t')$ and $-+T(t,t') \in effect_r(I)$, or
    - $-+T(t,t')$ and $-+T(t',t'') \in effect_r(I)$, or
    - $-+T(t,t')$ and $-+T(t,t'') \in effect_r(I)$, or
    - $-+T(t',t)$ and $-+T(t'',t) \in effect_r(I)$

2. For any variable v occuring in the action of r there are no distinct valuations θ and θ' such that:

    - $\theta(v)$ and $\theta'(v) \in effect_r(I)$

Given a rule r and its effect, $effect_r(I)$, one constructs the maximal consistent subset of $effect_r(I)$, noted $cons\_eff_r(I)$. The notion of firable rule can now be introduced.

DEFINITION   *Firable Rule.*

Let $r: C \to A$ be a rule and I a database instance.

1. If A contains some side effect or rollback action then r is said to be *firable* if $satisf_r(I) \neq \emptyset$.

2. If A only contains insertion, deletion, update, or variable assignment actions, then r is said to be *firable* if there exists a fact $T(t)$ or a variable instance $\theta(v)$ such that either:

- $+T(t) \in cons\_eff_r(I)$, and $T(t) \notin I$, or
- $-+T(t',t) \in cons\_eff_r(I)$, $T(t) \notin I_k$, and $T(t') \in I_k$, or
- $-T(t) \in cons\_eff_r(I)$, and $T(t) \in I$, or
- $\theta(v) \in cons\_eff_r(I)$ and $\theta'(v) \in I$, with $\theta \neq \theta'$.

A firable rule r is said to be *productive* in I if its effect is capable of changing I into a new instance I'. The semantics of a set of rules and a set of rule modules is now formally given.

DEFINITION   *Semantics of Virtual Definition Rules.*

Let $(\mathcal{R}, \leq)$ be a set of rules in a virtual definition module. $(\mathcal{R}, \leq)$ is also an operator that defines a relationship among database instances. For each state I_k, I_{k+1} is *reachable* from I_k using $\mathcal{R}$ if there is a firable rule $r \in \mathcal{R}$ in I_k such that no other firable rule precedes r, and I_{k+1} is defined as follows:

1. If r is not productive then $I_{k+1} = I_k$,

2. If r is productive then I_{k+1} consists of the facts $T(t)$, and variable instances $\theta(v)$, such that:

    - $T(t) \in I_k$, $-T(t) \notin cons\_eff_r(I_k)$, and $-+T(t,t') \notin cons\_eff_r(I_k)$, or
    - $+T(t) \in cons\_eff_r(I_k)$, or
    - $-+T(t',t) \in cons\_eff_r(I_k)$ and $T(t') \in I_k$, or
    - $\theta(v) \in cons\_eff_r(I_k)$ and $\theta(v) \notin I_k$

Given an initial database instance I_0, if there is a sequence of reachable states $I_1 \; I_2 \; \ldots \; I_k$ such that no rule of $\mathcal{R}$ is firable in I_k, then the sequence has a limit called a *partial fixpoint* of $\mathcal{R}$ on I_0, denoted $fix(\mathcal{R}, I_0)$. It can be shown that a set of rules may have several fixpoints or no fixpoint at all.

It is important to notice that the effect of each individual productive rule is deterministic. However, the computation of a set of rules is non-deterministic because the result depends on the actual ordering of rule execution.

DEFINITION   *Semantics of Virtual Definition Modules.*

Let $\{\mathcal{M}_1, \ldots, \mathcal{M}_n\}$ be a set of virtual definition modules. This set defines a relationship among database instances as follows. For each state I_k, I_{k+1} is reachable from I_k if there exists some $i, 1 \leq i \leq n$, such that

1. $I_{k+1} = fix(\mathcal{M}_i, I_k)$, and

2. there is no j such that $\mathcal{M}_j \prec \mathcal{M}_i$, and there exists a firable rule r $\in \mathcal{M}_j$ in I_k.

Thus, virtual definition modules are executed according to their ordering in the module hierarchy, and once it starts to execute, a module is executed until a fixpoint (if any) is obtained. Given an initial database instance I_0, if there is a sequence of reachable states I_1 I_2 ... I_k such that no rule of $\{\mathcal{M}_1, \ldots, \mathcal{M}_n\}$ is firable in I_k, then the sequence has a limit denoted *fix* $(\{\mathcal{M}_1, \ldots, \mathcal{M}_n\}, I_0)$.

5.4.3   Base Definition Modules

The semantics of base definition modules is now given. Compared to virtual definition modules, the semantics first differs in the definition of the set of satisfying instantiations of a rule.

In the following definition, *Virt* denotes the set of virtual definition modules.

DEFINITION   *Satisfying Instantiations.*

Let r: $C \to A$ be a rule and I a database instance. Let r' be an instantiation of r such that (i) each (tuple) variable ranging over a delta, a local, or an extensional relation is valuated to some fact in I, (ii) each variable ranging over a virtual relation is valuated to some fact in $fix(Virt, I)$, and (iii) condition C evaluates to true. Then r' is said to be a *satisfying instantiation* of r in I. The set of all satisfying instantiations of r in I is noted $satisf_r(I)$.

The definitions of the effect and consistent effect of a rule are the same as for virtual definition rules. However, a second difference in the semantics is that base definition modules are capable of changing delta relations' instances. For a given rule r and database instance I, assume that the set $cons\_eff_r(I)$ is partitioned into three sets e^+ of insertions, e^- of deletions, and e^{-+} of updates.

DEFINITION   *Semantics of Base Definition Rules.*

Let $(\mathcal{R}, \leq)$ be a set of rules in a base definition module. $(\mathcal{R}, \leq)$ is also an operator that defines a relationship among database instances. For each state I_k, I_{k+1} is *reachable* from I_k using $\mathcal{R}$ if there is a firable rule r $\in \mathcal{R}$ in I_k such that no other firable rule precedes r, and I_{k+1} is defined as follows:

1. if r is not productive then $I_{k+1} = I_k$,

2. If r is productive then for every intensional relation T and variable v, I_{k+1} consists of the facts $T(t)$ and variable instances $\theta(v)$, such that:

   - $T(t) \in I_k$, $-T(t) \notin cons\_eff_r(I_k)$, and $-+T(t,t') \notin cons\_eff_r(I_k)$, or

   - $+T(t) \in cons\_eff_r(I_k)$, or

   - $-+T(t',t) \in cons\_eff_r(I_k)$ and $T(t') \in I_k$, or

   - $\theta(v) \in cons\_eff_r(I_k)$ and $\theta(v) \notin I_k$

3. If r is productive then for every delta relation associated with an extensional relation T occurring in $cons\_eff_r(I_k)$, I_{k+1} consists of the facts defined as

$$(\dagger) \quad I_{k+1} = apply(e^{-+}, apply(e^{-}, apply(e^{+}, I_k)))$$

In the above definition, items 1 and 2 are the same as before. Only item 3 is added to specify how delta relations are changed. Note that since the effect of a rule is reduced to its consistent part, the *apply* function is associative in formula ($\dagger$) above.

The above definitions imply that the semantics of a base definition module is defined as a nested partial fixpoint operator. The inner fixpoint corresponds to the fixpoint of virtual definition modules and the outer to the fixpoint of the base definition modules. If no virtual relation is used in a base definition module then the fixpoint collapses to a single (flat) fixpoint. This is illustrated by Figure 5.1. $\mathcal{R}$ represents a set of rules in a base definition module, $\mathcal{M}_1, \ldots, \mathcal{M}_p$ are modules composing the set $Virt$ of virtual definition modules.

DEFINITION   *Semantics of Base Definition Modules.*

Let $\mathcal{M}_1, \ldots, \mathcal{M}_n$ be a set of base definition modules. This set defines a relationship among database instances as follows. For each state I_k, I_{k+1} is reachable from I_k if there exists some $i, 1 \leq i \leq n$, such that $I_{k+1} = fix(\mathcal{M}_i, I_k)$.

Thus, base definition modules are executed one after the other and when the execution of a module starts it continues until no more rules are firable.

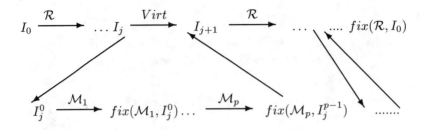

FIGURE 5.1
Nested Partial Fixpoint Operator.

5.4.4   Controlling the Execution of Rules

As described before, there is an implicit ordering between rules that governs the execution of rules. In addition, within a module, an explicit (i.e., user-defined) ordering of rules can be specified using a procedural language derived from RDL1 [KdMS90]. A desire to have control separated from rules as much as possible has influenced the design of a powerful control language. This language includes basic symbols that are rule names and four primitives: sequence, saturation, conditional, and disjunction. The syntax for control strings is given in Table 5.8.

TABLE 5.8
Syntax for control strings.

< exp >	:	<rule_name> | <sequence> | <saturation> | <disjunct>
<sequence>	:	**seq** $(< exp > [\{,< exp >\} \ldots])$
<saturation>	:	$[< exp > [\{,< exp >\} \ldots]]$
<conditional>	:	$(< exp > \backslash < exp >)$
<disjunct>	:	$(< exp > + < exp >)$

The *sequence* primitive expresses that argument expressions are evaluated in their specified order. The *saturation* primitive expresses that argument expressions are evaluated up to a fixpoint in any order. The *conditional* primitive expresses that an expression is evaluated only if the evaluation of another expression fails. Finally, the *disjunct* primitive specifies an exclusive "or" between argument expressions. More formally, the semantics of these primitives is given by means of the *eval* function:

$eval$ $(r) =$ if r is firable then fire r and return r otherwise return *nil*

$eval$ (**seq**($< \exp_1 >, \ldots, < \exp_n >$)) $= eval$ ($< \exp_1 >$); $\ldots$; $eval$ ($< \exp_n >$);
$eval$ ([$< \exp_1 >, \ldots, < \exp_n >$]) $=$
        repeat $eval$ ($< \exp_i >$), $i \in \{1, \ldots, n\}$
        until all $< \exp_i >$ evaluate to nil
$eval$ ($< \exp_1 > \backslash < \exp_2 >$) $=$
        $eval$ ($< \exp_2 >$) if $eval$ ($< \exp_1 >$) $= nil$
$eval$ ($< \exp_1 > + < \exp_2 >$) $=$
        $eval$ ($< \exp_1 >$) or $eval$ ($< \exp_2 >$)
$< \exp >$; $nil = < \exp >$

EXAMPLE 5.1
Consider the control string $s =$ **seq** ($r_1 + r_2$, r_3). This is interpreted as: r_1 or r_2 is evaluated first, then r_3 is evaluated.

Priorities between rules are easily expressed using the control language, as shown by the following example.

EXAMPLE 5.2
Suppose there are two rules r_1 and r_2 and one wants to express that r_1 has priority over r_2. This is specified by the control string [$r_1 \backslash r_2$]. As long as r_1 is firable it is fired first. If r_1 is not firable then r_2 is fired once then r_1 is evaluated again.
    Now, suppose r_1 also has priority over rule r_3. Then the control string becomes [$r_1 \backslash r_2 + r_3$]. Finally, if r_2 has priority over rule r_4 and r_3 has priority over rule r_5 then the control string is [$r_1 \backslash ((r_2 \backslash r_4) + (r_3 \backslash r_5))$].

For every rule module, the user-defined control string is automatically transformed, by the A-RDL system, into a system control string that includes all rules of the module. First, if no user-defined control string is specified in a rule module, rules are evaluated according to their implicit ordering and every rule is executed up to saturation. Now, suppose that a control string s only contains some of the rules composing the module and that rules $r_1 \ldots r_k$ do not occur in s. The system control string generated by the system is:

$$s \backslash ([r_1] + [r_2] + \ldots + [r_k])$$

Essentially, the system control string enforces that the user-defined control string always has priority over the other rules. The set of rules $\{r_1 \ldots r_k\}$ will be evaluated according to the implicit ordering.

5.5
System Architecture and Implementation Features

Two important decisions underly the architecture of the A-RDL system: (i) a rule base is compiled into an executable system called the *Trigger Monitor*, which automatically activates and executes rules depending on the actions taken by an application program, and (ii) the Trigger Monitor is coupled with a relational database system (rather than built-in).

As a basis, the system assumes a client-server architecture where an application program is linked with a library of communication procedures to interface with a DBMS server. A typical library is considered, including procedures like *SqlConnect, SqlDisconnect, SqlRead*, and *SqlExec*. The *SqlConnect* and *SqlDisconnect* procedures respectively open and close a connection between the application process and a DBMS process. The *SqlExec* procedure takes an SQL command as input and transmits it to the corresponding DBMS process. Such communication procedures may vary from one DBMS to another. However, the A-RDL library can be easily emulated on existing relational DBMSs.

5.5.1   Process Architecture

The Trigger Monitor is an executable program that automatically activates and executes rule modules according to the operations performed by an application program. The Trigger Monitor results from the compilation of a rule base. This section describes the process architecture of the Trigger Monitor.

An assumption in the A-RDL implementation is that it is not possible or desirable to change the underlying DBMS. Hence, the communication between an application process and a DBMS process must be intercepted by the Trigger Monitor. This is achieved by renaming the communication procedures. Within an application program, the *SqlConnect* procedure call is replaced by an *SqlConnect** procedure call that creates a Trigger Monitor process instead of a DBMS process at application start-up time. Communication with a local or remote DBMS process is then established by the Trigger Monitor. Thereafter, the Trigger Monitor intercepts all commands issued by the application program to the DBMS. A Trigger Monitor process is created for every application process; it interfaces with the DBMS process. Similarly, the *SqlDisconnect* procedure call is replaced by an *SqlDisconnect** procedure call that removes the Trigger Monitor process. Every call to *SqlExec* is replaced by an *SqlExec** call that transmits SQL statements to the Trigger Monitor instead of the DBMS process. Finally, every call to *SqlRead* is replaced by an *SqlRead** call that reads the result of the previous SQL statement received by the Trigger Monitor.

The Trigger Monitor and the application processes reside on the same client workstation. Figure 5.2 depicts the run-time process architecture.

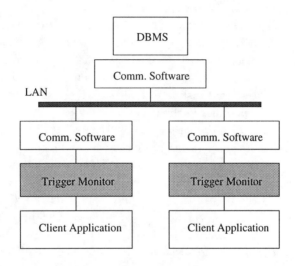

FIGURE 5.2
Run-time Process Architecture.

5.5.2 Functional Architecture

The Trigger Monitor is functionally decomposed into three main components: the environment initialization, the event handler, and the rule evaluator. This pseudo-code procedure describes the logical structure of the Trigger Monitor:

Trigger Monitor
begin
    create_DBMS_process();
    init_Environment();
    while (an *SqlDisconnect* command is not issued by the
        application) do
        event = read_Client_Event(SQL statement);

```
            handle_Event(event);
            reset_Context();
            send_Result_to_Client();
        endwhile
end
```

The *init_Environment* procedure performs two tasks. First, it builds a data structure describing all the delta relations that need to be managed for executing rules in the rule base. For instance, if there is a rule referencing any delta relation associated with T, then the delta relations associated with T have to be managed. Otherwise no delta relation associated with T needs to be managed. The second task is to build a data structure containing the names of all the rule modules in the rule base.

The *read_Client_Event* procedure is a SQL parser that analyzes incoming SQL statements. These statements are passed as arguments of the *SqlExec** invocations within the application program. The parser initializes a record-structured variable, *event*. A field *type* indicates the type of the event, field *statement* contains the text of the command, field *updated_relation* indicates the relation modified by a data modification event, and field *result* is a record-structured variable that describes the relation(s) returned by a select or a data modification command. Field *result.new* indicates the set of tuples inserted in the case of an insert command. Similarly, field *result.old* indicates the set of tuples deleted in the case of a deleted command. In the case of an update, *result.new* indicates the set of updated tuples and *result.old* indicates their old values.

Every invocation to procedure *handle_Event* corresponds to a rule processing phase. After each invocation, the *reset_Context* procedure reinitializes the context associated with the execution of rules at the previous rule processing phase. For instance, it releases the data structure describing the rules in main memory, and reinitializes the value of the *event* variable.

The Event Handler

The Event Handler, implemented by procedure *handle_Event*, performs a case analysis of the SQL commands read by the *read_Client_Event* procedure. If the command is a select involving virtual relations, then all virtual definition modules participating in the definition of the virtual relations are executed and the instances of the virtual relations are computed into temporary relations. A modified select statement, in which virtual relation names are replaced by the corresponding temporary relation names, is sent to the DBMS. If the select only involves extensional relations, it is merely issued to the DBMS and the result is returned to the client application. All temporary relations associated with virtual relations are dropped at the end of the transaction.

If the command is an update, it is sent to the DBMS. There is an assumption that the result of an SQL data modification command can be stored as a temporary relation using a special command, called "NAME," which assigns a relation name to the result of the last command. In the case of an insert (resp. delete) command, the temporary relation returned by the result is the set of tuples that can be inserted (resp. deleted). In the case of an update command, the temporary relation returned by the system only contains the updated tuples. A specific treatment is then necessary to construct the relation containing the old values of the updated tuples.

When the command "NAME" is used, a specific variable indicates the number of tuples in the temporary relation created by the command. This number tells the system if the data modification command produces a net change to the current database state. If so, the *manage_Update* procedure uses the temporary relations associated with the result of the data modification command to update the corresponding delta relations, if any. Then, the Rule Evaluator executes with immediate rules.

If the command issued by the application program is a commit or a checkpoint, deferred rules are evaluated and then the command is sent to the DBMS.

Here is a description of the analysis performed by the Event Handler.

```
handle_Event(event) {
switch (event.type)
    case UPDATE:
        send_Statement_to_DBMS(event.statement);
        receive_Result_from_DBMS(event.result);
        if (event.result.tupleCount > 0)
        {construct event.result.old;
        manage_Update(event.result, UPDATE);
        execute_Base_Modules(immediate);}
    /* DELETE similar to INSERT */
    case INSERT:
        send_Statement_to_DBMS(event.statement);
        receive_Result_from_DBMS(event.result);
        if (event.result.tupleCount > 0)
        {manage_Update(event.result, UPDATE);
        execute_Base_Modules(immediate);}
```

```
    case SELECT:
        if (event.statement involves deduced relations)
        {execute_Virt_Modules(); modify_query(event.statement);}
        send_Statement_to_DBMS(event.statement);
        receive_Result_From_DBMS(event.result);
    /* CHECKPOINT similar to COMMIT */ case COMMIT:
        execute_Base_Modules(deferred);
        send_Statement_to_DBMS(event.statement);
        receive_Result_rom_DBMS(event.result);
        reset_All_Events();
    case ROLLBACK:
        send_Statement_to_DBMS(event.statement);
        receive_Result_from_DBMS(event.result);
        reset_All_Events();
    default:
        send_Statement_to_DBMS(event.statement);
        receive_Result_from_DBMS(event.result);
}
```

Evaluation of Rules

The processing of the *execute_Base_Modules* and *execute_Virt_Modules* procedures are quite similar. For base modules, the procedure cycles over the set of base definition modules and successively executes every module until a fixpoint is reached (if any). For virtual modules, because modules are stratified, the procedure executes a module only once.

The processing of a module is now detailed. Three phases are distinguished. First, the status of delta relations is matched against the triggering events associated with the module. For instance, if ΔT^+ is the only relation that changed since the previous execution of the module (in the same rule processing phase), and "insertions into T" is not a triggering event for the module, then the module is not executed.

If the module passes the first phase then the next phase consists of building a specific data structure associated with the rules of the module. This structure (presented in [dMS88b]) describes the relationships between relations and rule conditions and actions.

The last phase is the execution of rules in a module. First, a rule is selected according to the control strategy specified in the module (augmented with defaults generated by the system) and evaluated. If the rule is fired then extensional and intensional relations that occur in the rule action, as well as module variables, are upated appropriately. Changes to an extensional relation yield changes to the delta relations associated with this relation (if any). This is performed by the *manage_Update* procedure. A next rule is selected, and so on, until no more rules are firable.

If a rule condition involves a virtual relation T, a specific processing arises in the *select_Firable_Rule* procedure. The query associated with the rule condition is constructed and a new variable of type *event*, say *internal_event*, is initialized. Then procedure *handle_Event* is invoked with *internal_event*. As a result, the virtual relation T will be computed and the relation defined by the query will be returned to the *execute_Base_Modules* procedure. This processing implements the nested partial fixpoint operator defined before.

Suppose that, within the same rule processing phase, a module which has already been executed is considered again for execution. The system verifies if the instances of the relations over which the module executes have changed since its last execution. If not, the system does not reexecute the module.

The overall processing of a module is summarized by the pseudo-code description of the *execute_Module* procedure:

```
execute_Module(coupling_mode); {
    if (module not loaded in main memory)
        {if (test_triggering_event is positive)
            {init_Data_Structure();
            init_Control_Strategy();}
        else {return}
    }
    else /* module has already been executed */
        {if (no relation changed since last execution time)
            {return}
        }
    select_Firable_Rule(coupling_mode);
    while there exists a firable rule do
        fire_Rule(); /* returns an event */
        manage_Update(event);
        monitor changes to module variables;
        select_Firable_Rule(coupling_mode);
    end while;
    maintain_Data_Structure() }
```

5.5.3 Generating the Trigger Monitor

Two levels of compilation are used to generate a Trigger Monitor from a set of rule modules. At the first level, a *Rule Compiler* compiles each rule module into executable code, and an *Environment Compiler* generates the *init_Environment* procedure mentioned before. In the second level of compilation, a standard makefile facility is used to generate a Trigger Monitor from the output of the first compilation phase, the Event Handler, the Interface Procedures (like *SqlConnect** described before), and the user-supplied C procedures invoked in rule modules.

Changes to rules require that the Trigger Monitor be rebuilt. Since rules are organized into modules, only those modules which have been updated need to be recompiled. The initialization procedure also has to be recompiled. The Trigger Monitor is then reassembled by linking together the set of compiled modules.

The functional architecture of Trigger Monitor generation is depicted in Figure 5.3. Square boxes represent the compilers and the makefile facility. Grey boxes represent the user-provided components.

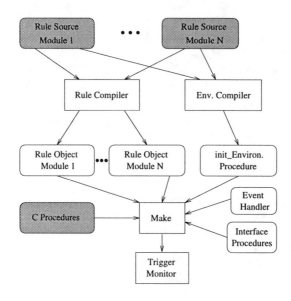

FIGURE 5.3
Generating the Trigger Monitor.

5.6
Summary and Future Directions

This chapter has presented an active rule language obtained as an extension of the RDL1 deductive database language. The system supports both extensional relations that are stored in the database, and intensional relations that are defined by means of rules. Transactions can access extensional and intensional relations but only extensional relations can be modified. Triggering events are either transactional events or data manipulation events. Transactional events correspond to the usual SQL transactional commands commit, rollback, and checkpoint. Data manipulation events consist of database access and modification events. The net effects of data modification events on extensional relations are recorded into delta relations.

The A-RDL language has the following features. First, rules are expressed at a high level. Triggering events need not be provided by the user but are derived from the rules by the system. Second, the rule system is formally described by means of a nested partial fixpoint operator, which encompasses both the deductive and active database paradigms. Hence, a rule module may consist of rules that deduce data and rules that modify the database as a reaction to some data modification events. Finally, a control language enables the user to specify a rich variety of rule execution orderings.

In the A-RDL architecture, a component responsible for detecting events issued by application programs and triggering rules is front-ended to an existing relational database system. This approach can be used over any relational DBMS that supports run-time interpretation of SQL commands. Hence, this approach enables users to rapidly develop and test rule modules over an existing database.

Several research issues are envisioned in the future. One is the development of an optimizer integrated within the Rule Compiler. Preliminary work into that direction is reported in [FRS93]. Second is the incorporation of error and exception handling mechanisms in the rule language, and exploring various alternative ways of implementing them. Third is a tool that helps the user write and understand rules; the need for such a tool was strongly felt during the debugging phase of A-RDL. Last is the removal of the limitation that intensional relations cannot be updated. Preliminary studies have shown that allowing updates to intensional relations presents many problems at both the semantics and implementation levels.

6

Active Rule Management in Chimera

Stefano Ceri, Piero Fraternali,
Stefano Paraboschi, and Letizia Tanca

Chimera is a novel database language integrating an object-oriented data model, a declarative query language based on deductive rules, and an active rule language for reactive processing.[1] In most active object-oriented databases, active rules are associated with objects through methods—rules are triggered by method activations, and are used as devices for testing pre- and post-conditions for method applications to individual object instances. The Chimera approach is substantially different: it uses *set-oriented* active rules, activated as the effect of several, logically indistinguishable events affecting multiple object instances. This approach is consistent with the rest of Chimera, which supports a set-oriented, declarative query and update language.

Object-orientation in Chimera guarantees important advantages over relational active rules, due to the use of *object identifiers*. In object-oriented databases, object identifiers are uniquely associated with each object instance. In Chimera active rules, object-valued variables (i.e., variables ranging over object identifiers) provide a powerful *binding passing* mechanism for linking events to conditions and conditions to actions, thus bridging the three syntactic components of active rules.

Active rules in Chimera have several innovative features:

- They support different models for processing events (called *event consumption modes*) when rules are activated.

- They optionally support event composition (called *net effect computation*) when the same object is the target of multiple operations.

- They support mechanisms for accessing *intermediate states* of affected object instances during transaction execution.

These features are orthogonal to each other and can be generalized to any active rule system. In Chimera, they yield a powerful language that supports a variety of applications, including integrity checking for both static and dynamic constraints, derived data and view materialization, monitoring, and bookkeeping.

---

[1] A chimera is a monster of Greek mythology with a lion's head, a goat's body, and a serpent's tail; each of them represents one of the three components of the language.

6.1
Syntax of Rule Language

The Chimera language provides *declarative expressions* and *procedural expressions*:

- Declarative expressions are composed of two main syntactic categories: terms and formulas. A term is an expression denoting either a value or an object. A formula is an expression that evaluates to either true or false.

- Procedural expressions are composed of primitive database statements, i.e., of updates, queries, and operation calls. The only means of forming more complex statements is to build chains of primitive statements. Variable bindings may be passed from one statement in a chain to another.

Declarative expressions are ubiquitous in Chimera: they are used in query primitives, passive rules, integrity constraints, and view declarations. Procedural expressions are used in transactions and in class operations (methods). Active rules in Chimera use declarative expressions for conditions and procedural expressions for actions. A full specification of Chimera expressions can be found in [CM93].

6.1.1   Active Rule Definition

Active rules in Chimera are called *triggers*. The definition of active rules is performed through a *trigger definition statement*, whose syntax is:

```
trigger_rule ::=
   "define" [trig_options] "trigger" trig_name ["for" class_name]
   "events" trig_events
   "condition" condition_formula
   "actions" reactions
   [priority_option]
   "end"
```

Active rules may be defined in the context of a single class, in which case they are called *targeted* rules, or in the context of multiple classes, in which case they are called *untargeted* rules. Syntactically, targeted rules include the **for** clause in the above definition. This distinction is relevant for schema design and modularization, but there is little syntactic difference and no semantic difference between targeted and untargeted rules.

Each active rule in Chimera consists of four components: events, conditions, actions, and priority.

Events indicate the primitive operations monitored by the active rule; they are denoted by the name of the primitive operation and of the schema element to which the operation is applied (either a class or an attribute of a class). Primitive operations are queries, object creation, modification, and deletion, object migration within generalization hierarchies, and change of persistence status of an object. Queries and modification may refer to specific attributes. In addition, active rules may monitor *operation calls* (methods), although rule execution remains set-oriented. A special event *change* denotes all events causing state changes of objects of a given class. Class names can be omitted when they are understood from the context, e.g., in targeted rules.

```
trig_events ::= event { "," event}

event ::= "create"
        | "create_tmp"
        | "delete"
        | "make_persistent"
        | "generalize" "(" class_name ")"
        | "specialize" "(" class_name ")"
        | "modify" [ "(" attribute_name ")" ]
        | "query" [ "(" attribute_name ")" ]
        | "change"
        | operation_name
```

Details of the Chimera primitives can be found in [CM93].

The *condition* is a conjunction of atomic formulas; some of the atomic formulas introduce variables ranging over the types and classes of a Chimera database, and some other atomic formulas specify conditions over those variables. The entire formula is interpreted as an expression of predicate calculus over typed variables. Conditions are computed over both the state of the database and relevant events (as will be explained below). If the variables of the formula can be satisfied (*bound*) by condition evaluation, then the condition is satisfied. Chimera also supports the constant condition *true*, that is always satisfied but produces no bindings.

```
condition_formula ::= simple_condition_formula
                      { "," simple_condition_formula }
                      | "true"

simple_condition_formula ::= [ "not" ] atomic_formula
                             | [ "not" ] event_formula

atomic_formula ::= class_formula
                   | type_formula
                   | comparison_formula
                   | membership_formula
                   | choose_formula
```

Details of atomic formulas in Chimera can be found in [CM93]; examples are given below. Event formulas are discussed later in this section.

The *reaction* is a sequence of procedure calls, including update or display primitives of the language, externally defined procedures, and the transactional commands *savepoint* and *rollback*. The reaction is executed only when the condition is satisfied. The reaction may share some variables with the condition; in this way, bindings produced by the condition evaluation are provided, as input parameters, to procedures of the reaction.

```
reactions ::= reaction { connector reaction }

reaction ::= display_cmd
             | for_each_cmd
             | select_cmd
             | create_cmd
             | create_tmp_cmd
             | delete_cmd
             | change_persistence_cmd
             | generalize_cmd
             | specialize_cmd
             | modify_cmd
             | population_cmd
             | operation_call
             | procedure_call
             | savepoint_cmd
             | rollback_cmd
```

Again, details of individual Chimera commands can be found in [CM93].

Syntactically, active rules must be *safe*. That is, the variables occurring as input parameters of procedures in the reaction part of the rule must be present in some positive literals of the condition part of the same rule (or be defined as output parameters of preceding procedures).

To control their run-time selection, active rules have an optional priority clause consisting of *before* and *after* declarations. These indicate the names of rules that have lower or higher priority than the rule being defined. Such specifications define a partial order on active rules; acyclicity of the precedence relation between rules is checked when a new rule is defined.

```
priority_option ::= [ "before" trigger_list ]
                  | [ "after" trigger_list ]


trigger_list ::= trigger_name { "," trigger_name }
```

Example

All of the features discussed above are illustrated by the following example. Assume a schema consisting of the two classes *employee* and *dept*; a set-valued attribute *members* connects each department to its member employees. The rule is triggered by inserts on *employee* or updates to the *salary* of *employee*, or by updates to *members* or *salary-budget* of *department*. The condition is satisfied if there are departments D for which the sum of salaries of their employees, assigned to a variable I, is greater than the department's salary budget. Variables D and I are shared by the condition and the reaction. If the condition evaluation produces some bindings for D and I, then the reaction applies the *modify* primitive of Chimera for each <D,I> pair of bindings produced by the condition. The set-oriented modify primitive has three arguments denoting, respectively, the attribute being modified, the OIDs of the objects being modified, and the value to be assigned to the relevant attribute after the modification. This rule is specified to have lower priority than a rule called *adjustSalary* defined in the context of the class *employee* (and specified in Section 6.3).

```
define trigger raiseBudget
  events    create(employee),
            modify(employee.salary),
            modify(dept.members),
            modify(dept.salaryBudget)
```

```
condition dept(D), integer(I),
          I = sum(E.salary where employee(E), E in D.members),
          I > D.salaryBudget
actions   modify(dept.salaryBudget,D,I)
after     employee.adjustSalary
```

Execution Modes

The options associated with each active rule indicate the rule's *consumption* and *execution* modes:

```
trig_options ::= [trigger_consumption] [trigger_execution]
trigger_consumption ::= "event_consuming" | "event_preserving"
trigger_execution ::= "deferred" | "immediate"
```

Two distinct *event consumption modes* are possible for each rule; this feature is relevant when a given rule is considered multiple times in the context of the same transaction.

- Events can be *consumed* after the consideration of a rule. In this case, each instance of an event is considered by a rule only at its next execution, and then disregarded.

- Events can be *preserved* after the consideration of a rule. In this case, all instances of the event since the transaction start are considered at each execution of that rule.

The *execution mode* of active rules is either *immediate* or *deferred*. Immediate rules are considered for execution after the completion of each *transaction line*, which is the smallest unit of execution in Chimera that can be considered as a transformation from one database state into another. Deferred rules are considered only after the issuing of the (user-controlled) *commit* primitive or after a *savepoint* primitive. Defaults for execution and consumption modes are set to *deferred* and *consuming*; alternative modes must be specified explicitly.

Event Formulas

Conditions of active rules may use *event formulas*, special formulas supported by the declarative language of Chimera, built by means of the binary predicates *occurred* and *holds*. These predicates are used to inspect the events that have occurred during a transaction. Syntactically, these predicates have as arguments: (1) a list of events, and (2) a variable, called the *event variable*, which ranges over the OIDs of the object instances affected by at least one of the events:

```
event_formula ::=
    event_token "(" event_list "," variable_name ")"
event_list ::= t_event { "," t_event }
event_token ::= "holds" | "occurred"
```

The computation of these special predicates occurs during condition evaluation:

- The predicate *occurred* binds the event variable to the OIDs of all objects affected by the specified events.

- The predicate *holds* binds the event variable to the OIDs of a subset of the objects affected by the specified events. The subset is based on the evaluation of *net effect*, explained next.

The computation of net effect is performed as follows:

- A sequence of *create* and *delete* primitives on the same object, possibly with an arbitrary number of intermediate *modify* primitives on that object, has a null net effect.

- A sequence of *create* and several *modify* primitives on the same object has the net effect of a single create operation.

- A sequence of several *modify* and a *delete* primitives on the same object has the net effect of a single delete operation on that object.[2]

Reference to Past States

Finally, it is sometimes useful in active rules to refer to past database states. This feature is supported by the special function *old*, which can be applied to simple terms computed in the condition part of the rule, indicating that the terms are to be evaluated in a previous database state.

```
old_term ::= "old" "(" var_or_oid_name [ opt_attrib ] ")"
```

---

[2]Other update primitives of Chimera, such as *create_tmp, make_persistent, specialize,* and *generalize* could be considered for net effect. Currently, the definition of net effect is limited to the primitives *create, delete,* and *modify,* which are more significant.

Which previous state is used depends on the event consumption mode:

- If the rule is event-consuming, then the old state is the state holding at the last consideration of the rule. For the first consideration of a rule, the old state refers to the state at transaction start.

- If the rule is event-preserving, then the old state always refers to the state at transaction start.

6.1.2   Other Rule Commands

Active rules can be deleted by means of a *drop* statement followed by a rule name. The drop statement has the effect of eliminating the rule, including all priority definitions which reference it from other rules.

Active rules can be replaced by a *redefine* statement having the same syntax as the *define* statement. The redefine statement preserves the priority definitions referencing the modified rule from other rules. However, all components of the rule must be completely redefined, including priority definition referencing other rules from the rule which is redefined.

The transactional command *savepoint* can be issued at any point of time during the course of a transaction, forcing the consideration of all active rules (both immediate and deferred) at the end of the transaction line containing the *savepoint* command. For example, when active rules maintain integrity constraints, savepoints are used to check the consistency of intermediate states during the transaction's execution.

6.2
Semantics of Rule Execution

This section describes the execution behavior of Chimera active rules by introducing the main features of a formal model; a complete description of the model is reported in [FMT94]. Informally, a rule is *activated* by the occurrence of any of its events. A rule processing mechanism, executed at the end of transaction lines and at *commit* and *savepoint* user commands, selects rules based on their priorities. The selected rule is *considered* when its condition is evaluated; if the condition is satisfied, then the rule reaction is *executed*. This process is iterated until a fixpoint is reached, when either normal transaction activity is resumed or the transaction is completed.

In previous approaches, the semantics of active rules was given either in a denotational [Wid92] or deductive style [Zan93]. The semantics of Chimera instead uses a two step approach: first Chimera rules are translated into a uniform "internal" format (called *core* format); then, an operational semantics is given for rules in this format by means of a rule execution algorithm. The rationale for this approach is to encode the different semantic options of Chimera rules (e.g., activation modes, event consumption modes, and various options for event formulas) into a low-level syntax. This provides two benefits:

- The operational semantics requires a simpler rule execution engine; there is no need to hard-wire in the algorithm the treatment of the semantic options mentioned above.

- The semantics is modular, and thus can be used to model other active rule systems—changing or adding features to the language requires a different encoding but no change of the execution engine.

Note that core rules are not intended to be a tool for programmers, as the translation into core rules is syntax-driven. Thus, the readability of core rules (which is admittedly worse than that of Chimera rules) is not an issue.

The main syntactic difference between rules in Chimera and core rules is that the latter extend the former: core rules include additional components (queries and/or updates) to explicitly express how events are consumed and rules are activated.

6.2.1   The Event Base

The *event base* is a repository of *event instances*, whose lifetime is the duration of a user transaction plus the execution of rules triggered by that transaction. The event base records two kinds of events: *internal* and *external*. Internal events are produced by update and query primitives of Chimera and concern database modifications. External events are due to Chimera transactional commands (such as *savepoint*, *commit*, or *rollback*). Note that this model could be augmented to support arbitrary kinds of external events (such as temporal events).

Each event instance in the event base is described by the following pieces of information:

- The *eid*, the unique identifier of the event.

- The *type*, one of the event types supported by Chimera.

- The *affected database information*, which links an event to the *OIDs* of target objects.

ACTIVE	
EID	SCOPE
e12	R_1

EVENT

EID	TYPE	DATAINFO	TS
e12	"create(P)"	#417, #582	4
e23	"delete(C)"	#555, #84, #123	8

FIGURE 6.1

An example event base.

- The *timing information*, which models the order of occurrence of events by means of timestamps.

- The *scope*, which concerns the visibility of events to rules.

This information is grouped into the relations *ACTIVE(eid, scope)* and *EVENT(eid, type, datainfo, ts)*. These tables are initially empty and become populated during the course of a transaction.[3]

Figure 6.1 shows an example event base, which records, in relation *EVENT*, two events. The first event is caused by the execution of an object creation primitive affecting two objects (with OIDs *#417, #582*) of class *P*. It has the event identifier *e12*, and has occurred at time *4*. From relation *ACTIVE* it can be deduced this event is still *"active"* for rule R_1, meaning that it is able to trigger R_1.[4] Relation *EVENT* also records an event *e23* caused by the execution of an object deletion, affecting three objects of class *C*; the event has occurred at time *8*. This event is not recorded in the relation *ACTIVE*, thus it is no longer able to trigger any rule. However, it can still be inspected to obtain information about past transaction history.

6.2.2   Translation from Chimera Rules into Core Format

This section informally describes the translation of Chimera rules into core format through an example; a formal treatment is given in [FMT94]. Consider rule **raiseBudget** of Section 6.1.1. Its translation into core format is:

---

[3]The event base is for semantic definition and need not be an implementation structure. See Section 6.4.2 for a discussion of implementation techniques.

[4]Note that *e12* may also have triggered other rules, but if so the event has already been consumed by such rules.

```
RULE raiseBudget
(* CORE EVENT PART *)
   ∃ V, TS1:  ACTIVE(eid1, "raiseBudget" ) ∧
              EVENT(eid1, type, V, TS1) ∧
              (type="create(Employee)") ∨
              (type= "modify(Employee.salary)" ) ∨
              (type= "modify(Dept.members)" ) ∨
              (type= "modify(Dept.salaryBudget)" ) ∧
   ∃ Z, TS2:  ACTIVE(eid2, raiseBudget ) ∧
              EVENT(eid2, "savepoint", Z , TS2)
(* CORE CONDITION PART: DATABASE QUERY *)
   dept(D), integer(I),
   I=sum(E.salary where employee(E), E in D.members),
   I > D.salaryBudget
(* CORE CONDITION PART: EVENT BASE UPDATE *)
   -(eid1, raiseBudget)
──→ (* CORE ACTION PART *)
   modify(dept.salaryBudget,D,I)
(* CORE PRIORITY *)
   after employee.adjustSalary
```

As shown by the above example, a core rule is still composed of four parts: event, condition, action, and priority.

When the rule is deferred, the *event part* is a conjunction of queries over the event base:

- The first part of the query looks for one or more "active" event instances of the types specified in the event part of the Chimera rule. If these event instances are present in the event base, their identifiers become bound to the variable `eid1` (so that they can be used to handle event consumption in the condition part of the core rule).

- The second part of the query looks for an active occurrence of the special event *savepoint*. This event is either produced by the *commit* command at the end of the transaction or by the *savepoint* command. This feature represents explicitly the deferred activation mode of the rule: Even if a triggering event has occurred, the rule is not activated until the execution of a *commit* or *savepoint* command.

An immediate rule is modeled by omitting the query on the *savepoint* event.

The *condition part* is divided into two distinct parts:

- The first part is a query on the database and/or the event base, obtained by translating the condition part of the Chimera rule. Since rule `raiseBudget` does not contain event formulas, this translation is straightforward.

- The second part is an update to the event base, which expresses the event consumption. Note that after the evaluation of a condition, the event base must be updated regardless of whether the reaction will be executed. The translated core rule contains the update `-(eid1, raiseBudget)`, by which the triggering event(s) bound to the variable `eid1` are deleted from relation $ACTIVE$ for rule `raiseBudget`, and thus cannot subsequently retrigger the rule. However, the triggering events can still be retrieved by queries on transaction events, since they remain in the relation $EVENT$.[5]

Finally, the *action* is a straightforward translation from the reaction of the Chimera rule.

Event Formulas, Net Effect and Past States

The translation of an event formula in the condition part of a Chimera rule relies on the event base relations $ACTIVE$ and $EVENT$. A literal *occurred(event-type, X)* is translated into an event base query as follows:

- If the rule is *consuming*, then the query is: $\exists Y, TS : (ACTIVE(Y, R) \wedge EVENT(Y, \text{"event-type"}, X, TS))$, which binds the variable X to the objects affected by active events of the specified type.

- If the rule is *preserving*, then the query is: $\exists Z, TS : EVENT(Z, \text{"event-type"}, X, TS)$, by which objects affected by all (active and processed) events of the specified type are bound to the variable X.

Net effect is represented by defining the interpretation of the predicate *holds* so that a different version of the event base (call it *net-EB*) is queried. Net-EB contains only those events that are valid according to the net effect criteria described earlier.

Net-EB is computed by *auxiliary core rules*, generated by the translation of Chimera rules containing an occurrence of the predicate *holds*. Auxiliary rules are given a priority higher than the rule from which they are generated

---

[5] *Savepoint* events are removed only at the end of rule processing, before resuming transaction execution. This can be done, e.g., by an ad hoc lowest priority core rule.

so that the evaluation of the predicate *holds* in the original rule can take place correctly.

As an example, the following core rule is generated for a Chimera rule **r** containing the event formula *holds("create(Employee)", X)*:

```
RULE auxRuleforR
(* CORE EVENT PART: EVENT BASE QUERY *)
∃ X: ACTIVE(e1, r) ∧ EVENT(e1, create(Employee), X, ts1) ∧
    ACTIVE(e2, r) ∧ EVENT(e2, delete(Employee), X, ts2) ∧
    ts1 < ts2;
(* CORE CONDITION PART: EVENT BASE UPDATE *)
    -(eid1, r), -(eid2, r)
⟶
(* CORE ACTION PART *)
    NULL
(* CORE PRIORITY *)
    before r
```

This auxiliary rule simply discards from the net-EB, through operation `-(eid, rule)`, two subsequent events whose composite effect is null. The same events are unaffected for rules other than **r**.

Note that this approach guarantees generality and extensibility: The rule execution algorithm does not depend on the net effect evaluation, whose semantics could easily be redefined.

The semantics of the function *old* requires extending the database to include an auxiliary data structure, called *LOG*, which contains past states of objects. The *LOG* for a given class C is required only for those rules R whose condition contains a literal which uses the function *old* and refers to class C (such as *old(X.a)*, where X is a variable ranging over objects of class C). Logging is conventional: states are accumulated together with their validity timestamps. Occurrences of the function *old* are translated into queries, with suitable timestamp-based predicates, that inspect the *LOG* rather than the database.

6.2.3   Core Rule Execution Algorithm

Execution of core rules proceeds in three steps: *triggering, consideration,* and *execution*. A core rule is *triggered* when the event base query in its event part yields a nonempty result. A core rule is *considered* when the query in its condition part is evaluated (independently of the result) and the updates on the event base are processed. Finally, a core rule is *executed* when its action part is performed.[6]

These three stages constitute the core rule execution algorithm that expresses the semantics of rule processing in Chimera. The three stages together are called an *Elementary Production Step (EPS)*. EPS (see Figure 6.2) takes as input a database and event base and produces as output the database and event base generated by executing one of the triggered rules. In addition, EPS computes the *triggering set*, i.e., the set of triggered rules left behind by the round of rule processing.

If the input event base E contains an occurrence of the event *rollback* (e.g., due to the execution of a rollback statement in the action part of a previously executed rule or in the user transaction), then the output is the original database prior to the user transaction (S_{or}) and the empty event base and triggering set. A *rollback* can also be forced when the number of EPS executions exceeds a given threshold.

When there is no *rollback* event, the behavior of EPS is:

1. analyze the event part of all rules to get the current triggering set,

2. choose nondeterministically one activated rule (this is done by procedure *Choose*, which thus implements the *conflict resolution strategy*),

3. compute the bindings (Θ') for the condition part of the selected rule

4. perform event consumption, and

5. possibly execute the action part of the selected rule.

Note that since event consumption occurs whenever a rule is considered, the output event base may differ from the input event base even if no rule is executed.

Based on the illustrated rule execution algorithm, the semantics of rule processing is described by means of a binary relation Γ, defined as follows:

$$\langle\langle S, E\rangle, \langle S', E'\rangle\rangle \in \Gamma \quad \Leftrightarrow \quad \exists \tau, \tau' : \langle\langle S, E, \tau\rangle, \langle S', E', \tau'\rangle\rangle \in \overline{EPS}$$
$$\wedge \langle S', E', \tau'\rangle \text{ is a fixpoint of } EPS$$

where

---

[6]The above states of core rules also correspond to the states of Chimera rules: A Chimera rule is activated when at least one of its triggering events occurs, is considered when its condition is evaluated (irrespective of the result), and is executed when its reaction is performed.

GLOBAL CONSTANTS: the rule set $\mathcal{R}$, the original state S_{or}.
INPUT: a database S, an event base E, a triggering set τ.
OUTPUT: a new triple $\langle S, E, \tau \rangle$.
BEGIN
    IF*rollback* $\in E$ THEN   (*Rollback detected*)
      $S := S_{or}$; $E = \emptyset$; $\tau := \emptyset$; RETURN(S, E, τ)
    ELSE   (*Process rules*)
      FORALL R_j IN $\mathcal{R}$ DO   (*Triggering*)
        Θ_j := Event-bindings(R_j, E);   (*Evaluate event query*)
        IF $\Theta_j \neq \emptyset$ THEN $\tau := \tau \cup R_j$ END (*IF*)
      END (* FORALL*)
      Selected-rule := NIL; (*Consideration*)
      WHILE $\tau \neq \emptyset \wedge$ Selected-rule = NIL DO   (* Not found and still candidates *)
        Candidate := *Choose*(τ); $\tau := \tau -$ Candidate;   (* Pick next candidate *)
        Θ' := Condition-bindings(Candidate, S, E); (* Evaluate condition *)
        E := Perform-EB-update(Candidate,E) (* Consume events *)
        IF $\Theta' \neq \emptyset$ THEN Selected-rule := Candidate(Θ') END (*IF*)
      END (*WHILE*)
      IF Selected-rule $\neq$ NIL THEN
        $\langle S, E \rangle$:= Perform-action(Selected-rule, S, E); (*Execution*)
      END (*IF*)
      RETURN $\langle S, E, \tau \rangle$
    END (*IF*)
END

FIGURE 6.2
The Elementary Production Step.

- EPS is a binary relation that associates the input and output of the EPS algorithm (i.e., EPS contains a tuple $\langle\langle S, E, \tau\rangle, \langle S', E', \tau'\rangle\rangle$ iff $\langle S', E', \tau'\rangle$ is a possible output of EPS applied to $\langle S, E, \tau\rangle$;

- a triple $\langle S, E, \tau\rangle$ is a fixpoint of EPS, if $\not\exists\, \langle S', E', \tau'\rangle \neq \langle S, E, \tau\rangle$ such that $\langle\langle S, E, \tau\rangle, \langle S', E', \tau'\rangle\rangle \in EPS$.

- $\overline{EPS}$ is the transitive closure of EPS.

Intuitively, Γ describes state transformations of the database and event base from an initial state a to a *quiescent state* b, obtained from a by a finite number of applications of the rule execution algorithm. Thus the tuple $\langle a, b\rangle$ must be in the transitive closure of the input/output relation EPS. In addition, for b to be a quiescent state, it is necessary that rule processing halts when b is reached; thus b must be a fixpoint of EPS, i.e., a state from which the rule execution algorithm cannot evolve.

Note that relation Γ gives a clean representation of the nondeterminism of rule computation when the conflict resolution procedure *Choose* is nondeterministic. The *Choose* procedure, not described in detail here, reflects the partial order induced by the priorities explicitly defined in Chimera rules and in auxiliary core rules. Due to nondeterminism, relation EPS may contain several tuples corresponding to one input state, one for each possible choice of the next rule to execute. Accordingly, $\overline{EPS}$ contains "branches" for each nondeterministic choice, and hence Γ lists all the possible quiescent states reached from the initial state of rule computation.

6.2.4   Rules and Transactions

To complete the semantic description, it is necessary to define how rule execution is intermixed with the operations of user transactions. Each transaction is subdivided into transaction lines. Execution is started by performing the instructions of the first transaction line; after that, the first round of rule processing is done (limited to immediate rules). If rule processing reaches a quiescent state S_1, then the second transaction line is applied to S_1. Execution proceeds in this fashion until the last transaction line is completed. Then a final round of rule processing is performed, this time including deferred rules. The quiescent state eventually reached is taken as the final state of the transaction.

6.3
Examples

The first example rule reacts immediately to violations of an integrity constraint specifying that a manager's salary must be greater than each of his employees' salaries. The rule sets employee salaries that are too high equal to the salary of their managers.

```
define immediate trigger immAdjustSalary for employee
   events    create, modify(salary)
   condition Self.salary > Self.mgr.salary
   actions   modify(employee.salary,Self,Self.mgr.salary)
```

Note that in this targeted rule the variable Self is implicitly defined on the target class *employee*.

The next example illustrates the use of event formulas and of the function *old*. The rule selects all employees who get, in the course of the transaction, a high salary raise (possibly caused by several small salary raises due to individual modify operations). Note that the rule is event-preserving, therefore all modifications since the transaction start are accumulated at each rule consideration. Further, note that the condition part evaluates the salary difference between the state before transaction execution and the new state determined at rule processing time. The reaction calls the external procedure *monitor-Salary*.

```
define event-preserving trigger modifySpecialEmp for employee
   events    modify(salary)
   condition occurred(modify(salary),X), integer(Y),
             Y = X.salary - old(X.salary), Y > 50000
   actions   monitorSalary(X,Y)
```

The last example shows how active rules can automatically process orders. The schema includes classes for *order* and *client*; the attribute *issuer* maps each *order* to the corresponding *client*. Orders have an *amount* and a *status* which becomes "accepted" after successful processing. Clients have a *credit* and a Boolean attribute *trusted*. Orders are processed regardless of their amount if clients are trusted, otherwise the client must have sufficient credit for the order. When the credit of a trusted client drops below 50,000, the client is no longer trusted. This behavior is coded by the following four deferred rules.

```
define trigger process-trusted-order for order
  events    create
  condition occurred(create, X),
            X.issuer.trusted = "true"
  actions   modify(order.status, X, "accepted"),
            modify(client.credit, X.issuer,
                    X.issuer.credit - X.amount)

define trigger process-N/A-untrusted-order for order
  events    create, modify(amount)
  condition occurred(create, modify(amount), X),
            X.client.trusted = "false",
            X. status != "accepted",
            X.amount - X.client.credit > 0
  actions   modify(order.status, X, "accepted"),
            modify(client.credit, X.issuer,
                    X.issuer.credit-X.amount)

  define trigger process-A-untrusted-order for order
  events    modify(amount)
  condition occurred(modify(amount), X),
            X.client.trusted = "false",
            X. status = "accepted",
            Integer(D), D = X.amount - old(X.amount)
            D - X.client.credit > 0
  actions   modify(client.credit, X.issuer,
                    X.issuer.credit - D)

define trigger drop-trust for client
  events    modify(credit)
  condition Self.credit < 50,000
  actions   modify(client.trusted, Self, "false")
```

Several applications have been prototyped in Chimera, including *EMS* (Energy Management System of ENEL, the Italian Energy Board), *ODD1* (an Oncology Database), and *TMS* (Test Management System for Software Engineering). Some of these applications are described in Chapter 10.

6.4
Architecture and Implementation Features

A prototype of Chimera focused on active rules has been developed at the Politecnico di Milano. The Chimera prototype is implemented on Sun workstations running the SUN-OS 4.1.3 Operating System. The code is written in GNU C++ and uses the GNU standard libraries; the user interface is implemented in *Motif*. Figure 6.3 represents the overall architecture of the prototype. The target DBMS used in the implementation is *ALGRES* [CCL⁺90], an extended relational DBMS characterized by a rich schema (supporting orthogonal type constructors such as sets, multisets, and lists) and a powerful algebraic language (supporting operations over complex relations).

6.4.1   Compilation Techniques

Due to the complexity of the Chimera language, a new compiler construction technique has been adopted: the grammar is decomposed into subgrammars, and a family of compilers has been developed, one for each of the subgrammars. Interaction among compilers is maintained by a *federated compiler's compiler*.

Chimera transactions and active rules are submitted to compilers which perform lexical analysis and produce their representations in an Intermediate Graphical Language called *Igloo* [PP93]. Igloo graphs are translated into blocks of ALGRES instructions. Every transaction line corresponds to a single ALGRES block, while the compilation of a rule generates a pair of blocks, one corresponding to the condition and the other one to the action. This permits ALGRES to execute the condition part of a rule without executing the corresponding action. The event base is stored by means of ALGRES relations and is manipulated by the ALGRES blocks generated by compilers.

6.4.2   Run-Time System

The run-time system is responsible for invoking the ALGRES executor on the blocks generated by the compilers. In addition, the run-time system reacts to user-level commands issued directly from the system interface, such as *commit* or *rollback*.

Events that don't trigger any rules need not be handled by the run-time system. In order to determine relevant events for each rule, the run-time system inspects an *Event/Rule Table*, which is updated by the rule compiler whenever a new rule is added.

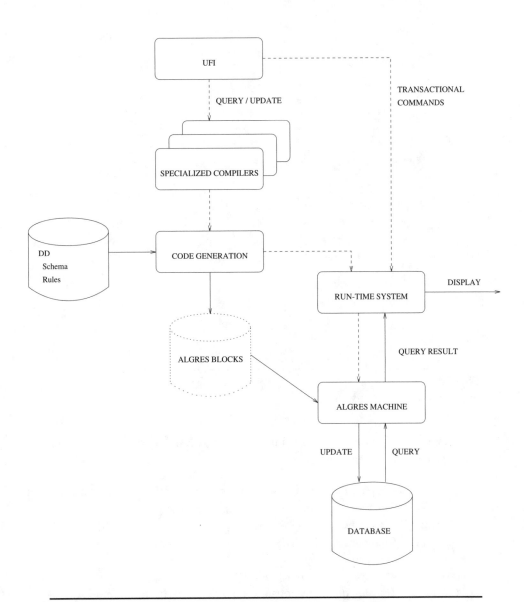

FIGURE 6.3
Compilation and execution of Chimera statements.

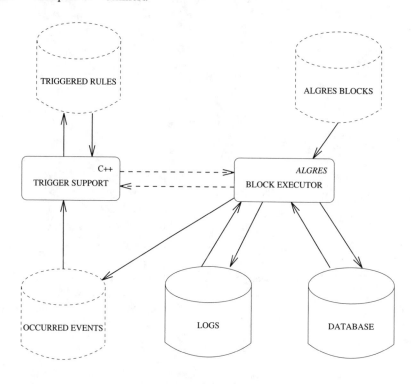

FIGURE 6.4
Architecture of the run-time system.

Figure 6.4 expands the run-time system block of Figure 6.3. The run-time system has two major components:

- The *Block Executor* retrieves the correct ALGRES block and invokes an ALGRES Executor for processing the relevant compiled code. It is activated either by the user interface (which has invoked the suitable compiler to generate ALGRES blocks from Chimera transaction lines) or by the *Trigger Support*.

- The *Trigger Support* is responsible for selecting the next rule for consideration. It receives control from the user interface at the end of a transaction line (or at *commit* or *savepoint* evaluation), and returns control when rule processing has terminated (either at a fixpoint or due to a *rollback*).

The *Trigger Support* algorithms implement, in an efficient way, the rule semantics defined in Section 3. In order to keep track of event processing, two data structures are used:

- The *Occurred Events* table records all the event instances relevant to a particular transaction.

- The *Triggered Rules* table records the evolution of event processing for each individual rule. In particular, *Triggered Rules* is implemented as a timestamp pointing into *Occurred Events* for each rule, which separates already processed events from events that still need to be considered. Timestamp management reflects the mode of consumption of each individual rule.

Tables *Occurred Events* and *Triggered Rules* were first introduced in the implementation of Starburst (see Chapter 4). Their design in Chimera does not incorporate multi-user features, but it does incorporate some optimization due to OID exploitation.

6.4.3 Debugger

The Chimera prototype includes a sophisticated *debugging mode* for development of active rule applications. Debugging mode can be entered at any time during transaction rule processing by issuing a special command. When the command is intercepted, execution of the current rule is completed (if rules are being processed), after which execution proceeds interactively. Interactive execution of rules is available at two levels of granularity:

- At the *rule step* level: After each rule execution, rule processing is halted and the situation is presented to the user. At this level there is no possibility of interrupting the run-time system during the computation of triggered rules and the evaluation of rules' conditions.

- At the *intra-rule step* level: Rule processing is halted at each of the three fundamental moments of rule execution: triggering, condition evaluation, and action execution. The user can obtain information on the state of rule processing and influence (in a limited way) the behavior of the rule executor.

The following functionalities are available in either mode:

- *Inspection of the Conflict Set*: After execution of a transaction line or of a rule, the set of triggered rules (called the *Conflict Set*) is displayed in a scrollable list in order of priority.

- *Inspection of the Deferred Conflict Set*: Displays those triggered rules whose execution is deferred.

- *Information on Rules*: Displays information about a selected rule.

- *Rule Activation/Deactivation*: Rules can be explicitly deactivated during debugging, so that they are disregarded during subsequent rule processing. A deactivated rule can be reactivated at any time.

- *Information on Occurred Events*: All events since the beginning of a transaction are displayed in a scrollable list. Each event is described by its event type, the list of the OIDs of the objects affected by the event, and the indication of the database state in which the event has occurred. For identifying the various states of the database, all intermediate states since the beginning of the transaction are numbered progressively. Events are listed in order of occurrence.

- *Rule Source Code*: Displays in a pop-up text window the source code of any rule.

When the debugging mode is intra-rule step, the following additional options are available:

- *Processing Status*: A graphical icon is used to show the current point of execution, either the computation of triggered rules, the evaluation of a rule's condition, or the execution of a rule's action.

- *Detection of First Executable Rule*: Finds the rule with highest priority, among those that have not been considered yet, whose condition is satisfied in the current database state.

- *Modification of Dynamic Priorities*: Alters the chosen priority of triggered rules with equal static priority. In this way, it is possible to force the selection of a different rule from the one that would be chosen using the built-in conflict resolution strategy.

- *Information on Condition Bindings*: Allows inspection of the objects that are bound by the evaluation of the rule's condition; these are presented through the graphical interface of ALGRES.

6.5
Summary and Future Directions

This chapter described the active rule language of Chimera, a new-generation database language integrating object-oriented, deductive, and active components. The distinguishing features of active rules in Chimera are integration with object-orientation and availability of alternative semantics. Integration with object-orientation provides both a structuring mechanism (defining active rules in the context of classes) and a powerful mechanism for tracking events (by means of object identifiers). Offering a rich spectrum of alternative semantics for active rules enables the use of rules for many different applications.

The prototype implementation of Chimera, completed in June 1994, has yielded several interesting observations:

1. The set-oriented nature of active rules in Chimera has proved to be useful for the compilation and optimization of rules. For example, optimization techniques for the condition part of rules are identical to those used for the *select* query primitive.

2. Early evaluation of event predicates (*occurred* and *holds*) has proved to be useful for immediately suspending the evaluation of a rule condition if the relevant predicates are empty. This built-in optimization reinforces the generally held principle that rules should be *incremental*, i.e., they should use state changes (deltas) in their condition whenever possible [CW90].

3. In deciding how to compute event instances, a trade-off analysis was performed between doing most work at compile-time or doing some of it at run-time. As a result of this analysis, most of the work (including the computation of events propagating due to generalization hierarchies) is done at compile-time. However, the computation of event predicates from event instances was left to the run-time component.

4. To implement active rules easily and efficiently there is a need for mechanisms in the underlying DBMS that automatically and transparently select objects affected by operations and store their identifiers in appropriate collections.

5. Preliminary measures of performance are encouraging: Active rule selection is very fast and thus the overall execution times are dominated

by execution time of the ALGRES code produced for transactions and for rules.

The current Chimera prototype will be extended in at least two directions:

- The user interface will gradually evolve into a complete design tool for active rules. Such a tool can be used for understanding rule behavior at a conceptual level, then mapping the behavior into a set of Chimera rules or rules that can be supported by commercial relational products.

- The system will incorporate design techniques and tools for mapping views and constraints defined in Chimera into suitable rules, thereby implementing missing parts of the full Chimera language on top of a prototype which is already available.

7

The HiPAC Project

Umeshwar Dayal, Alejandro P. Buchmann,
and Sharma Chakravarthy

The initial goal of the HiPAC project was to provide the necessary infrastructure for event-driven applications where timely response to monitored situations is critical. It was recognized early in the project that this implied two major lines of research: active database capabilities provided through ECA rules, and time-constrained data management. Both were novel technologies for which few results existed at the time the HiPAC project was started in 1987. Therefore, it was decided to separate work on the two areas but provide for links between them. For example, the active portion of HiPAC considers temporal events and includes facilities for specifying timing constraints as part of the rule language. The time-constrained data management portion of the HiPAC project, in turn, includes the notion of a contingency plan that is triggered whenever a transaction cannot be completed in time.

The HiPAC project concentrated on the development of basic abstractions that would be useful for a variety of applications. To this effect, the requirements of many different applications were analyzed and their common features extracted. Examples of such applications were power- and communication-network management, chemical plant control, flight control, battle management, shop-floor control, and automated trading. In addition to these applications, the utility of the ECA-rule paradigm for internal DBMS use was studied. Examples include materialized view maintenance, integrity control and access control, and as support for blackboard systems.

The resulting rule language and the execution model reflect, in their flexibility, this extensive requirements analysis. HiPAC has a clear separation of events, conditions, and actions. Further, through the definition of various coupling modes between a triggering transaction and the condition and action portions of triggered rules, a powerful execution model is used. The use of the various features of the rule language and execution semantics has been illustrated through various applications, among others, the handling of complex integrity constraints in computer-aided design applications, and transactional workflow management.

7.1
Rule Model and Language

HiPAC is an active object-oriented database management system. It extends a basic object-oriented database management system with ECA rules. The underlying object model is based on the semantic model DAPLEX [Shi81] extended with object-oriented features in PDM [MD87] and OODAPLEX

[Day89]. Only those aspects of the underlying object model needed to understand the semantics of rules are presented here (for details, see [MD87, Day89]). The main ingredients of the model are **entities**, which model objects; **functions**, which model the structure and behavior of objects, the attributes of objects, operations on objects, and relationships among objects; and **entity types**, which group objects with similar structure and behavior. Entity types are organized in a type hierarchy. Subtypes inherit functions from their supertypes, but may redefine the inherited functions and their implementations. Although multiple inheritance is supported, inheritance conflicts are disallowed. Type-specific **create**, **modify**, and **delete** functions may be defined over some entity types, and like other functions may be inherited and overridden.

Rules, like all other forms of data, are treated as entities. There is a **rule** entity type, and every rule is an instance of this type. Special functions are defined over the rule type to **fire**, **enable**, and **disable** rules (the syntax and semantics of these functions will be defined presently). Like other entities, rules can be created, modified, or deleted (by invoking the appropriate functions defined over the **rule** type). Furthermore, rules are subject to the same transaction semantics as other data objects: a transaction must obtain a read lock in order to **fire** or **enable** it, and a write lock in order to **modify**, **delete**, or **disable** it. Hence, a rule that is in the process of being fired or enabled by one transaction cannot be concurrently modified, deleted, or disabled by another. Rules are subject to the same authorization mechanisms as other data objects: a user must have the appropriate privileges to invoke a desired function on a rule.

Treating rules as first class objects also allows for organizing the collection of rules in the database. Subtypes of the **rule** type can be defined. These provide named subsets of rules that not only inherit useful functions such as **fire**, but can additionally introduce new functions to model attributes of rules or to relate rules to other objects in the database.

7.1.1 The Rule Type

The **rule** type is defined as a subtype of the most generic type **entity**. The event, condition, and action parts of a rule are defined by three functions over the **rule** type:

- **event**, which maps the rule entity to an **event** entity;

- **condition**, which maps the rule entity into a pair consisting of a **coupling_mode** and a set of queries; and

- **action**, which maps the rule entity into a pair consisting of a **coupling-mode** and a program.

Queries are written in the query language of the HiPAC system (details are omitted here; see [CBB$^+$89]). Programs may be written in one of several host languages with embedded data manipulation commands.

A coupling-mode is one of **immediate, deferred, decoupled,** or **causally-dependent-decoupled** (abbreviated **CD**), and specifies the execution scope in which the rule's condition is evaluated relative to the transaction in which the event occurred, and, similarly, the execution scope in which the action is evaluated relative to the transaction in which the condition was evaluated. Coupling modes will be explained more clearly in Section 7.2.

7.1.2   Operations on Rules

The operations on **rule** entities include the redefined operations **create, delete,** and **modify**. The **create** operation takes the specification of an event, a pair consisting of a coupling mode and a set of queries, and a pair consisting of a coupling mode and a program, and inserts a new rule into the database. The **delete** operation deletes the specified rule. The **modify** operation takes a rule and a specification of changes to be made to its event, condition, or action, and produces a modified rule.

Two additional operations, **enable** and **disable**, are defined on rules. These operations selectively enable and disable a rule for a specified set of entities. If a rule r is disabled for entity e, this means that e will not participate in the evaluation of r's condition or action, even if r's triggering event occurs.

The operations on rules described so far are invoked on behalf of applications. The **fire** operation is performed automatically by the system when the event specified in the rule occurs. It creates a **rule-firing** entity to record the parameters of the event occurrence; then, it causes the rule's condition to be evaluated; if the condition is satisfied, it causes the rule's action to be executed. The rule's condition is satisfied if at least one of its queries returns a nonempty answer. The queries' results are inserted into the rule-firing entity and passed to the action.

Note that these operations have been defined on individual rules. HiPAC's data manipulation language provides statements to operate on collections of entities. Thus, for example, the following statement selectively disables a set of rules of type R for some entities of type E. (P and Q are predicates specified over entities of type R and E respectively.)

for each r **in** R **where** $P(r)$
    disable $(r, \{\ e$ **in** E **where** $Q(e)\ \})$
endfor

7.1.3   The Event Type

Events in HiPAC are also first-class entities; they are instances of the type **event**. Associated with each event is a **parameters** function, which returns a tuple of typed formal parameters, each of which is a pair of a variable name and an entity type. The event type has a single operation **signal**, which is usually executed by event detector components of the system, but may also be explicitly executed by users or application programs. This function returns an **event_occurrence** entity, in which the formal parameters specified for the event are bound to actual entities of the specified types.

The **event** type has two subtypes: **primitive-event** and **composite-event**. The primitive events are of three subtypes: **data-manipulation-events**, **clock-events**, and **external-notification-events**.

Since HiPAC is an object-oriented DBMS, all data manipulation occurs through the execution of functions on entities. To cause rules to be triggered when some data manipulation function is executed, a **data-manipulation-event** associated with the function has to be defined. In fact, since functions do not execute instantaneously, it is possible to associate events with the beginning and the end of a function execution. Thus, each **data-manipulation-event** has a function **on** that identifies the function f whose execution causes the event to be signaled; a function **at** that specifies whether this event is to be signaled at the **beginning** of f's execution or at the **end**; and the **parameters** function, which typically includes the formal arguments of f, but may also include other environment variables (such as the time of invocation or the identifier of the transaction in which f was invoked).

Note that events can be defined for the generic data manipulation operations **create**, **delete**, and **modify**, as well as for type-specific operations. Also, since HiPAC's object model allows operations for manipulating individual entities and operations for manipulating collections of entities, events may be defined for any of these. For **modify** operations (and similarly, for operations that **insert** into or **delete** from collections), the parameters of the event include **old** and **new** values of the operation's arguments.

Events are also associated with the beginning and end of transactions. The arguments of such events include the transaction, user, and session identifiers.

A second subtype of **primitive_event** is the **clock_event**. Clock events can be **absolute**, **relative**, or **periodic**. Associated with an **absolute** event is a time point. The event is signaled when this time point occurs. Associated with a **relative** event is another event (the **reference event**), and a time interval. The event is signaled when the time interval elapses after the reference event has been signaled. Associated with a **periodic** event is also a **reference** event and a time interval (the **period**). The event is signaled first when the reference event is signaled, and then at intervals equal to the period thereafter. Clock events can have arguments, which are bound at the time the event is signaled.

The third subtype of **primitive-event** is the **external_notification_ event**. These have no special functions other than **parameters**. They are signaled explicitly by a user or application program rather than automatically by components of the HiPAC system, and the signal operation specifies how to bind the parameters.

Additional subtypes of events, with special parameters or special semantics for the signal operation, can be defined.

The composite events are defined by three parameterized types: **disjunction**, **sequence**, and **closure**. HiPAC's query language is extended with an expression language for denoting composite events. Let $E1$ and $E2$ be two events. Then, **disjunction(E1,E2)** (denoted $E1|E2$) is an event that is signaled whenever $E1$ is signaled or $E2$ is signaled. The parameters of $E1|E2$ are the discriminated union of the parameters of $E1$ and $E2$ (i.e., the parameters of $E1|E2$ are bound to the parameters of $E1$ or of $E2$ depending on which one occurred).

The event **sequence(E1,E2)** (denoted $E1; E2$) is signaled when $E2$ is signaled provided that $E1$ had previously been signaled within some interval. The default interval in HiPAC is a transaction. The parameters of $E1; E2$ are bound to the concatenation of the parameters of $E1$ and $E2$.

The event **closure(E1)** (denoted $E1^*$) is signaled when $E1$ has been signaled one or more times within an interval. Again, the default interval in HiPAC is a transaction. The parameters of $E1^*$ are bound to the minimal set containing the parameters of all occurrences of $E1$ that comprise $E1^*$. The closure event is useful if one wants a rule to fire only once per transaction, no matter how many times the event $E1$ occurred during the transaction (provided it occurred at least once). This is especially useful for integrity checking, where a constraint is typically evaluated at the end of a transaction rather than every time an update occurs.

7.2
Semantics of Rule Execution

Underlying HiPAC's rule execution semantics are two important concepts: *coupling modes* and *extended nested transactions*. Coupling modes are covered in Section 7.2.1, while extended nested transactions are covered in Section 7.2.2. Section 7.2.3 explains how the execution order of rules can be influenced, and Section 7.2.4 discusses the semantics of failure handling and recovery in HiPAC.

7.2.1 Coupling Modes

Coupling modes give the rule definer fine control over how a rule is to be processed relative to the transaction that triggered the rule. The rule definer specifies a coupling mode between the event and condition, and another (possibly different) coupling mode between the condition and action; these determine where transaction boundaries should occur. Three basic coupling modes are supported: **immediate**, **deferred**, and **decoupled**, plus a variant of the decoupled mode, **causally-dependent decoupled**.

Suppose that transaction T executes an operation E, and a rule R has been defined, with event E, condition C, and action A. If the E-C coupling mode is **immediate**, then C is evaluated within T immediately when E is detected, preempting the execution of the remaining steps of T. If the mode is **deferred**, then C is evaluated within T, but after the last operation in T and before T commits. If the mode is **decoupled**, then C is evaluated in a separate transaction. The same options are available for the C-A coupling. The deferred mode is especially useful for checking integrity constraints. The decoupled mode is useful for breaking up a long cascading sequence of triggers into short transactions. For example, in an inventory control application, there might be a rule that checks the quantity on hand of some item in the database, and triggers an action to restock the item when the quantity on hand falls below some threshold. There is no need for the restocking action to be executed within the transaction that caused the quantity on hand to fall below the threshold. Another example is the maintenance of replicas in distributed database systems: If a transaction updates the primary copy of a data item stored at one server, the updates have to be propagated to replicas stored at other servers. It may be acceptable to perform these updates in transactions that are separate from the original transaction (to avoid expensive commit processing).

When the condition or action is decoupled, the triggered transaction (call it T') can execute concurrently with the triggering transaction T. If serializability is the only correctness criterion, then it might happen that T' is serialized before T. This, however, may violate some notion of *causality* in the real world: T "sees" the results of T'; also, T may abort after T' committed. For applications where causality is important, the HiPAC model allows the rule definer to specify that the decoupled transaction is *causally dependent*, i.e., T' must be serialized after T, and T' can commit only if T commits. This mode is useful for the replica maintenance example above.

Note that sometimes causality is not necessarily desirable. For example, consider a rule that writes a record in the security log whenever a user accesses some data object. The security log record must be written irrespective of whether the original transaction that accessed the data object commits or aborts. Also, it doesn't matter if the triggered transaction is serialized ahead of the original transaction.

7.2.2   An Extended Nested Transaction Model

The execution of rules under the various coupling modes is governed by an extension of the *nested transaction* model of [Lis85] and [Mos82]. HiPAC's extended nested transaction model is appropriate for modeling the execution of a user transaction coupled with the execution of rules for three reasons. First, its structure accommodates nicely the hierarchical relationship between a triggering transaction and rules triggered by it, including the cascaded triggering of rules. Second, it allows a set of rules triggered by the same event to be executed concurrently within a transaction. Finally, it allows rule execution to be modularly committed or undone without requiring the entire transaction to be committed or undone as well.

A nested transaction is a transaction that is started from inside another transaction (the *parent transaction*). In the original nested transaction model of [Lis85, Mos82], nested transactions are created explicitly by the parent transaction. These nested transactions are called *subtransactions* of the parent. A transaction may contain any number of subtransactions, some of which may be required to execute sequentially, others may execute concurrently. Subtransactions may recursively spawn subtransactions of their own, forming a transaction tree of arbitrary depth. While a subtransaction is executing, its parent is suspended. Sibling subtransactions, however, may execute concurrently. Sibling subtransactions are serializable at every level of the transaction tree. However, this intra-transaction concurrency is not visible to other transactions, i.e., the entire transaction tree still executes as a single atomic transaction. Subtransactions commit relative to their parents, so if a subtransaction commits but its parent aborts, the effects of the subtransaction will be undone. Thus, the effects of a subtransaction are not visible until all its ancestors up to and including the root have committed. A subtransaction may be aborted without causing its parent to abort. Thus, upon failure of a subtransaction, its parent can either go on with the computation or create another subtransaction to retry the computation that was aborted.

Nested transactions are used for rule execution as follows. If the triggering event occurs inside a transaction (the *triggering transaction*), the system scheduler, or the transaction manager, creates a nested transaction (the *triggered transaction*) of the triggering transaction to execute the rule. Since HiPAC also allows events (e.g., clock events and external notification events) to be signaled by processes or humans outside transactions, for these events a new top transaction is started to execute the rule (and all four E-C coupling modes have identical semantics in this case).

The triggered transaction T' does the following: first, it creates a nested transaction C that evaluates the condition part of the rule; then, if C commits and the condition is satisfied, it starts another nested transaction A that executes the action part of the rule. If the E-C coupling mode is immediate, then T' is a subtransaction of the triggering transaction T (and C is a subtransaction of T'). If the C-A coupling mode is also immediate, then A is also a subtransaction of T' and is executed sequentially after C.

The deferred and decoupled modes require extending the basic nested transaction model to allow three more types of nested transactions.

First, *deferred subtransactions* can be created. The execution of deferred subtransactions is explicitly delayed until the end of the user's top transaction T, a point that is referred to as the *cycle-0 end*. (At this point, all the operations of the original transaction and of immediate rules triggered by it have been executed.) When T reaches its cycle-0 end, a deferred subtransaction is started, and runs as a proper subtransaction of T. If several deferred subtransactions are created before T reaches its cycle-0 end, then all these subtransactions are started as concurrent subtransactions in *cycle-1* at cycle-0 end. If the processing of subtransactions in cycle-1 causes more deferred transactions to be created, the latter are started when all subtransactions in cycle-1 have finished, and are started as concurrent subtransactions of T in cycle-2. The cycles of execution of T continue until no more deferred subtransactions are created. Like a regular subtransaction, the commit of a deferred subtransaction is conditional on its triggering transaction committing through the top.

Thus, if the E-C coupling mode for a rule is deferred, then the triggered transaction T' that executes the rule is started as a deferred subtransaction. Similarly, if the C-A coupling mode is deferred, then the action A is executed in a deferred subtransaction.

The second extension to the nested transaction model allows top transactions to be started from within another transaction (the *creator*). Such a *nested top transaction*, unlike a subtransaction, has no special privileges relative to its creator; for example, it cannot read an object modified by its creator. Furthermore, the commit of a nested top transaction is not relative to its creator, but rather independent. Note that the nested top transaction is not constrained to follow its creator in serialization order. When the E-C coupling mode is decoupled, then the triggered transaction is executed as a nested top transaction (and similarly for the C-A coupling mode).

Finally, a *causally-dependent-top*, (or *CDtop*, for short) transaction can be spawned from inside another transaction. This type of "nesting" imposes the causality constraint. Let T be the user's top transaction and T' be the causally-dependent transaction created either by T or by one of its descendants. Then T' is serialized after the execution of T. A nested CDtop transaction, unlike a nested top transaction, is *commit-dependent* on its creator, i.e., T' commits only if its creator commits through the top.

7.2.3   Controlling Rule Execution Order

An event may trigger more than one rule. In the HiPAC model, these rules are executed as concurrent nested transactions of the triggering transaction (regular or deferred subtransactions, or top or CDtop nested transactions). As concurrently running siblings, their execution is serializable. Note that this is in contrast to many other active rule systems, in which rules are executed sequentially, using some conflict resolution mechanism to select a single rule if multiple rules are triggered by the same event.

The HiPAC model supports three mechanisms for controlling the execution order of concurrent triggered transactions. First, priorities can be assigned to rules (via a *priority* function defined for the **rule** object type). Instead of numerical priorities, the model supports a definable number of ordered priority classes or *urgencies* (e.g., high, medium, low). Triggered transactions of the highest urgency are executed first, then those of the next highest urgency, and so on. Within an urgency, transactions are executed concurrently. The model can easily be extended to partially ordered urgencies.

Second, the cycle mechanism described earlier orders the execution of deferred rules. This is useful for rules that evaluate integrity constraints and attempt to repair the database state when a constraint is violated. Cycling ensures that the first "generation" of repair actions is completed before the constraints are reevaluated; this could make it easier to write the repair actions. The cycle mechanism interacts with urgencies: Within each cycle, the subtransactions are executed in urgency order.

Third, for decoupled transactions, there is a *pipelining* mechanism. A decoupled transaction T', triggered by transaction T, satisfies the *pipelining* property if for all transactions T_i that are serialized before (after) T, any decoupled transaction T_i' triggered by T_i is serialized before (respectively, after) T'. Pipelining allows the execution order of triggered transactions to reflect that of the triggering transactions. For example, suppose the output of a sensor is displayed on a screen, and a (causally dependent) decoupled rule is used to update the display every time the sensor's output changes. If many sensor update transactions occur within a short period, several decoupled display update transactions may be queued. For the display to correctly reflect the sequence of updates, the display update actions should be pipelined.

7.2.4   Failure Semantics and Recovery

The HiPAC model supports two options for handling the failure of a rule: Either the execution of that rule alone is aborted and the triggering transaction continues from the point where the rule was triggered, or the whole transaction in which the rule execution occurs is aborted. Note that in the basic nested transaction model, the failure of a subtransaction results only in aborting the failed subtransaction. The parent of the aborted subtransaction waits for its child's termination at a point at which it can take appropriate measures. In the extended model, however, rules may be executed as nested transactions anywhere in the program without the parent (creator) explicitly starting them or even being aware of their execution. As a result, the normal failure semantics must be extended to allow a subtransaction or deferred subtransaction to request that the top transaction and all its descendants (excluding nested top transactions) be aborted. For nested top or CDtop transactions, the failure of the nested transaction cannot affect the creator, since the creator may already have terminated.

The recovery of triggered transactions after a system failure is also an important issue. In HiPAC, events signaled by committed transactions are automatically recovered as part of normal transaction recovery. For temporal

events and those external events that are signaled outside transactions, the
definer of the event can specify whether or not to recover the signals. (This
is done via a function *recoverable* associated with the **event** object type.)
Then, uncommitted transactions triggered by these recovered event signals
are restarted.

7.3
Examples

This section illustrates event and rule definition, and the use of the various coupling modes, in a simplified stock trading application. The database
schema includes the entity types *stock* and *customer*. For stock entities, the
database records an identification code, the current price, and the price at
the close of the previous day. For customer entities, the database records a
taxpayer identifier, the current balance in the customer's account, and a set
of stocks currently being monitored for this customer's account.

> **type** stock **is** entity
> **function** stockid: stock $\rightarrow$ string
> **function** price: stock $\rightarrow$ money
> **function** closingprice: stock $\rightarrow$ money
> **type** customer **is** entity
> **function** custid: customer $\rightarrow$ string
> **function** balance: customer $\rightarrow$ money
> **function** monitored: customer $\rightarrow$ {stock}
> **function** trade: (customer, stock, signed_integer) $\rightarrow$ customer

Stock price quotes are received from an external source (an on-line feed,
for example). For those stocks that are being monitored for some customer,
a transaction updates the database to reflect the new price. (Also, if this
is the last quote of the day, then the closing price is updated.) When the
price is updated, if some specified condition is true of the price, then trade
(buy or sell) actions are initiated. These actions cause the customers' account
balances to change, subject to the integrity constraint that balances cannot
drop below 0.

To achieve this functionality, several events and rules are defined. An
external notification event, *quote*, is signaled when a new price quote for a
stock is received; its parameters include the *stockid* and *price*. The event
is signaled explicitly by an external application (within or outside a transaction). It is defined to be recoverable, so that even occurrences signaled outside

transactions can be reconstructed after a system crash. Two data manipulation events, *update_price* and *update_balance*, track changes in stock prices and customers' accounts balances, respectively; the parameters of *update_price* include the *stockid* of the stock whose price has changed and the old and new prices; the parameters of *update_balance* include the *custid* of the customer whose account balance has been modified, and the old and new values of the account balance.

```
quote := create external_notification_event
            (recoverable := true
            parameters := [stockid:string, price:money, time:time])
update_price := create data_manipulation_event
            (on := update_stock(s:stock, p:money)
            at := end
            parameters := [stockid:string, oldprice:money,
                              newprice:money])
update_balance := create data_manipulation_event
            (on := update_customer(c:customer, amount:money)
            at := end
            parameters := [custid:string, oldbalance:money,
                              newbalance:money])
```

Several rules are created, of which three are shown.

```
R1 := create rule
      (event := quote [stockid, price, time],
      condition := [mode := immediate, cond :=
                        {s in stock where stockid(s) = stockid and
                        for some c in customer (s in monitored(c))} ],
      action := [mode := CD-decoupled pipelined, act :=
                        update_stock (s, price)] )
R2 := create rule
      (event := update_price [stockid, oldprice, newprice],
      condition := [mode := CD-decoupled, cond :=
                        {c in customer where for some s in stock
                        (stockid(s) = stockid and s in monitored(c)
                        and newprice < 50 and closingprice(s) > 60)} ],
      action := [mode := immediate, act :=
                        for each c in cond
```

trade(c, stockid, +100)

endfor])

R3 := create rule

(event := update_balance [custid, oldbalance, newbalance] *,

condition := [mode := deferred, cond :=

{c in customer where custid(c) = custid

and balance(c) < 0}],

action := [mode := immediate, act := abort-top])

Rule $R1$ fires when a *quote* event is signaled. It checks if this stock is being monitored for some customer; if so, then it updates the stock price in the database. The E-C coupling mode is specified to be **immediate**. The C-A mode is specified to be **CD-decoupled**, so as not to hold the signaling transaction until the database has been updated. However, if for some reason the signaling transaction aborts, the database should not be updated. Furthermore, the actions are declared to be pipelined, so that changes are recorded in the order in which the quotes came in.

Rule $R2$ fires when the *update_price* event is signaled for some stock (as a result of an *update_stock* transaction). If this stock is being monitored for some customer, the price at close the previous day exceeded 60, and the current price drops below 50, then, for each such customer, the rule invokes the *trade* function to buy 100 shares of this stock. The E-C coupling mode is **CD-decoupled** so as not to delay the transaction that updated the stock price. The C-A mode is **immediate**, because it is important to do the trade as soon as possible after the condition is satisfied. The *trade* function presumably updates the customer's account balance. There is likely to be a whole family of such rules for triggering *trade* operations.

Rule $R3$ checks the integrity constraint that customers' account balances should be nonnegative. Since the account balance may be updated several times during a transaction and the constraint needs to be checked only at the end of a transaction, the triggering event is specified to be the closure of the *update_balance* event, and the E-C coupling mode is specified to be **deferred**. A constraint violation causes the entire transaction to be aborted.

7.4
System Architecture and Implementation

The goal of the HiPAC project was to develop the basic primitives for active and time-constrained data management. This included the development of a conceptual architecture for active object-oriented DBMSs. The concepts have been illustrated through three simple prototypes, each of which implemented a subset of the capabilities. It is necessary to differentiate between the conceptual architecture proposed for HiPAC, its extension to accommodate timing constraints, and the actual implementations of the proof-of-concept prototypes. This section first describes the conceptual architecture, then describes implementation approaches for some components of the architecture, and finally briefly sketches the three implementations; extensions of the architecture for time-constrained processing are omitted (for details, see [CBB+89]).

The HiPAC architecture is based on an object-oriented DBMS, adding functions to the object manager and transaction manager, and introducing new components. The added functionality beyond that of a passive DBMS is the following:

- event detection;

- rule selection and firing;

- condition evaluation; and

- support for multiple coupling modes and nested transactions.

A rule fires when its event is signaled. HiPAC must include mechanisms for event detection and signaling. After an event is signaled, HiPAC must determine which rules to fire (i.e., which rules include this event and are enabled). Depending on the coupling mode, it must create one or more nested transactions in which to evaluate the conditions of the selected rules. It must include mechanisms for efficiently evaluating conditions. For those conditions that are satisfied, it must create nested transactions to execute the actions. Since actions can include calls to application procedures in addition to database operations, HiPAC must include "call-out" mechanisms.

Figure 7.1 shows the conceptual architecture of HiPAC, which will be described shortly. The remainder of this System Architecture and Implementation section proceeds as follows. Sections 7.4.1 and 7.4.2 respectively describe the functionality and interaction of the architectural components. Section 7.4.3 discusses various alternatives for detecting data manipulation events. Methods for efficient condition evaluation are discussed in Section 7.4.4. Finally, the three HiPAC prototypes are described in Section 7.4.5.

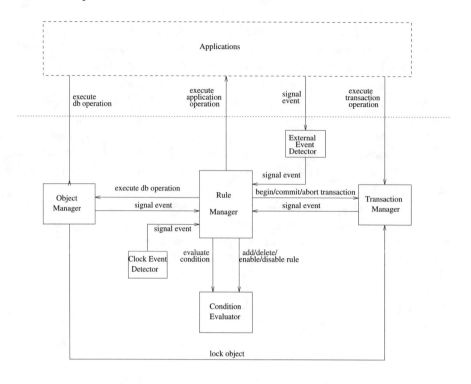

FIGURE 7.1
HiPAC architecture

7.4.1   Component Functionality

Event detection in HiPAC is distributed across several components, due to the variety of events allowed by the HiPAC rule language: database events, which may be data manipulation events or transaction events; temporal events; and arbitrary notification events signaled by external applications. Data manipulation events are detected by the object manager, and transaction events by the transaction manager. A clock event detector detects temporal events, and a separate application event detector is used for external events as shown in Figure 7.1. Each of these event detectors is capable of detecting a class of primitive event. Event composition is performed by the rule manager.

All the event detectors share a common interface, consisting of four functions: *define_event*, *delete_event*, *deactivate_event*, and *activate_event*. The *drop_event* function accepts a description of an event entity and programs the event detector to detect and signal the event; it returns an event identifier. Conversely, *drop_event* accepts an event identifier, and has the effect of dropping the event permanently from the list of events that are monitored by the detector. These two functions are invoked by the object manager in response to **create** and **delete** operations on the event type. When an event entity is created in the database, the appropriate event detector is programmed, using the *define_event* function, to detect and signal the event. When the event entity is deleted from the database, the *drop_event* function is used to delete it also from the event detector. The other two functions are for temporarily deactivating and reactivating the signaling of an event, and are invoked by the rule manager in response to operations on rules. Note that although an event may be defined independently of any rules, it need not be signaled unless there are rules for which it is the triggering event. Thus, an event is activated when the first rule that uses it is created. When a rule is deleted or disabled, if there is no other enabled rule with the same event, the event is deactivated. When the rule is enabled again, the event is (re)activated.

The rule manager controls the firing of rules. Its interface includes a *signal_event* function, which is used by event detectors to report event occurrences. The rule manager is also responsible for aggregating composite events from primitive events that are signaled by the various event detectors. Rule firing begins when an event detector signals an event. The rule manager determines which rules are to be fired. It invokes the transaction manager to create the appropriate nested transactions. It invokes the condition evaluator to initiate condition evaluation. If the condition evaluator signals success, then the rule manager initiates action execution. For database operations, it calls on the object manager to execute the action; for executing external actions, it calls out to client application programs. The rule manager also creates and maintains temporary rule firing entities, which contain all the data needed for condition evaluation and action execution; it collects the data needed by calling on the object manager.

The rule manager also participates in other operations on rules. When rules are created, deleted, enabled, or disabled, it notifies the appropriate event detectors to activate and deactivate event detection. Similarly, when a rule is created, it notifies the condition evaluator to optimize the rule's condition and add it to its "condition graph." When a rule is deleted, it notifies the condition evaluator to remove the rule from the condition graph.

The condition portion of a rule is a query. It has been a special concern within the HiPAC project to investigate efficient approaches to condition evaluation using incremental evaluation and multiple query optimization techniques. Also, the semantics of the various coupling modes lead to interesting optimization questions. These issues prompted the decision to break out the condition evaluator as a separate component in the HiPAC architecture. Its interface includes functions to add, delete, and evaluate conditions. Like a query optimizer, it compiles conditions into graphs, which it optimizes, and generates efficient execution plans. Condition evaluation is discussed in more depth in Section 7.4.4.

Finally, the transaction manager and object manager components of the passive DBMS must be extended. The concurrency control and recovery algorithms of the transaction manager are extended to implement the different types of nested transactions. (For details of the algorithms, see [HLM88].) The transaction manager maintains the commit dependencies for causally-dependent decoupled transactions. It also serves as an event detector, and signals the **BOT** (beginning of transaction), **EOT** (end of transaction), **commit**, and **abort** events for top and nested transactions.

The object manager executes operations on objects, including the definition of new entity types. Events and rules are objects, and as such are stored and retrieved by the object manager. The object manager includes event detector subcomponents, with which it interacts when events are defined or deleted. It also interacts with the rule manager component when rules are defined, modified, or deleted.

7.4.2   Component Interaction

This section shows in detail how the components of the architecture interact to perform two of the rule operations: rule creation and rule execution. More detail for other operations are available in [MD89, CBB+89]. Refer to Figure 7.1.

Rule creation:

1. The object manager receives a request to apply the **create** function.

2. When the creation of the rule object is complete, the object manager signals the rule manager, which adds the rule definition to its internal data structures. The **create** operation is suspended.

3. The rule manager passes the rule's event, condition, and coupling mode to the condition evaluator in an *add_rule* request.

4. The condition evaluator adds the rule to its condition graphs and returns the events that must be signaled for this rule.

5. The rule manager activates the appropriate event detectors to signal the events specified by the condition evaluator. The rule manager records the association between these events and the rule.

6. The rule manager responds to the event signaled for the rule creation and the operation resumes.

Rule execution:

1. An event occurs and is signaled by an event detector. If the event is a database operation, then the operation is suspended.

2. The rule manager determines which rules are fired by the event. For each of these, it creates a **rule_firing** entity to hold data that will be needed later in condition evaluation and action execution.

3. If the E-C coupling mode for any of the rules that are fired by the event is **immediate**, then the rule manager proceeds as follows:

   (a) The rule manager invokes the transaction manager to create a subtransaction for evaluating each of these rules, and a subtransaction of each rule transaction for evaluating the condition part.

   (b) The rule manager passes the **rule_firing** entities to the condition evaluator.

   (c) The condition evaluator executes the plan that it constructed for the rules that were selected. Execution of the plan might require invoking the object manager to query the database within the subtransaction that was created for condition evaluation. The condition evaluator returns the list of rules whose conditions are satisfied to the rule manager.

   (d) The rule manager commits the condition evaluation subtransaction.

   The rule manager determines which of the rules whose conditions are satisfied have the **immediate** coupling mode for the action part. The rule manager calls on the transaction manager for setting up subtransactions of the rule transaction for each of these. Then, the rule manager invokes the object manager to execute the actions. If the action parts have a **deferred** coupling, the rule manager programs the event detector in the transaction manager to signal the end of the triggering transaction. If the action part is **decoupled**, the rule manager prompts the transaction manager to set up a separate top transaction (with commit dependencies for CD decoupled).

4. If any of the rules that are fired by the event have the **decoupled** mode for condition evaluation, then the rule manager proceeds as follows for each rule:

   (a) The rule manager calls on the transaction manager to create a new top transaction.

   (b) The rule manager passes the **rule_firing** entity for the rule to the condition evaluator.

   (c) The condition evaluator evaluates the condition and returns the result to the rule manager.

   (d) If the condition is satisfied, then the rule manager calls on the transaction manager to set up either a subtransaction for the action part (immediate or deferred coupling) or a separate top transaction (decoupled).

5. If any of the rules that are fired by the event have **deferred** condition evaluation, then the rule manager proceeds as follows:

   (a) The rule manager programs the event detector in the transaction manager to signal the end of the triggering transaction.

   (b) The rule manager stores the event occurrence with its bindings in the **rule_firing** entity for each rule, and the triggering transaction resumes.

   (c) When the triggering transaction tries to commit, the event detector of the transaction manager signals the rule manager.

   (d) The rule manager retrieves the **rule_firing** entity and passes it to the condition evaluator.

   (e) The condition evaluator evaluates the rule's condition and returns the result to the rule manager.

   (f) If the condition is satisfied, the rule's action is executed. The rule manager calls on the transaction manager to create the corresponding (sub)transaction in which to execute the action, and calls the object manager to execute it.

6. When all deferred rule firings have been processed, the triggering transaction is allowed to terminate.

7.4.3 Detection of Data Manipulation Events

Data manipulation events in HiPAC correspond to the execution of functions. As described in Section 7.1, a data manipulation event includes a specification of the function **on** whose execution the event must be signaled, and the point in the execution **at** which the event must be signaled. Three basic techniques for detecting data manipulation events have been developed and incorporated into the HiPAC prototypes.

1. Hardwired: Incorporate code as part of the function's implementation (method) to signal the beginning or the end of function execution, to package the parameters of the event occurrence, and to return an **event_occurrence** entity to the rule manager. This code is executed only if the event has been activated. For system-defined functions such as **create**, **delete**, **insert**, and **modify**, the code is provided by the system implementor. For user-defined functions, it is provided by the user who implements the function.

2. Wrapper-based: Wrap the function with additional code. This wrapping is done either by a preprocessor or dynamically at run time. This technique is especially useful for user-defined functions that were not written to be incorporated into an active DBMS (for instance, functions imported from a library).

3. System-supported: Modify the function invocation (dispatch) mechanism of the object manager to signal **beginning** events. This mechanism resolves the parameters of the function call, determines which implementation method of the function to use (based on the parameters' types), and then passes the parameters to the chosen method. The mechanism is modified to signal the event occurrence before invoking the method. Analogously, **end** events are signaled upon return from the method execution.

7.4.4 Condition Evaluation

Since conditions are pure queries, all of the traditional techniques for query optimization and evaluation are relevant. However, HiPAC conditions have some unique characteristics that provide additional challenges and opportunities for optimization. First, a condition may refer to the event parameters captured in the **event_occurrence** entity, in addition to data stored in the database. Second, since data manipulation events most often correspond to database state transitions, a condition may refer to multiple database states (see [CBB+89]). Third, there might be a large number of rules with the same event, whose condition parts have to be evaluated concurrently.

HiPAC reexamined the applicability of currently used query evaluation techniques and developed new ones to suit the requirements of condition evaluation.

1. Signal-driven evaluation: Since a condition can be defined over **event_occurrence** entity sets, which are are likely to be small in comparison to stored data, there is scope for optimizing event detection, parameter computation, and condition execution as a unit (subject to coupling mode specifications).

2. Materialization of intermediate results: Since conditions are evaluated over and over again as events occur, it may be beneficial to materialize and cache partial results, especially of subexpressions that are expensive to compute.

3. Incremental evaluation: Often, it is necessary to determine if the result of a query has changed as a result of some update event. For this purpose, HiPAC introduced a **Changes** operator. Let Q be a query defined over an entity set E (in addition to possibly other entity sets). Let $R = Q(E)$ be the result of evaluating Q. Let U be an update on E. Then, if $E' = U(E)$ and if ΔE expresses the symmetric difference between E and E', then the expression $Changes(Q; [E, \Delta E])$ expresses the symmetric difference between R and R'. A brute force method for computing $Changes(Q; [E, \Delta E])$ is to compute $R' = Q(E')$, and then to compute the symmetric difference between R and R'. Incremental evaluation computes these changes directly from ΔE and the expression for Q. Since ΔE is likely to be much smaller than E', this computation should be less expensive. The **Changes** operator is useful for maintaining the cached partial results of subexpressions, so incremental evaluation can be used in conjunction with materialization of incremental results. Also, the **Changes** operator is a useful shorthand for conditions that users often want to express, and hence it is exposed to users for defining rules.

4. Multiple Condition Optimization: If a large number of rules have been

created, it may be beneficial to analyze the interactions between rules and to optimize rules collectively where possible. For instance, several rules' conditions may have common subexpressions. Multiple query optimization techniques have been described for passive DBMSs. In an active DBMS, the problem is more complicated, because the rules must be triggered by similar events and must have compatible coupling modes.

The remainder of this subsection further discusses conditions graphs and signal-driven evaluation. In addition, techniques for combining rules for more efficient evaluation are discussed. Details for all of the above condition evaluation techniques can be found in [CBB+89, RCBB89, RC88].

Condition Graphs and Signal-driven Evaluation

Queries in HiPAC's object-oriented query language are mapped into an extended relational algebra (as described in [Day89]) and represented by query graphs:[1] entity sets are mapped to relations, function application to a sort of join, subset formation to selection, and tuple formation to projection. To understand the techniques described in this section, it is sufficient to think of the conditions as if they were expressed in relational algebra.

Conditions are compiled into variants of query graphs, called *condition graphs*. Since conditions can refer to event parameters, the leaves of a condition graph may represent **event_occurrence** entities in addition to entity sets stored in the database. Figure 7.2 shows the condition graph for Rule *R2* of Section 7.3. The nodes corresponding to **event_occurrence** entities and paths directed from these nodes are shown in solid lines (these are called "active"); others (called "passive") are shown in dashed lines.

Because condition evaluation imposes overhead on potentially every data manipulation operation and other primitive events, it must be very efficient. Conventional query optimization techniques can be used to reorder joins and move selections and projections past joins. In fact, the graph of Figure 7.2 already reflects some optimization: Since the event occurrence entity sets are small, it is probably more efficient to evaluate the join between *update_price* and *stock* before the join between *stock* and *customer*.

Additional techniques have been developed to exploit the special semantics of condition graphs. One such technique is signal-driven evaluation, which focuses on the operations along active paths, since their inputs are likely to be

---

[1] A query graph is a rooted directed acyclic operator graph, in which leaves represent stored relations, internal nodes represent intermediate relations computed by relational operators, and the root represents the result of the query.

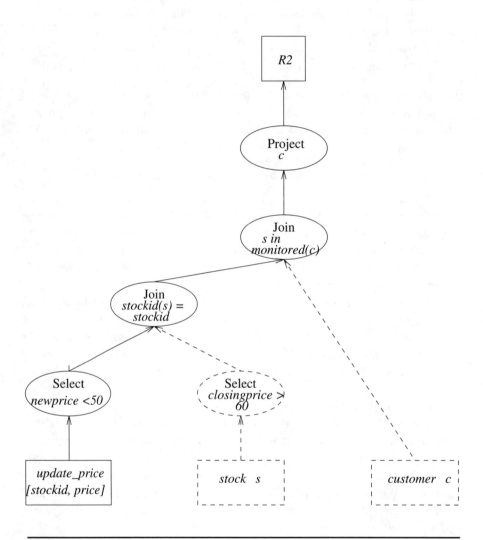

FIGURE 7.2
Condition Graph for Rule R2

small and they often produce empty results. The operations along the active paths are evaluated bottom-up as long as the result is nonempty. Passive subgraphs are evaluated top-down (by subqueries), but only if needed by a node that appears on an active path. This prevents the unnecessary computation of large intermediate results. In the example, the selection on *newprice* will only infrequently produce a nonempty result. When it does, this result is used as the "outer" operand in a nested loop join with the selection subquery on *stock* as the "inner" operand. Of course, indexes or other available access paths can be exploited to perform the nested loop join more efficiently. This is better than a purely bottom-up approach, which would always compute the selection of *stock* on *closingprice* > 60; since *stock* might be a large entity set, this operation could be expensive. Similarly, the result of this first join, if nonempty, is used as the "outer" operand in the next join with *customer* as the "inner" operand. An alternative plan considered by the optimizer makes the "inner" operand of the first join a subquery that evaluates the join of *stock* and *customer*.

A second technique developed for HiPAC combines event detection and the evaluation of selections that are purely on **event_occurrence** entities. For example, the selection *newprice* < 50 can be evaluated when the **event_occurrence** entity *update_price* is created. This saves the cost of additional disk I/O.

The **enable** and **disable** operations are efficiently implemented using condition graphs. Each edge of the graph is labeled with a list of enabled rules on whose behalf the operation is executed. Unconditional enabling and disabling of rules is implemented by modifying these lists. During condition evaluation, an operation is evaluated only if this list is nonempty. Run-time overhead is thus minimized. Selective enabling and disabling of rules for certain values of the parameters is implemented by a selection node with predicate "**event_occurrence** parameters are not in the disabled set," and treating this like any other selection in the condition graph. Thus, no extension is needed to the optimizer or to the run-time evaluation algorithms.

Rule Combination

Since a large number of rules may be defined, it is important to consider techniques that allow several rules to be evaluated together. Several such techniques have been devised for HiPAC.

One technique, derived from multiple query optimization in passive databases, is to identify common subexpressions in the conditions of a collection of rules, and to evaluate these common subexpressions only once. Of course, this is only possible if the triggering events and coupling modes for these conditions permit the concurrent evaluation of the conditions. Consider rules $R1 = (E, C1, A1)$ and $R2 = (E, C2, A2)$. If the E-C coupling modes are the same, then these rules will execute concurrently. Furthermore, if $A1$ does not conflict with $C2$, then the sequence $(E, C1, C2, A1, A2)$ is serializable, and so $C1$ and $C2$ can be optimized together.

A second technique is to combine rules end-to-end. This is useful when it is known at optimization time that one rule's action triggers another rule. Sometimes, it may be possible to move operators from the second rule's condition graph into the first rule. Such a transformation may make it unnecessary to trigger the second rule at all (which can be particularly valuable if the rules are evaluated at different sites in a distributed system). Consider rules $R1 = (E1, C1, A1)$ and $R2 = (E2, C2, A2)$. Suppose that $A1$ includes an operation that causes event $E2$ to be signaled, and that $A2$, $E2$, and $C2$ are all required to execute in the same transaction. Then, $C2$ can be moved into $A1$.

7.4.5   Prototypes

To demonstrate the feasibility and effectiveness of the HiPAC architectural concepts, three small prototypes have been developed. Each prototype implemented a subset of the functionality proposed for HiPAC, along with an application to illustrate the use of the features supported.

The first prototype was developed in Common Lisp with Flavors [CN90]. This system compared the performance of polling with that of active event detection and condition monitoring. It used the *whopper* capability provided by the Common Lisp system [Cor88] to detect data manipulation events. This mechanism permits the binding of a *whopper* (essentially, a wrapper) around any function at link time. The whoppers were used to detect read and write events associated with functions on objects stored in the database. Higher level events corresponding to insert, delete, and modify operations were built using this primitive facility.

This first prototype confirmed the hypothesis that active monitoring is, in general, better than polling when the entity set being monitored is large or when real-time response is important. However, experiments with the prototype also indicated that a naive implementation of active monitoring will not provide the performance advantage that one would expect of an active database system. Event detection itself is not sufficient. Good condition evaluation techniques are also important. For instance, if after an event is signaled an entire entity set has to be scanned to evaluate a condition, then this may be no better than polling. This observation led to the development of techniques for incremental and multiple condition evaluation.

The second prototype was built on top of the PROBE object-oriented DBMS prototype [D+87] and a threat assessment application was modeled using it. Complex events and conditions could be specified, but only the immediate coupling mode was supported. Event detection code was incorporated (by "hardwiring") into the functions that manipulated objects in the database. Rules could be defined for object classes or for specific instances. The system supported the selective enabling and disabling of rules for a given object. Conditions were specified using the full power of the PROBE query language, including operations over spatial and temporal data. For example, rules were written to monitor the movement of enemy ships around a friendly platform. The output of the application was a display that showed the position of enemies with respect to the friendly platform, and a panel of aggregate information such as the distance to the nearest enemy. An example rule from the application was "Whenever an enemy ship moves, calculate the individual and aggregate threats to the friendly platform, and update the display." Complex spatial conditions were evaluated using the PROBE query optimizer.

This implementation focused on event detection and the evaluation of complex conditions. It showed that all the primitive event types of the HiPAC model could be detected by reducing them to one of three system events: the invocation of a function with the appropriate parameters passed to it, the return from a function call with the appropriate parameters, and simulated events or explicitly invoked interrupts.

The third prototype, which was implemented in SmallTalk-80, demonstrated the usefulness of the coupling modes and the extended nested transaction model. A Securities Analyst's Assistant (SAA) application was implemented. It simulated a typical stock-trading situation by implementing a ticker to update the current prices of selected stocks from a wire service; a display module to display prices, portfolios, etc.; and a trader, which transmitted requests to a trading service and updated the clients' portfolios. Several rules for buying and selling stocks, updating the display, and checking integrity constraints were defined with different coupling modes. (The example rules in Section 7.3 were derived from this application.)

The architecture of this implementation resembled the general architecture shown in Figure 7.1, but was restricted in the power of the rule language:

only primitive external notification and data manipulation events were supported. The conditions and actions of rules were defined as SmallTalk-80 blocks, and there was no optimization of condition evaluation. Concurrently executing transactions were implemented using "lightweight" SmallTalk-80 processes. The application and HiPAC layers were clearly separated, with a well-defined interface between them that included functionality for invoking data manipulation operations and transaction operations, for signaling events, and for calling out to application procedures from the HiPAC layer. Messages were used for signaling events to the HiPAC layer from the application layer.

This prototype helped in the development of the HiPAC overall architecture by clarifying the interactions between the various components of the HiPAC subsystem (the rule manager, object manager, transaction manager, and the condition evaluator) as well as between the subsystem and the application. It also established the utility of various coupling modes. Finally, it demonstrated that it is possible to code the high level logic for a complex application in rules rather than in the application software, thus making the application more modular and maintainable.

7.5
Applications

The HiPAC project included two phases that were particularly concerned with applications: an early phase in which many different application domains were analyzed to extract the basic primitives needed for an active DBMS, and a second phase in which HiPAC's rule model and execution semantics were tested against particular application scenarios. The implementation of two typical applications, threat assessment and stock trading, was outlined briefly in Section 7.4.5. Additionally, the concepts of HiPAC have been extended to three other application domains: time-constrained data management, consistency in computer-aided design (CAD) environments, and specification and management of transactional workflows. Since HiPAC's handling of time-related issues is considerably more sophisticated than most other active database systems, the next subsection describes extensions related to time-constrained data management. Details of consistency management and transactional workflows can be found in [BD88] and [DHL90], respectively.

7.5.1 Time-constrained data management

Early in HiPAC's requirements gathering phase, it was noticed that many applications that could profit from active database capabilities must also deal with timing constraints. An important common characteristic of many of these applications, among them power and communication network management, command and control applications, brokerage, plant and reactor control, and air traffic control, is that deadlines must be met, and timeliness is an integral part of the correct behavior of the system.

The ECA rules of HiPAC have been extended to include the specification of timing constraints such as hard and soft deadlines. A hard deadline implies that a task has no value if it is completed past its deadline. Catastrophic consequences may result from missing a hard deadline. A soft deadline implies that a task's value is diminished but still positive if it is completed after the deadline. Each action in a rule is allowed to have an associated value function that gives the value of the triggered action as a function of the expected time of its completion. The HiPAC architecture has been extended to include a time-constrained scheduler that schedules transactions to satisfy the serializability requirement and to maximize their aggregate value. Several scheduling algorithms have been analyzed and taxonomized [BMHD89]. When the system is overloaded (i.e., many transactions miss their deadlines), some overload management policy must be followed. In HiPAC, this policy is to execute contingency plans, which may require the substitution of less expensive, but lower quality, alternate actions, adding resources selectively, or relaxing constraints, thus trading off consistency for timeliness. ECA rules can be used to specify the contingency plans.

7.6
Summary

The goal of the HiPAC project was to develop flexible abstractions to support a wide range of time-constrained applications. The central abstraction is that of Event-Condition-Action rules. HiPAC is an object-oriented database system; events and rules are treated as first class objects, with the many advantages described earlier in this chapter. Many classes of events are supported: method invocation events, temporal events, external application events, and combinations of these. Coupling modes were introduced to allow flexible specification of where a rule is to be executed relative to transaction boundaries. The semantics of rule execution in the presence of the various coupling modes are described using an extended nested transaction model. A conceptual architecture has been developed for HiPAC. This architecture extends an object-oriented database system with capabilities for event detection and rule evaluation. Several alternative techniques have been developed for detecting events and evaluating conditions. Three prototypes have been constructed to demonstrate different subsets of features.

8

Active Database Facilities in Ode

Narain Gehani and H. V. Jagadish

The Ode object-oriented database [AG89a, AG89b] is based on the C++ object paradigm. The primary interface for the Ode database is the database programming language O++, which is an upward-compatible extension of the object-oriented programming language C++ [Str91]. O++ extends C++ by providing facilities suitable for database applications, including the association of constraints and triggers with objects. This chapter describes the design and implementation of active database facilities in Ode. More details can be found in [GJ91, GJS92c, GJS92b, JQ92, JS92].

Ode provides two kinds of active facilities: "constraints" for maintaining database integrity and "triggers" for automatically performing actions depending upon the database state. Ode supports two kinds of constraints: "hard" and "soft." Hard constraints are checked after each object access while soft constraints are checked just before a transaction commit. Ode supports three kinds of triggers: "once-only," "timed," and "perpetual." Triggers, unlike constraints, must be activated explicitly.

The trigger and constraint facilities in Ode were designed with the following goals in perspective:

1. Triggers, which cause arbitrary actions to be executed upon the occurrence of an event, and constraints, which maintain the consistency of an object (or objects), should be specified separately.

2. Triggers and constraints should be specified declaratively.

3. Triggers and constraints should be associated with class definitions to reflect object orientation.

4. Triggers and constraints should work with the inheritance mechanism (including multiple inheritance).

5. Trigger and constraint condition checking should be minimized. It is clearly infeasible to check every trigger and constraint before a transaction commits. In an object-oriented environment where the operations can be user defined, the system cannot determine automatically which operations will affect the trigger and constraint predicates. Consequently, it must be possible to narrow sufficiently the points at which the predicates have to be checked [BZ87].

6. Constraint violations should be able to abort a transaction, raise an exception, or take any other specified recovery action.

7. Immediate, deferred, and separate execution modes should all be supported.

Although constraints and triggers can be implemented using similar techniques, separate facilities have been provided for them since the two are conceptually and semantically different. In particular:

1. Constraints ensure consistency of the database state. If this consistency cannot be maintained (on an object update basis or on a transaction basis), then the transaction is aborted. Triggers are not concerned about object consistency. They are fired whenever the specified conditions become true.

2. Constraints apply to an object from the moment it is created to the moment it is deleted. Triggers must explicitly be activated after an object has been created.

3. The condition specified in a constraint refers to the state of the object while the condition specified in a trigger can involve events that do not affect the state of an object but which nevertheless cause some action associated with the object to be executed. For instance, a read access cannot cause a constraint violation since it does not update the state of the object. However, it could cause a trigger to fire.

4. All objects of a given type have the same constraints. But this is not true for triggers: Different triggers may be activated for different objects even though the objects may be of the same type.

5. Actions associated with a constraint violation are executed as part of the transaction violating the constraint. The reason for this is that the transaction violating a constraint must be aborted if the violation cannot be fixed. On the other hand, there are no such restrictions on triggered actions, and indeed it is often useful to allow a triggering transaction (such as one recording the approach of an enemy aircraft) to commit even if the triggered transaction (such as one to fire a missile at the enemy aircraft) aborts. Ode permits a wide choice in the type of coupling between triggering transactions and the triggered action.

6. Constraints do not have parameters because they are intended primarily to ensure object integrity. Triggers have parameters to allow trigger firing to take place using user-specified values.

7. Conceptually, constraints can be considered a special case of the very general trigger facility. However, they are an important enough special case that Ode provides a carefully tailored syntax as well as a specifically optimized implementation for them.

The primary user interface to Ode is O++, which is now described in more detail. The O++ object facility is based on the C++ object facility and is called the *class*. Class declarations consist of two parts: a specification (type) and a body. The class specification can have a private part holding information that can only be used by its implementor, and a public part which is the class user interface. The body consists of the bodies of the *member* functions (methods) declared in the class specification but whose bodies were not given there.

C++ supports inheritance, including multiple inheritance [Str87]. O++ extends C++ by providing facilities to create persistent objects. O++ visualizes memory as consisting of two parts: volatile and persistent. *Volatile* objects are allocated in volatile memory and are the same as those created in ordinary programs. *Persistent* objects are allocated in persistent storage and they continue to exist after the program creating them has terminated. Each persistent object is identified by a unique identifier, called the object identity [KC86]. The object identity is referred to as a *pointer to a persistent object*.

Transactions in O++ have the form:

```
trans { ... }
```

Transactions are aborted using the `tabort` statement. Transactions provide atomicity, isolation, and durability only with respect to items in the database (persistent objects). None of the above is provided for any non-database variables that may be updated.

8.1
Constraints

8.1.1   Hard Constraints

Hard constraints are specified in the constraint section of a class definition as follows:

```
constraint:
    constraint₁:    handler₁
    constraint₂:    handler₂
```

$$...$$

$$constraint_n: \quad handler_n$$

$constraint_i$ is a Boolean expression that refers to components of the specified class and $handler_i$ is a statement that is executed when a constraint is violated. Optionally, the handler can be absent. Hard constraints are checked only at the end of constructor and member (friend) function calls (but not at the end of destructor calls). Although accessing the public data components of an object directly is not prohibited, it is the programmer's responsibility to ensure that such accesses do not violate any constraints because no constraint checking is performed for such accesses.

If any constraint associated with an object is not satisfied and there is no handler associated with it, then the transaction of which this access is a part is aborted (and rolled back). If there is a handler associated with the constraint, then this handler is executed and the constraint is reevaluated. If the constraint is still not satisfied, then the transaction is aborted.

The granularity of hard constraint checking is at the member function level. This has two important advantages: objects are always in a consistent state (except possibly during an update operation) and the implementation of constraint checking is simplified. The notion is that each public member function must leave the object in a consistent state.

8.1.2   Soft Constraints

Ode also provides a *deferred* or *transaction-level* constraint checking mechanism. Transaction-level constraint checking is supported with *soft* constraints in Ode. Soft constraints are specified like hard constraints except that the keyword `soft` precedes the keyword `constraint`:

```
soft constraint:
```
$$constraint_1: \quad handler_1$$
$$constraint_2: \quad handler_2$$
$$...$$
$$constraint_n: \quad handler_n$$

$constraint_i$ is a Boolean expression that refers to components of the specified class and $handler_i$ is a statement that is executed when a constraint is violated.

In general, soft constraints are used when other objects are involved in the constraint. Hard constraints are likely to be used when the constraint condition does not involve other objects.

8.1.3   Special Constructs

Two types of integrity constraints that are commonly required are referential integrity and relational integrity. Special constructs are introduced to make these particular cases of integrity constraints easy to express.

Referential Integrity

Referential integrity requires the existence of an object referenced by another object. Ensuring referential integrity requires ensuring that there are no references to a deleted object. Suppose that an object to be deleted still has a reference to it. There are three options (policies) that can be used to enforce referential integrity [Dat81]. The reference can be deleted as part of the transaction deleting the object, the referencing object can be deleted, or the deletion of the object can be disallowed. These polices are specified using the keywords `nullify`, `ripple`, and `abort`. By default, referential integrity is not maintained.

Relational Integrity

A binary relationship, known at schema definition time, is stored in an object-oriented database as a directional reference (or set of references) from either participant in the relationship to the other. When such a relationship is to be updated, multiple updates have to be performed, one for each participant in the relationship, giving rise to the possibility that the relation is recorded differently at the different logical locations. *Relational integrity* in an object-oriented database is the proper maintenance of relationships recorded at multiple logical locations, ensuring that the recording is consistent. For example consider a "husband-wife" relationship. Relational integrity ensures that if (object) A records (object) B as his wife, then B records A as her husband and vice versa.

As in the case of referential integrity maintenance, there is a choice of actions that can be taken if a relational integrity constraint is violated. The keywords `ripple` and `abort` are used once again, meaning respectively that the action is to fix the reverse pointer and that the action is to abort the transaction. While it is required that a pair of inverse attributes each declare the other as its inverse, it is permissible to have two different action policies for the two directions.

The Syntax

The general form of these special integrity constraints is to modify the definition of a class as follows:

```
class classname {
    ...
    persistent attribute-type attribute-name
            [inverse inverse-attribute-name abort|ripple|nullify]
            [reference abort|ripple];
    ...
};
```

The material in square brackets is optional, and is the specification of the special constraints discussed above.

8.1.4   Discussion

Where there are multiple constraints associated with an object, the placement of constraints does not specify the order in which the constraints will be checked. It is in the spirit of declarative semantics not to specify any ordering, even though many programming languages such as Prolog do not follow this principle. Users should write the action parts of the constraints without making assumptions about the order of execution. However, it is guaranteed that the condition checking and action parts of each constraint execute atomically (with respect to the other constraints). Repeatability in the order of consideration also is guaranteed, to make debugging easier.

A derived class inherits the constraints of its parent class and new constraints can be added. Consequently, constraints can be used to specialize classes. Such constraint-based specializations are useful in many applications, e.g., in frame-based knowledge representation systems [BL85].

Constraints specified in a class definition can conflict with other constraints in the same class definition or with inherited constraints. For example, one constraint may be the negation of another constraint. In general, it is not possible to automate the detection of such conflicts. It is the programmer's responsibility to ensure that such conflicts do not happen. Otherwise, transactions involving objects of a class with conflicting constraints will always abort.

8.1.5   Inter-Object Constraints

A constraint is said to be *intra-object* if:

1. It is associated with a (single) specific object, and

2. the condition associated with it is evaluated only when this object is updated.

Otherwise, a constraint is said to be *inter-object*. An intra-object constraint can refer to other objects both in evaluating the condition and in the subsequent action. However, updates to these referenced objects do not require the condition part of the constraint or trigger to be checked.

Intra-object constraints are used in Ode for several reasons. First, by associating constraints with class definitions, they are incorporated in the framework of C++ without violating its object-oriented philosophy. Secondly, when an object is updated only the constraints associated with it, through its class definition, need to be checked. Moreover, the condition predicates in most of these are likely to involve members of the updated object and hence are likely not to require too much disk activity.

Nonetheless, inter-object constraints are important, and good mechanisms for dealing with them are required. One solution is to convert each inter-object constraint into one or more equivalent intra-object constraints manually or with the help of a pre-processor. See [JQ92] for a systematic technique to perform this conversion. An instance where this has been done is the "employee's salary no greater than the manager's salary" example shown below in Section 8.1.6.

8.1.6   Examples
Hard Constraint

Here is an example of a hard constraint:

```
class supplier {
  Name state;
  ...
constraint:
  state == Name("NY") || state == Name(""):
  printf("Invalid Supplier State \n");
};
```

After a `supplier` object has been created or accessed, the constraint is checked. The constraint is violated if the supplier's location is specified and it is not in New York (NY). The action associated with the constraint will be executed and the constraint checked once again. Since the action is simply a print statement, the constraint will still not be satisfied, so the transaction is aborted. Any database updates performed by the constraint handler are rolled back along with updates performed as part of the transaction code. Non-database actions, such as the print statement in this example, are not rolled back.

Inter-Object Constraint

The code fragment in Figure 8.1 specifies that an employee's salary must always be less than the manager's salary. This is clearly an inter-object constraint, involving two objects: an employee and a manager. This inter-object constraint has been converted into two complementary intra-object constraints, one to be associated with the employee and the other to be associated with the manager.

Soft Constraint

Here is an example of a soft constraint:

```
class person {
  ...
  persistent person *spouse;
public:
  ...
soft constraint:
  (spouse == NULL) || (this == spouse->spouse);
};
```

Note that if specified as a hard constraint, it would never be possible for two individuals to get married or to have a divorce.

Referential Integrity

Here is an example of a referential integrity constraint:

```
class Dept {
  ...
  persistent Mgr *head reference abort;
  persistent Emp *emps<50> reference nullify;
  ...
};
```

The third line specifies that if an attempt is made to delete a `Mgr` object, the transaction will be aborted if this object is referenced by the `head` attribute in some `Dept` object in the database. The fourth line specifies that when a `Emp` object is deleted, any reference to this object from a `Dept` object should be nullified (removed from the set `emps`) and the deletion allowed to commit.

```
class manager;
class employee {
      ...
      persistent manager *mgr;
      float sal;
public:
      ...
      float salary() const;
constraint:
      sal < mgr->salary();
};

class manager : public employee {
      persistent employee *emp<MAX>;
      int sal_greater_than_all_employees();
      ...
public:
      ...
constraint:
    sal_greater_than_all_employees();
};

int manager::sal_greater_than_all_employees()
{
      persistent employee *e;
      for (e in emp)
          if (e->salary() > salary())
              return 0;
      return 1;
}
```

FIGURE 8.1
Inter-object constraint

Relational Integrity

Here are some example inverse declarations:

```
class Emp {
   ...
   persistent Dept* dept inverse emps<> abort;
   persistent Emp* officemates<4> inverse officemates<> abort;
   ...
};
```

```
class Dept {
   ...
   persistent Emp* emps<50> inverse dept
       ripple reference nullify;
   persistent Mgr* head inverse dept
       abort reference abort;
   ...
};
```

The first declaration in each of the classes `Emp` and `Dept` relates employees to the department they work in. This is a many-one relation. The actions specified to maintain relational integrity are different in the two directions. If a `Dept` object modifies its **employee** set **emps**, then a corresponding modification is automatically made to the **dept** attribute of each employee affected, as part of constraint maintenance. On the other hand, an `Emp` object is not permitted to change its **dept** attribute unilaterally: an attempt to do so will cause the transaction to abort.

Officemates is declared to be an inverse of itself; that is, if a records b as an officemate then b must record a as an officemate as well.[1] Finally, there is a constraint relating a manager and the department he or she heads. There has to be a complementary inverse declaration in the definition of class `Mgr`, not shown here. Notice that `head()` is a computed attribute. Notice also that attributes can have both inverse and reference constraints attached, if desired.

---

[1]Relational integrity does not ensure transitivity. Thus, if a records b and c as officemates, then b and c each record a as an officemate. However, b and c need not record each other as officemates.

Comprehensive Example

Consider a row of adjacent cells on a chip that are placed next to each other. Except for the end cells, each cell has two neighbors. A cell must always satisfy the following conditions:

1. It must be on the chip.

2. It should be adjacent to but must not overlap its left neighbor (if any).

3. It should be adjacent to but must not overlap its right neighbor (if any).

These conditions must be satisfied when a cell is created and when a cell is moved. They are specified in the **constraint** section of class **cell**, shown in Figure 8.2. The three constraints ensure that the three conditions for row cells listed above are satisfied when a cell is created or moved. When a constraint is violated the statements associated with the constraint, if any, are executed in an attempt to rectify the violation. In particular, the constraint actions in the second and third constraints attempt to fix the constraints by shifting the neighbors. To ensure that its constraint is satisfied, the cell must move its appropriate neighbor, which in turn will violate the neighbor's constraint. And so on. Notice that if any cell is moved outside the chip (x-coordinate of left-end is less than **XMIN** or x-coordinate of right-end is greater than **XMAX**), then the resulting constraint violation cannot be repaired, and the entire transaction aborts.

Figure 8.3 shows the code for the member functions of class **cell**. Note the simplicity and the declarative nature of the specification, and compare it to the fairly complex procedural description (not shown here) that would have been required had the constraint mechanism not been available.

8.2
Triggers

Triggers are associated with objects; they are activated explicitly after an object has been created. A trigger T_i associated with an object whose id is *object-id* is activated by the call

object-id->T_i (*arguments*)

The trigger activation returns a trigger id (value of the predefined class **TriggerId**) if successful;[2] otherwise it returns **null_trigger**. The object id

---

[2] Trigger activation can be unsuccessful due to a variety of possible system errors.

```
class cell {
    persistent cell *left, *right;
    ...
public:
    int x, y; //Coordinates of the center point
    int width, height;
    cell(int x1, int y1, int width1, int height1);
    void neighbors(persistent cell *left1,
                   persistent cell *right1);
    void shift(int dx);
    ...
constraint:
    x-width/2 >= XMIN \&\&  x+width/2 < XMAX;

    (right == NULL) || x+(width+right->width)/2 == right->x:
        right->shift((width+right->width)/2 - (right->x-x));

    (left == NULL) || x-(width+left->width)/2 == left->x:
        left->shift((x-left->x)-(width+left->width)/2);
    ...
};
```

FIGURE 8.2
Constraints for class `cell`

can be omitted when activating a trigger from within the body of a member function.

An active trigger "fires" when its predicate becomes true (as a result of updates by a transaction). Firing means that the action associated with the trigger is "scheduled" for action as a separate transaction. Only active triggers can fire. No performance penalty is incurred for triggers that have not been activated.

Triggers can be deactivated explicitly before they have fired using the **deactivate** function:

deactivate(*trigger-id*)

```
cell::cell(int x1, int y1, int width1, int height1)
{
    x = x1; y = y1;
    width = width1; height = height1;
    left = NULL; right = NULL;
}
void cell::neighbors(persistent cell *left1,
                     persistent cell *right1)
{
    left = left1; right = right1;
}
void cell::shift(int dx)
{
    x += dx;
}
```

FIGURE 8.3
Member functions of class `cell`

The trigger with identifier *trigger-id* is deactivated. If successful,[3] `deactivate` returns one; otherwise, it returns zero. Multiple activations of the same trigger associated with an object (possibly with different arguments) are allowed.

Ode supports two kinds of triggers: *once-only* (default) and *perpetual* (specified using the keyword `perpetual`). A once-only trigger is automatically deactivated after the trigger has "fired," and it must then explicitly be activated again, if desired. On the other hand, once a perpetual trigger has been activated, it is reactivated automatically after each firing.

Triggers are specified within class definitions:

```
trigger:
```
   $[$perpetual$]$ $T_1(parameter - decl_1)$:   *trigger-body$_1$*
   $[$perpetual$]$ $T_2(parameter - decl_2)$:   *trigger-body$_2$*
      ...
   $[$perpetual$]$ $T_n(parameter - decl_n)$:   *trigger-body$_n$*

---

[3]Trigger deactivation can be unsuccessful due to a variety of possible system errors or if the specified *trigger-id* is invalid.

T_i are the trigger names. Trigger parameters can be used in trigger bodies, which have one of the following two forms:

> *event-expression* ==> *trigger-action*

> **within** *expression* ?   *event-expression* ==> *trigger-action*
> $\big[$: *timeout-action* $\big]$

The second form is used for specifying *timed* triggers. Once activated, a timed trigger must fire within the specified period (a floating-point value specifying the time in seconds); otherwise, the timeout action, if any, is executed.

The *trigger-action* (and the *timeout-action*) have the form

$\big[$ *mode* $\big]$ *statement*

By default, in the absence of an explicitly specified "mode," a trigger action is executed as a separate transaction with a commit dependency. Alternative modes can be specified as:

1. **independent**: execute action as a separate transaction with no dependencies.

2. **immediate**: execute action immediately as part of the triggering transaction.

3. **deferred**: same as semantics as **immediate** except that the action is executed just before transaction commit.

The form of an *event-expression* is described in the next section.

8.2.1   Event Specification Facilities

The following keywords, in conjunction with the qualifiers **before** and **after**, are used to specify the basic events:

- **create** (object creation),

- **delete** (object deletion),

- **update** (object update),

- **read** (object read),

- `access` (object access),

- `tbegin` (transaction begin),

- `tcomplete` (execution of the transaction code is complete but the transaction has not as yet attempted to commit),

- `tcommit` (transaction commit), and

- `tabort` (transaction abort).

An *event expression* is formed using primitive events and the operators (connectives) described below. An event expression can be $NULL$, any primitive event a, or an expression formed using the operators $\wedge$, ! (not), *relative*, and *relative*+. Formally, an event expression is a mapping from a history h of events to another history, a subset of h, comprising the points at which the event expression was satisfied. The semantics of event expressions are defined as follows (E and F are used to denote event expressions):

1. $E[null] = null$ for any event E, where $null$ is the empty history.

2. $NULL[h] = null$.

3. $a[h]$, where a is a primitive event, is the maximal subset of h composed of a event occurrences.

4. $(E \wedge F)[h] = h_1 \cap h_2$ where $h_1 = E[h]$ and $h_2 = F[h]$.

5. $(!E)[h] = (h - E[h])$.

6. $relative(E,\ F)[h]$ are the event occurrences in h at which F is satisfied assuming that the history started immediately following *some* event occurrence in h at which E takes place. Formally, $relative(E,\ F)[h]$ is defined as follows. Let $E^i[h]$ be the ith event occurrences in $E[h]$; let h_i be obtained from h by deleting all event occurrences whose eids are less than or equal to the eid of $E^i[h]$. Then $relative(E,\ F)[h] = \bigcup_i F[h_i]$ where i ranges from 1 to the cardinality of $E[h]$.

7. $relative+(E)[h] = \bigcup_{i=1}^{\infty} relative^i(E)[h]$ where $relative^1(E) = E$ and $relative^i(E) = relative(relative^{i-1}(E),\ E)$.

Any event occurrence, whether primitive or composite, can optionally be qualified by a *mask* predicate. Thus, multiple predicates can be part of the specification of a single composite event.

Regular expressions are widely used for specifying sequences. The above event expression language has the same expressive power as regular expressions.

8.2.2   More Operators for Specifying Events

Some additional operators (connectives) are presented that make composite events easier to specify. These operators do not add to the expressive power provided by the operators introduced in the previous section.

Let h denote a non-null history, and E, F, and E_i denote event expressions. The new operators are

1. $E \lor F = !(!E \land !F)$.

2. any denotes the disjunction of all the primitive events.

3. $prior(E, F)$ specifies that an event F that takes place after an event E has taken place. E and F may overlap. Formally, $prior(E, F) = relative(E, any) \land F$.

4. $prior(E_1, \ldots, E_m)$ specifies occurrences, in order, of the events $E_1, E_2, \ldots, E_m$. $prior(E_1, \ldots, E_m) = prior((prior(E_1, \ldots, E_m-1), E_m))$.

5. $sequence(E_1, \ldots, E_m)$ specifies immediately successive occurrences of the events $E_1, E_2, \ldots, E_m$:

   (a) $sequence(E_1, \ldots, E_m) = sequence((sequence(E_1, \ldots, E_m-1), E_m))$.

   (b) $sequence(E_1, E_2) = relative(E_1, !(relative(any, any))) \land E_2$. The first operand of the conjunction specifies the first event following event E_1. The second operand specifies that the event specified by the complete event expression must satisfy E_2.

6. $first$ identifies the first event in a history. $first = !relative(any, any)$.

7. $(E|F)[h] = F[E[h]]$; i.e., F applied to the history produced by E on h. Operator $|$ is called *pipe*, with obvious similarity to the UNIX pipe operator.

8. $(< n > E)$ specifies the nth occurrence of event E. Formally, $((E|seq(any_1, any_2, \ldots, any_n))|first)$, where each any_i is simply any.

9. $(every < n > E)$ specifies the $n^{\text{th}}, 2n^{\text{th}}, \ldots,$ occurrences of event E. Formally, $(every < n > E) = (E|relative + (< n > any))$.

10. $(F \ / \ E)[\ h\ ] \ = \ F[\ h'\ ]$ where h' is *null* if $E[h] = null$ and other-
    wise h' is the history obtained from h by eliminating all the event
    occurrences before and including $(< 1 > E)[h]$. Formally, $F/E \ = \ $
    $relative((!prior(E, \ any) \wedge E), \ F)$, equivalently, $F/E \ = \ relative$
    $((E|first), F)$.

11. Suppose that E takes place m times in h. $F \ /+ \ E \ [\ h\ ] = \bigcup_{i=1}^{m} F[\ h'\ _i]$.
    h'_i, $1 \leq i < m - 1$, is obtained from h by eliminating all event occur-
    rences before and including event $(< i > E)[h]$ and all event occurrences
    including and following $(< i+1 > E)[h]$. h'_m is obtained from h by elim-
    inating all event occurrences before and including event $(< m > E)[h]$.
    E is used to delimit sub-histories of h, where the "delimiters" are event
    occurrences at which E takes place. F is applied to each such sub-
    history, and the results of these applications are combined (unioned) to
    form a single history.

12. $firstAfter(E_1, \ E_2, \ F)[h]$ specifies events E_2 that take place relative to
    the last preceding occurrence of E_1 without an intervening occurrence
    of F relative to the same E_1. Formally, $firstAfter(E_1, \ E_2, \ F) = $
    $(E_2 \wedge !prior(F, \ any)) \ /+ \ E_1$.

13. $before(E) \ = \ prior(E, \ any)$.

14. $happened(E) \ = \ E \ \vee \ prior(E, \ any)$.

15. $prefix(E) \ [h]$ is satisfied by each event occurrence e such that there
    exists a history h' identical to h up to event occurrence e, and E is
    satisfied in h' at some event occurrence following e. In other words,
    $prefix(E)$ is recognized at each event occurrence as long as a possibility
    exists that an E event will be recognized eventually. This operator is
    normally used in the form $!prefix(E)$, which occurs as soon as it is
    known that E cannot occur.

16. $E * T$ is a series of zero or more E events followed by a T event.
    $E * T \ = \ T \wedge !prior(!E, \ T)$.

8.2.3   Discussion

Triggers, like constraints and members of a class, are inherited when
one class is derived from another. Also, like constraints, neither the order of
placement of triggers in a class definition nor the order in which the triggers

are activated determines the order in which triggers are evaluated or executed. In fact, since the action part of each trigger may execute as a separate transaction, it is impractical to control the execution schedule to force these transactions to be serializable in a specified order.

Trigger activation must be done explicitly for each individual object. However, the class designer can automate trigger activation by putting the trigger activation code in constructors. Since a constructor function is called at object creation time to initialize the object, the trigger automatically gets activated when an object is created. Because triggers are activated explicitly (by the programmer or by the class designer), different objects of the same type may have different sets of triggers active at any given time.

A trigger can be fired no more than once by a given transaction, even if the transaction causes several updates to the associated object, any one of which could by itself have satisfied the trigger predicate and caused it to fire. However, there is no limit on the number of activations of the same trigger that could be fired by a single transaction. Trigger predicates may overlap. Consequently, updating an object may result in the firing of one or more active triggers.

The Ode trigger model is an event-action (E-A) model. When an event occurs, the associated action is executed. Given the powerful event specification facilities, predicate evaluation can naturally be folded into the event specification. In the Ode E-A model, only one kind of coupling is needed—it is not necessary to support the multiple couplings of the E-C-A model. Any E-C-A desired coupling can be implemented by selecting an appropriate event specification, incorporating the required transaction events.

For instance, here is how to get deferred coupling between E and C, and immediate coupling between C and A, using constructs with only immediate coupling. Let E be a (composite) event expression, C be a condition (predicate) to be evaluated when e occurs, and A be the action to be executed if the condition evaluates to true (the trigger fires).

```
firstAfter(E,before tcomplete,after tbegin) & C ==> A
```

To ease the programmer's burden, explicit keywords have been provided to specify the type of coupling desired between the event and the action.

When the action part of a trigger is executed as a separate transaction, it is possible that the predicate causing the trigger to fire is no longer true at the time the triggered action is actually executed. For example, the stock price, after falling to a level at which a customer's buy order is triggered, could rise above the trigger threshold price before the buy transaction can complete. To prevent purchase of the stock at this now changed (higher) price, the trigger action must check (again) that the stock price is at or below the threshold; otherwise, it should deal with it appropriately.

There could, in general, be a delay between the occurrence of an event, say an update, that causes a trigger to fire, and the the actual execution of the action part. This is especially the case when the action executes as a separate transaction. In the meantime, it is possible for the trigger to be fired again, if it is defined to be perpetual. This may be exactly what is desired in many situations, but it is necessary that the action part of a perpetual trigger take this possibility of multiple firings into account. This problem does not arise in a once-only trigger, since the trigger is atomically deactivated when it is fired, and has to be activated again explicitly, in the action part of the trigger or elsewhere.

8.2.4   Examples
Triggers with Predicates

Consider the class `inventitem` in Figure 8.4, derived from class `stockitem` that was shown earlier. Trigger `order` is activated in the constructor function `inventitem` and in the member function `deposit`. The action associated with the trigger `order` will be executed after its condition becomes true (as a result of executing the `withdraw` operation). The bodies of some of the member functions of class `inventitem` are shown in Figure 8.5.

Now suppose that a complaint should be written if the supplier does not fill the order within the promised lead time. This can be achieved using a timed trigger as shown in Figure 8.6.

Basic Events

Some examples of basic events are:

```
after read
```

specifies an event that occurs immediately after the execution of a public member function that accesses an object for reading only. Similarly,

```
before tcomplete
```

specifies an event that occurs just before a transaction attempts to commit after having accessed the object. Note that the specification of the event

```
before tcommit
```

```
class inventitem: public stockitem {
public:
    inventitem (Name iname, double iwt, int xqty,
                int xconsumption, double xprice, int xleadtime,
                Name sname, Addr saddr);
    void deposit(int n);
    void withdraw(int n);
    \ldots
trigger:
    order(): qty < reorder_level() ==>
                    place_order(this, eoq());
                    //"this" refers to the object itself
};
```

FIGURE 8.4
Class definition for inventitem

is not allowed because it is not possible to be sure that a transaction is going to commit until it actually does so. An event can be scheduled to occur after a specified period (from the current time, when the trigger is armed) has elapsed as follows:

```
after time(HR=2, M=30)
```

Mask Predicates

An example of a basic event with a mask predicate is:

```
before withdraw(Item, int q) & q>1000
```

Composite Events

Here are some examples of composite events:

1. All occurrences of an event a:

    ```
    a
    ```

2. The 5th occurrence of deposit:

    ```
    (<5>deposit)
    ```

```
inventitem::inventitem(Name iname, double iwt, int xqty,
    int xconsumption, double xprice, int xleadtime,
    Name sname, Addr saddr):
    stockitem(iname, iwt, xqty, xconsumption, xprice,
            xleadtime, sname, saddr)
{
    \ldots
    order();   //trigger activation
}
void inventitem::deposit(int n)
{
    qty += n;
    order(); //trigger activation
}
void inventitem::withdraw(int n)
{
    qty -= n; //might fire trigger
}
```

FIGURE 8.5
Member functions of class `inventitem`

3. deposit followed immediately by `withdraw`:

    `sequence(deposit, withdraw)`

4. deposit followed eventually by `withdraw`:

    `prior(deposit, withdraw)`

5. deposit followed eventually by `withdraw` with no intervening `interest`:

    `relative(deposit, !before(interest)) && withdraw`

6. Event expression that is satisfied when an E occurs provided there is no "non-E" event before it. This essentially recognizes a series of E events:

```
class cinventitem: public stockitem {
public:
    \ldots
    TriggerId checkarrival;
    int delivered;
    void deposit(int n);
trigger:
    order(): qty < reorder_level()
      ==> {
        place_order(this, eoq());
        delivered = 0;
        checkarrival = complain(); }
    complain(): within leadtime ? delivered ==>;
                                : write_complaint_letter();
};
```

FIGURE 8.6
Timed trigger

```
    E && !prior(!E, E)
```

A particularly important composite event is when an object reaches a specified state, described as

```
(after update | after create) &&
    Boolean-expression-specifying-object-state
```

Since this form of event will probably be used often, it can be specified simply as

Boolean-expression-specifying-object-state

Here is an example of an event that occurs when the **balance** (say of a bank customer's account) falls below 500 dollars:

```
balance < 500.00
```

Complex Composite Event

Here is an example financial history (Figure 8.7) with discount rate cut events labeled by D (decrease) and increases labeled by I (increase). Many

FIGURE 8.7
Discount rate cut

other events can occur, for example, the prime rate may be cut and the stock market can crash, but these events are not of interest here. The problem is to write an event expression that is satisfied by three or more successive cuts in the discount rate without an intervening increase.

The composite event of interest occurs at the last two D events (marked with #). This composite event is specified in steps. First, the event expression

    prior(I, D)

specifies D events that are preceded by an I event. Expression

    !prior(I, D)

specifies all events except the occurrences of D that are preceded by I. Expression

    !prior(I, D) && D

specifies D events that are not preceded by an I event. The expression

    relative(D, !prior(I, D) && D)

specifies a D event followed eventually by another D event with no intervening I events. This expression gives a pair of D events with no intervening I events. Note that in this case, the **relative** operator is used to look at the history starting after a D event.

Finally, the event of interest can be specified as

    relative(relative(D, !prior(I, D) && D), !prior(I, D) && D)

The outermost **relative** finds another D without a preceding I, giving three D events without an intervening I event.

Using the pipe operator, the composite event for the three successive discount rate cuts is written simply as

    (I || D) | sequence(D, D, D)

8.3
Implementation

Currently, constraint and trigger facilities have not yet been implemented in the Ode object database. However, a subset of the the trigger facilities have been implemented in a stand-alone prototype [GJS92a] in order investigate implementation issues such as data structures appropriate for fast access, efficient techniques for implementing masks, and handling events with parameters.

The planned implementation strategy is based on the premise that object updates are performed only by calling public member functions. Constraints and trigger conditions are not checked if objects are updated by directly changing values of the data members.

Events specified by the event expressions in triggers are recognized using finite automata. Each basic event in an event expression is posted to the corresponding automaton. Automata are advanced to reflect the partial occurrence of the (composite) events. An event is recognized immediately after the basic event satisfying the event expression is posted. The recognition is immediate because only one state transition is needed to move the automaton to a final state (in case of a mask, two transitions are required along with the evaluation of the mask).

Each basic event is recognized in a "context." Thus method executions, object accesses and updates, etc., are recognized at the affected object. Transaction events are recognized at all objects affected by the transaction. (Event **tbegin** is posted to an object just before it is first accessed by a transaction; this scheme limits the posting of **tbegin** to only objects that will be accessed by a transaction.)

At each object there is one automaton per active trigger. When an event occurs, each appropriate automaton is advanced. If any automaton enters an accepting state, the corresponding trigger fires. Note that the code for the automaton is generated only once per trigger definition (part of the class definition). A single variable records the state of the automaton for each active trigger instance.

8.4
Summary and Future Directions

The Ode object-oriented database provides powerful facilities for specifying triggers and constraints. These are associated with class (object type) definitions. In an active database, a trigger "fires" (executes its action part) upon the occurrence of the event specified in the trigger. These events may be composite, and may involve the evaluation of predicates.

In keeping with the static nature of O++, new constraints and new types of triggers cannot be created without changing the class definition. Adding, deleting, or modifying triggers and constraints requires changing the class definition, i.e., it requires changing the database schema. So far the issue of schema evolution has not been addressed. However, trigger parameters can be altered, and individual triggers can be activated or deactivated at will.

Composite event specification is based on a set notation identical in expressive power to a notation based on regular expressions. These expressions can be translated into finite state automata in an efficient way.

A stand-alone prototype has been built implementing the constraint and trigger facilities. The issues in implementing composite events are now better understood, and the constraint and trigger facilities will soon be added to Ode. The current implementation of composite events also will be extended by permitting events to have arbitrary attributes, and for arbitrary temporal predicates to be specified over these.

9

Standards and Commercial Systems

Stefano Ceri and Jennifer Widom

Several commercial relational database management systems support active database rules, usually referred to as *triggers*. The functionality of commercial database trigger systems is generally rather limited as compared to the active database research prototypes described in the previous chapters. Nevertheless, the capabilities of many commercial systems are already sufficient to provide relatively complex active database behavior.

Currently, commercial active database capabilities suffer from four main shortcomings:

1. They lack standardization. Consequently, the various products have a wide variance in both the syntax and execution behavior of triggers. This results in a lack of uniformity, and the inability to use trigger applications on differing products.

2. They lack a clearly defined execution semantics. A number of alternative constructs may be provided (such as both tuple-level and statement-level triggering, or both immediate and deferred execution), but often it is not specified precisely how triggers will behave when multiple triggers with different options are present.

3. They lack a number of useful "advanced features" that have been included in research prototypes, such as application-specific events, event composition techniques, binding of events to conditions and of conditions to actions, use of net effects, use of enhanced transaction models to support sophisticated coupling modes or parallelism, lack of external procedure calls, and so on.

4. They often incorporate a number of restrictions, such as limitations on the number of triggers that may be defined, or on the interactions between triggers.

Despite these shortcomings, the existence of triggers in many relational database products (and the expectation that triggers are forthcoming in those products that don't currently support them) indicates that the field of active database systems is affecting real-world applications already, and it will likely expand to embrace many more of them.

This chapter first reviews the standardization efforts being pursued by the *ANSI* and *ISO* standards bodies to alleviate the first shortcoming mentioned above. Triggers won't be incorporated until the forthcoming standard, referred to as *SQL3*. However, triggers in SQL3 will be based upon integrity constraint (called *assertion*) features in the most recent standard, referred to as *SQL-92*. Hence, Section 9.1 reviews the SQL-92 features for integrity constraints, providing a basis for SQL3 triggers which are covered in Section 9.2.

In Section 9.3, a number of commercial relational database trigger systems are discussed. The systems covered are: Oracle, Informix, Ingres, Rdb, Sybase, Allbase, and InterBase. The descriptions of these systems in Section 9.3 do not serve to provide a complete specification of trigger capabilities, but rather to give a flavor of the basic trigger functionality in each system. For each system, the description includes at least the syntax for creating triggers (when it has been specified in publicly available manuals) and an example of trigger usage. Other issues, such as limitations on rule interaction, error handling, and authorization, are covered briefly as well.

Note that the material in this chapter is current based on the available material at the time of this writing. The field is moving rapidly, and the details of standards and commercial systems are sure to change quickly over time. This material should by no means be taken as a guide or manual for the standards or the commercial systems.

Note also that the descriptions of trigger execution behavior in this chapter are sometimes sketchy and incomplete, as compared to the descriptions of execution semantics for the research prototypes described in the previous chapters. This incompleteness is due, unfortunately, to the fourth shortcoming mentioned above: many products—and even the proposed SQL3 standard—simply do not provide a complete specification of trigger behavior for all possible scenarios.[1]

9.1
Integrity Constraints in the SQL-92 Standard

Although triggers were apparently too "new" to be incorporated into the SQL-92 standard, the specification of a rich collection of integrity constraints is one of the standard's main contributions. Constraints in SQL-92 can be classified into three categories: *table constraints*, *referential integrity constraints*, and *general assertions*. These three types of constraints are summarized briefly here, since they serve as an introduction to triggers in the

---

[1] The authors consider this lack of attention to execution semantics as a substantial problem which must be addressed.

proposed SQL3 standard and in commercial systems. Additional details on the SQL-92 standard can be found in, e.g., [CO92, MS93].

9.1.1   Table Constraints

Table constraints in SQL-92 are used to enforce restrictions on the data allowed in particular columns of particular tables. Table constraints are specified as part of the CREATE TABLE statement.

Any column in a table may be declared as NOT NULL. This indicates that null values are not permissible for that column. In addition, a set of one or more columns may be declared as UNIQUE. This indicates that no two tuples may have the same values for all of the designated columns (i.e., the columns must form a key for the table). Each table also can have at most one designated PRIMARY KEY, consisting of a set of one or more columns. Primary keys must be both unique and not null.

The permissible values of a column may also be restricted by means of a CHECK constraint. A CHECK clause specifies a condition involving the column whose values are restricted. Syntactically, the condition may reference the column (by name), other columns of the same tuple (by name), and it may involve other tables or other tuples of the same table by specifying an arbitrary SQL query. Semantically, a CHECK constraint is valid if the condition evaluates to true for every tuple in the table.

Table constraints are checked after any SQL statement that inserts into the table or modifies the constraint's column. If the constraint is violated, then the SQL statement causing the violation is rolled back and an error is raised. Note that CHECK constraints could also become violated if multiple tables are referenced in the condition and a table other than the constraint's table is modified, or even if other columns in the same table are modified. It is the understanding of the authors that a CHECK constraint is monitored only for the relevant column, so constraint violations due to modifications of other columns or tables may go unnoticed. Consequently, it is preferable to use general assertions (described below) for constraints involving multiple columns or tables.

9.1.2   Referential Integrity Constraints

A referential integrity constraint involves two tables, called the *referencing* table and the *referenced* table. Intuitively, every tuple in the referencing table must be a "child" of some tuple in the referenced table. Referential integrity disallows "orphans," which could be created by insertions (of child tuples), updates (of child or parent tuples), or deletions (of parent tuples).

Referential integrity constraints are specified by means of `FOREIGN KEY` clauses, included as part of the `CREATE TABLE` statement for the referencing table. Each table can reference an arbitrary number of tables, including itself. A syntax for the `FOREIGN KEY` clause is:[2]

```
<foreign key clause> ::= FOREIGN KEY (<referencing columns>)
                         REFERENCES <table name>
                            [(<referenced columns>)]
                         [<foreign key actions>]
```

Referencing columns must be specified; they constitute the *foreign key*. Referenced columns may be omitted, in which case the primary key of the referenced table is implicitly assumed as the referenced columns. Referential integrity is violated by a tuple in the referencing table if the tuple's referencing columns constitute a set of values that does not also appear in the appropriate columns of the referenced table.

Referential integrity can be violated by inserts or updates to the referencing table or by updates or deletes to the referenced table. In the SQL-92 standard, inserts or updates to the referencing table that violate the constraint are disallowed. Updates or deletes to the referenced table are handled by the specification of "referential trigger actions," one for updates and one for deletes. The following syntax is used:

```
<foreign key action> ::= <event> <action>
<event> ::= ON UPDATE | ON DELETE
<action> ::= CASCADE | SET DEFAULT | SET NULL | NO ACTION
```

Note that this treatment of referential integrity falls into the active database *event-condition-action* paradigm: the events are the operations causing the integrity violation, the condition is the constraint itself, and the action repairs the constraint's violation. The four possible actions are as follows.

- `CASCADE` "propagates" the update or the delete. When updates are propagated, changes to the referenced table's columns are also performed on the corresponding foreign keys of all referencing tables. When deletes

---

[2] A concise grammar-like notation is used throughout this chapter. Optional constructs are denoted by square brackets and alternatives by curly brackets. When a grammar production name is pluralized (such as `<referencing columns>` above), this indicates one or more repetitions of that grammatic construct separated by commas. For presentation, many of the syntaxes given are simplifications of the actual syntax, with unimportant features omitted.

are propagated, the tuples of all referencing tables whose foreign keys correspond to the deleted referenced tuples are also deleted.

- SET NULL sets to the null value all foreign key columns whose values are no longer matched in the referenced table. (It is not permitted to specify the SET NULL option for columns with a NOT NULL table constraint; recall Section 9.1.1.)

- SET DEFAULT sets to a specified default value (for each column) all foreign key columns whose values are no longer matched in the referenced table. (It is not permitted to specify the SET DEFAULT option for columns that do not have a default value.)

- NO ACTION disallows the updates or deletes to the referenced table that caused the referential integrity violation. (Sometimes this option is denoted instead by the keyword RESTRICT.)

Referential integrity is checked, and referential trigger actions are performed, after every SQL statement that might violate a referential integrity constraint. When disallowed actions are detected (inserts or updates to the referencing table that violate the constraint), or violating actions with the NO ACTION option occur, then the SQL statement causing the violation is rolled back and an error is raised.

9.1.3   SQL-92 Assertions

Assertions in SQL-92 provide the capability for expressing general constraints which may involve multiple tables. A syntax for assertions is:

```
<SQL92 assertion> ::= CREATE ASSERTION <constraint name>
                      CHECK (<condition>)
                      [<constraint evaluation>]


<constraint evaluation> ::= [NOT] DEFERRABLE
                            [{INITIALLY DEFERRED |
                              INITIALLY IMMEDIATE}]
```

As in CHECK constraints (Section 9.1.1), the condition can be an arbitrary SQL predicate, although here there is no implicitly referenced column, tuple, or table. The assertion is satisfied if the condition evaluates to true.

A constraint's evaluation is said to be *immediate* if the constraint is evaluated after every SQL statement that may affect the constraint. A constraint's evaluation is said to be *deferred* if constraint checking is not performed until the commit point of a transaction. (Note the direct correspondence to the *coupling modes* of active database systems; recall Chapter 1.) Table constraints and referential integrity constraints always have immediate evaluation. However, general assertions may instead have deferred evaluation. If an assertion is specified as `DEFERRABLE`, then a transaction may explicitly request that the constraint's evaluation be deferred. In this case, the assertion can also specify either `INITIALLY IMMEDIATE` or `INITIALLY DEFERRED`, to set the default evaluation mode for each transaction. The mode is changed by a transaction using the statement:

```
<constraint mode> ::= SET CONSTRAINTS <constraint names>
                      {IMMEDIATE | DEFERRED}
```

As with table and referential integrity constraints, if an assertion violation is detected during immediate evaluation, then the SQL statement causing the violation is rolled back and an error is raised. If a constraint violation is detected during deferred evaluation, then the entire transaction is rolled back.

9.2
Assertions and Triggers in SQL3

Since the completion of SQL-92, ANSI and ISO have been working towards a new SQL standard, currently referred to as SQL3. The proposed SQL3 standard incorporates an impressive list of new features. At the time of this writing, it is uncertain when SQL3 will be released (or even some fraction of what is currently a massive specification), although expectations are for 1996 or 1997.

This section covers assertions and triggers in SQL3 as interpreted by the authors from the latest available document [ISO94] at the time of this writing. The presentation here is based on the current standard proposal, which will almost certainly be modified. Nevertheless, this presentation is relevant even if the specification ultimately changes, because many relational database system vendors have already used the specification as a basis for their trigger capabilities and, conversely, trigger capabilities already available in products have influenced the proposed standard. Consequently, the description given here also serves as an introduction to commercial systems, which are discussed in Section 9.3.

9.2.1   SQL3 Assertions

Assertions in the proposed SQL3 standard extend the general assertions of SQL-92 in two ways:

1. They introduce explicit *assertion events*—specification of data modification or transactional events that cause the constraint to be evaluated.

2. They introduce *tuple-level evaluation*—the option of evaluating the constraint for each tuple of a given table instead of for the entire table.

These changes make assertions in SQL3 become quite similar to triggers (introduced in the next section), which is probably the main motivation for the change. A syntax for assertions in SQL3 is:

```
<SQL3 assertion> ::= CREATE ASSERTION <constraint name>
                     {BEFORE COMMIT | AFTER <assertion events>}
                     CHECK (<condition>)
                     [FOR [EACH ROW OF] <table name>]
                     <constraint evaluation>


<assertion event> ::= {INSERT | DELETE |
                       UPDATE [OF <column names>]}
                       ON <table name>
```

The syntax as currently proposed permits assertions to be checked either BEFORE COMMIT or AFTER one or more data modification operations (possibly referring to different tables). If the FOR clause is present, then the specified table may be referenced directly in the condition. When the EACH ROW OF option is used, the condition is evaluated once for each tuple of the specified table (*tuple-level granularity*); otherwise, the condition is evaluated exactly once for the entire table (*statement-level granularity*).

The time of constraint evaluation and the handling of violations is the same as in SQL-92. The default value for <constraint evaluation> is NOT DEFERRABLE INITIALLY IMMEDIATE (recall Section 9.1.3). Note, however, that there is a certain amount of redundancy between the <assertion events> and the <constraint evaluation> clauses, since they both indicate when a constraint should be checked. In particular, there could be an inconsistency, e.g., if both BEFORE COMMIT and NOT DEFERRABLE are specified. The current SQL3 proposal does not indicate how such inconsistencies are handled.

9.2.2 Triggers

In the proposed SQL3 standard, each trigger reacts to a specific data modification operation on a specific table. The trigger may be executed before, after, or instead of the operation. A syntax for triggers is the following:[3]

```
<SQL3 trigger> ::= CREATE TRIGGER <trigger name>
                   {BEFORE | AFTER | INSTEAD OF} <trigger event>
                   ON <table name>
                   [ORDER <order value>]
                   [REFERENCING <references>]
                   WHEN (<condition>)
                   <SQL procedure statements>
                   [FOR EACH {ROW | STATEMENT}]


<trigger event> ::= INSERT | DELETE | UPDATE [OF <column names>]


<reference> ::= OLD AS <old value tuple name> |
                NEW AS <new value tuple name> |
                OLD_TABLE AS <old value table name> |
                NEW_TABLE AS <new value table name>
```

SQL3 triggers follow the active database *event-condition-action* paradigm. The event is the monitored database operation, the condition is an arbitrary SQL predicate, and the action is a sequence of SQL procedure statements. The procedure statements are executed serially iff the event occurs and the condition evaluates to true. Transaction, connection, and session statements are disallowed in trigger action procedures.

Like assertions in SQL3, a trigger can execute FOR EACH ROW, i.e., once for each modified tuple, or it can execute FOR EACH STATEMENT, i.e., only once for an entire SQL statement. Note that only in the latter case will the trigger execute even if no tuples are actually modified. The default setting is FOR EACH STATEMENT.

References to values before or after the triggering operation, respectively called *old* and *new* values, are available by means of the REFERENCING clause.

---

[3]The current SQL3 specification for triggers is rather long and difficult to understand. One source of confusion is the differences between the proposals considered by the two standardization committees (ANSI and ISO). At the time of this writing, some features proposed by ANSI are not being considered by ISO (including the INSTEAD OF alternative and the table-level references to OLD_TABLE and NEW_TABLE), while some features proposed by ISO are not being considered by ANSI (such as the ORDER clause).

This clause is used to associate names with the old and/or new values of the modified tuple (if the trigger is FOR EACH ROW) or of the entire table (if the trigger is FOR EACH STATEMENT).

A trigger is specified to execute either BEFORE, AFTER, or INSTEAD OF the triggering operation. In addition to determining when a trigger executes, these alternatives influence which tuples are visible during trigger condition evaluation and action execution.

- Triggering on INSERT: With BEFORE or INSTEAD OF, the inserted tuples are not visible as part of their table, but they may be accessed using the REFERENCING clause for NEW tuples or tables. With AFTER, the inserted tuples are visible in their table as well as through the REFERENCING clause.

- Triggering on DELETE: With BEFORE or INSTEAD OF, the deleted tuples are visible in their table, as well as through the REFERENCING clause for OLD tuples or tables. With AFTER, the deleted tuples are not visible in their table, but they may be accessed using the REFERENCING clause.

- Triggering on UPDATE: With BEFORE, AFTER, and INSTEAD OF, the old and new values of the updated tuples are visible through the REFERENC- ING clause for OLD and NEW tuples or tables. Note that even if execution of the trigger takes place before or instead of the update operation, the update must be evaluated in order to produce bindings for OLD and NEW references. With BEFORE and INSTEAD OF, the effect of the update is not visible in the relevant table, while with AFTER the effect of the update is visible.

A REFERENCING clause for OLD is not allowed with INSERT triggers, and a REFERENCING clause for NEW is not allowed with DELETE triggers.

Note that with three possible triggering operations on each table (INSERT, DELETE, and UPDATE), three possible triggering times for each operation (BEFORE, AFTER, and INSTEAD OF), and two possible evaluation granularities (FOR EACH ROW and FOR EACH STATEMENT), there are eighteen distinct types of triggers available for each table. In addition, UPDATE triggers may be spec- ified separately for the different columns of a table.

The SQL3 proposal introduces the concept of a *trigger action graph* in order to model interactions between triggers. The graph includes nodes for tables and for data modification operations on tables, and edges derived from triggers' events and actions. Restrictions are imposed on the allowable structures in the graph for a set of triggers, which translate to restrictions on possible trigger interactions. The graph is constructed and checked when triggers are defined.[4]

The trigger action graph guarantees that trigger execution will always terminate. In some cases, the graph also guarantees that trigger execution will have a unique final database state. In particular, the graph ensures that "conflicts" (multiple triggers activated at the same time) can occur only when there is more than one trigger defined on the same table and operation. The execution order of such triggers can be controlled by using ORDER clauses to specify numeric priorities; triggers without an ORDER clause are assigned a priority based on their time of definition. Note that the property of having a unique final state also may be lost due to FOR EACH ROW executions: triggered actions resulting from two distinct tuple modifications may set some other tuple to two different values, in which case trigger execution order is relevant. However, if this behavior occurs, an exception condition called TRIGGERED DATA CHANGE VIOLATION is raised.

An additional restriction prohibits triggers on tables for which referential integrity constraints are defined, so that referential integrity and trigger actions are not in conflict.

In the case where there are both tuple-level and statement-level triggers on the same operation and table for the same time (BEFORE, AFTER, or INSTEAD OF), the order of trigger execution is given by the following rules:

- If the triggers are BEFORE or INSTEAD OF, then the statement-level triggers precede the tuple-level triggers.

- If the triggers are AFTER, then the tuple-level triggers precede the statement-level triggers.

Finally, when an SQL operation has both triggers and immediate assertions, then trigger execution precedes assertion checking.[5] Note that it is possible to execute transactions with a special cursor mode called CASCADE OFF, in which case all assertions and triggers are deferred until commit time.

---

[4]The trigger action graph is a particularly weak part of the current standard document. It is difficult to understand, and the exact rationale for the graph is never explained.

[5]This important decision regarding triggers and assertions has been addressed by ANSI but apparently not by ISO.

The current standard proposal does not indicate the relative order of assertion and trigger processing in this case.

The proposed standard also supports a statement for dropping triggers:

```
<drop trigger> ::= DROP TRIGGER <trigger name>
```

9.3
Triggers in Commercial Relational Systems

This section reviews several commercial relational database management systems that support triggers. The description of products given here is based on the authors' understanding of systems from the relevant sections of manuals available at the time of this writing. Again, due to the fast evolution of this field, the reader should be aware that some features described here may already be obsolete, or may become obsolete in a short time. Also note that the descriptions given here are not fully comprehensive. Rather, they briefly describe the general capabilities of each system.

The syntax and execution behavior of the systems span a broad spectrum in their variance from the proposed SQL3 standard, and they vary widely among themselves. Most systems share at least some features with the proposed standard; such features are stated with little discussion. More attention is paid to the non-standard features of each system, and to issues such as limitations on rule interaction, error handling, and authorization. Note that all systems support a command for dropping existing triggers that is similar to the proposed SQL3 command (above); such commands will not be discussed for the individual systems.

There is considerable variation in the handling of referential integrity constraints in systems that also include triggers. Most trigger languages are powerful enough to encode the referential integrity policies discussed in Section 9.1.2. Consequently, in some systems little support is provided for referential integrity on the assumption that it will be implemented using triggers. In other systems a full suite of referential integrity capabilities is provided separately from triggers. The issue of interactions between triggers and referential integrity is an important one, dealt with in the proposed SQL3 standard by prohibiting triggers on tables with referential integrity constraints. However, most commercial systems do not (yet) have such a strict restriction; unfortunately, the systems often do not specify exactly how triggers and referential integrity will interact. Referential integrity is not discussed further in this section.

9.3.1 Oracle

Oracle System 7 supports triggers that are executed either before or after the triggering operation, and with either tuple-level or statement-level granularity. This yields four possible combinations:

```
BEFORE ROW
BEFORE STATEMENT
AFTER ROW
AFTER STATEMENT
```

One trigger can monitor multiple operations on the same table, but each operation (including updates to any column) can be monitored by at most one trigger. Thus, at most twelve triggers per table are allowed. (The difference between the twelve triggers expressible in Oracle and the eighteen expressible in the proposed SQL3 standard is due to the fact that Oracle—and in fact every commercial system discussed here—omits the INSTEAD OF option.) A syntax for triggers in Oracle is:

```
<Oracle trigger> ::= {CREATE | REPLACE} TRIGGER <trigger name>
                     {BEFORE | AFTER} <trigger events>
                     ON <table name>
                     [[REFERENCING <references>]
                     FOR EACH ROW
                     [WHEN <condition>]]
                     <PL/SQL block>


<trigger event> ::= INSERT | DELETE | UPDATE [OF <column names>]


<reference> ::= OLD AS <old value tuple name> |
                NEW AS <new value tuple name> |
```

The condition is supported only in conjunction with the FOR EACH ROW option, and is restricted to be a simple predicate on the modified tuple. The triggered action is a procedure block written in *PL/SQL*, a special database programming language supported by Oracle. PL/SQL procedures in trigger actions may include variable declarations and/or calls to external procedures, but they may not include DDL or transaction control statements. The OLD and NEW references are handled similarly to SQL3, except they are restricted to FOR EACH ROW triggers only. When the REFERENCING clause is omitted, old and new values are implicitly available through built-in variables called

OLD and NEW. When a trigger monitors multiple operations, special predicates INSERTING, DELETING, and UPDATING may be used in the action to detect which triggering event actually occurred.

As an example consider the following Oracle trigger, taken from [ORA92b], which automatically inserts into a table of pending orders the part number, reorder quantity, and current date for those parts whose quantity on hand has fallen below the reorder point for that part (and for which there is no pending order already).

```
CREATE TRIGGER reorder
AFTER UPDATE OF parts_on_hand ON inventory
WHEN (NEW.parts_on_hand < NEW.reorder_point)
FOR EACH ROW
  DECLARE NUMBER X
  BEGIN
    SELECT COUNT(*) INTO X    /* X=1 if already ordered */
    FROM pending_orders       /* X=0 otherwise */
    WHERE part_no = NEW.part_no;
    IF X=0 THEN
      INSERT INTO pending_orders
        VALUES (NEW.part_no, NEW.reorder_quantity, SYSDATE)
    END IF;
  END;
```

Now consider Oracle's execution behavior. Suppose all four kinds of triggers are specified for the same SQL operation, and the operation occurs. The following algorithm is used for trigger processing:

1. Execute the BEFORE STATEMENT trigger.

2. For each row affected by the SQL operation:

   (a) Execute the BEFORE ROW trigger.

   (b) Lock and change the row, then perform row-level referential integrity and assertion checking. (The lock is not released until the transaction is committed.)

   (c) Execute the AFTER ROW trigger.

3. Perform statement-level referential integrity and assertion checking.

4. Execute the AFTER STATEMENT trigger.

It is important to note that steps 1, 2(a), 2(c), and 4 could call the entire algorithm recursively if there are triggers defined on the SQL operations executed by the trigger actions. If an error occurs during trigger execution that is not handled explicitly by the system, then all database changes performed as a result of the original SQL operation and the subsequent triggered actions are rolled back.

Triggers may "cascade" as a result of recursive trigger processing, but there is a maximum number of cascading triggers set at 32. This number can be modified by setting the initialization parameter MAX_OPEN_CURSORS. Note that since the system does not guarantee any particular order for the rows processed by an SQL operation, the result of trigger processing may be nondeterministic.

A specific **CREATE TRIGGER** system-level privilege is required for creating triggers. In addition, trigger creators must either be the **OWNER** of the table on which the trigger is defined, or be granted an **ALTER** privilege on that table. Triggers can be *replaced*; this option permits a new version of a trigger to substitute for an old version without changing any authorizations already granted. Finally, triggers can be selectively *disabled* and *enabled*.

In [ORA92a], applications of Oracle triggers are described for:

- Auditing and event logging

- Automatically computing derived data

- Enforcing referential integrity, business rules, or authorization rules for security

- Maintaining replicated tables synchronously

Reference [ORA92a] also provides some suggestions for trigger design. For example, since triggers are not compiled until they are executed, it is suggested that pre-compiled stored procedures should be used for complex trigger actions. Also, **AFTER ROW** triggers are reported to be somewhat more efficient than **BEFORE ROW** triggers.

9.3.2   Informix

Informix Version 6 provides triggers with a somewhat nonstandard syntax in which multiple triggers are defined within a single rule. Separate condition-action pairs are defined together, one pair to be triggered **BEFORE** a statement, one pair to be triggered **FOR EACH ROW** affected by a statement, and one pair to be triggered AFTER a statement. Statements may be INSERT, DELETE, or UPDATE operations on a given table. There may be at most one rule for each of INSERT and DELETE on a table. For UPDATE there may be multiple rules, provided they refer to mutually exclusive columns. When an update operation modifies multiple columns and triggers multiple condition-action pairs, the order of trigger execution is based column numbers in the table's schema.

A syntax for triggers in Informix is:

```
<Informix trigger> ::= CREATE TRIGGER <trigger name>
                       <trigger event> ON <table name>
                       [BEFORE [<condition>] (<actions>)]
                       [[REFERENCING <references>]
                        FOR EACH ROW [<condition>] (<actions>)]
                       [AFTER [<condition>] (<actions>)]


<trigger event> ::= INSERT | DELETE | UPDATE [OF <column names>]


<reference> ::= OLD AS <old value tuple name> |
                NEW AS <new value tuple name>


<condition> ::= WHEN (<predicate>)


<action> ::= <insert statement> | <delete statement>
             <update statement> | <procedure call>
```

Although each of the BEFORE, FOR EACH ROW, and AFTER clauses are optional, at least one must be present. The REFERENCING clause with an INSERT event may define a variable name for NEW tuples only, while the REFERENCING clause with a DELETE event may define a variable name for OLD tuples only. Conditions may be arbitrary predicates and may include calls to stored procedures. If a condition is omitted, it implicitly returns *true*. The action is executed if condition evaluation produces *true*, while the action is not executed if condition evaluation produces *false* or *unknown*. Actions are arbitrary sequences of insert statements, delete statements, update statements, or procedure calls. Procedures called from trigger actions may not include transaction control statements.

An example of an Informix trigger, taken from [Inf94b], is shown below. The trigger monitors changes to the unit price of stocks. It inserts into a

warning table information about any stock whose unit price has been updated to more than double its original value as the result of a purchase order. CURRENT refers to current date and time.

```
CREATE TRIGGER up_price
UPDATE OF unit_price ON stock
REFERENCING OLD AS pre, NEW AS post
FOR EACH ROW WHEN (post.unit_price > pre.unit_price * 2)
  (INSERT INTO warning
   VALUES(pre.stock_num, pre.order_num, pre.unit_price,
          post.unit_price, CURRENT))
```

Like Oracle, triggers in Informix can cascade but with a built-in limit: The maximum number of cascading triggers in Informix is 60. In Informix, logging may or may not be enabled. When logging is enabled, if an error occurs during trigger execution then the triggering operation and all subsequent triggered actions are rolled back. When logging is not enabled, handling of errors during trigger execution is the application's responsibility. Triggers can be traced and their failure can raise exceptions and generate error messages.

Triggers may be defined by the table's owner or by the database administrator. Applications that cause triggers to be fired must have suitable privileges to execute the queries, database modifications, and stored procedures invoked by the triggers.

Reference [Inf94a] gives suggestions for how to ensure that trigger execution with the BEFORE and FOR EACH ROW clauses cannot affect the outcome of the triggering operation (so that the affect of the operation remains the same with or without triggers), and for achieving deterministic trigger behavior. Informix triggers on external databases in a client-server environment may interact, but a trigger will generate an error if it involves writing to multiple, distributed servers.

9.3.3 Ingres

Ingres supports triggers, referred to as rules, as part of its *Knowledge Management Extension*. Each rule is executed AFTER its triggering operation and with a tuple-level granularity. That is, a rule is defined on and fired immediately after insert, delete, or update operations to individual tuples only. A syntax for rules in Ingres is:

```
<Ingres rule> ::= CREATE RULE <rule name>
                  AFTER <rule events> ON <table name>
                  [REFERENCING <references>]
                  WHERE <predicate>
                  EXECUTE PROCEDURE <procedure call>


<rule event> ::= INSERT | DELETE | UPDATE [(<column name>)]


<reference> ::= OLD AS <old value tuple name> |
                NEW AS <new value tuple name>
```

The predicate may reference constants and it may reference current, NEW, or OLD attributes of the tuple that caused the rule to fire. These same values may also be passed as parameters to the procedure in the rule's action.

The following example, taken from [ASK92], shows an Ingres rule that executes after each deletion of an employee. The rule updates the tuple of the employee's manager by decreasing the number of managed employees by one, then it logs the manager-employee pair into a `mgrlog` table.

```
CREATE RULE emp_delete
AFTER DELETE ON EMPLOYEE
EXECUTE PROCEDURE
  manager_emp_track(ename = OLD.name, mname = OLD.manager)

CREATE PROCEDURE manager_emp_track
  (ename VARCHAR (30),  mname VARCHAR (30)) AS
    BEGIN
      UPDATE manager
        SET employees = employees - 1
        WHERE name = :mname;
      INSERT INTO mgrlog VALUES (:mname, :ename);
    END;
```

Like Oracle and Informix, rule triggering may cascade, with a maximum cascading in Ingres of 20 rules. If an error occurs during rule execution, then the triggering operation and all subsequent triggered actions are rolled back. There is no explicit authorization privilege for rules, but rule creators must own the rule's table and must have an EXECUTE privilege for the procedure invoked by the rule's action.

Reference [ASK92] provides several examples of Ingres rules used for maintaining referential integrity, for enforcing general-purpose business policies, and for managing authorization violations.

9.3.4 Rdb

In *VAX Rdb/VMS*, each trigger is executed either before or after the triggering operation, and with either tuple-level or statement-level granularity, yielding the same four possible combinations as in Oracle. Insert and delete operations on a given table may have at most one trigger of each type, but there may be multiple triggers for update operations as long as the column lists are mutually exclusive for multiple triggers of the same type. A syntax for triggers in Rdb is:

```
<Rdb trigger> ::= CREATE TRIGGER <trigger name>
                  {BEFORE | AFTER} <trigger event>
                  ON <table name>
                  [REFERENCING <references>]
                  WHEN <predicate> (<statement>)
                  [FOR EACH ROW]


<trigger event> ::= INSERT | DELETE | UPDATE [OF <column names>]


<reference> ::= OLD AS <old value tuple name> |
                NEW AS <new value tuple name>
```

The REFERENCING clause is permitted only for statement-level triggers, and it is not permitted for BEFORE INSERT or AFTER DELETE triggers of any form. BEFORE UPDATE and AFTER UPDATE triggers may reference both OLD and NEW, AFTER INSERT triggers may reference NEW only, and BEFORE DELETE triggers may reference OLD only.

The following example, taken from [Rdb91], illustrates how an Rdb trigger can be used to implement the "cascaded update" form of referential integrity enforcement: When status codes in a work_status table are updated, employees' status codes are changed to reflect the new values.

```
CREATE TRIGGER sc_cascade_update
BEFORE UPDATE OF status_code ON work_status
REFERENCING OLD AS old_work_status,
            NEW AS new_work_status
```

```
(UPDATE employee E
 SET E.status_code = NEW.status_code
 WHERE E.status_code = OLD.status_code)
```

In Rdb there is no limit on cascaded triggering. However, a trigger is not allowed to fire itself either directly or indirectly. This restriction guarantees that during trigger processing only a finite number of triggers can fire. If an error occurs during trigger execution, then an error message is produced, and the triggering operation and all subsequent triggered actions are rolled back. There is no special authorization associated with triggers, but trigger creators must have a **CREATETAB** access privilege on the trigger's table.

9.3.5   Sybase

In *Sybase SQL Server Release 10.0*, each table may have at most three triggers, one each for insert, delete, and update operations. All Sybase triggers are statement-level, and triggers always execute after the triggering operation. There are two variants of triggers in Sybase, depending on whether or not update triggers may monitor specific columns. A syntax for the first variant of Sybase triggers, in which specific updated columns are not allowed, is:

```
<Sybase trigger1> ::= CREATE TRIGGER <trigger name>
                      ON <table name>
                      FOR <trigger events>
                      AS <SQL statements>


<trigger event> ::= INSERT | DELETE | UPDATE
```

In the second variant, update events may be specified for given columns, and Boolean connectives **AND** and **OR** may be used for triggering columns, but triggering on deletion is disallowed. A syntax for the second variant of Sybase triggers is:

```
<Sybase trigger2> ::= CREATE TRIGGER <trigger name>
                      ON <table name>
                      FOR <trigger restricted-events>
                      AS [IF <trig-upd-exp>] <SQL statements>


<trigger restricted-events> ::= INSERT | UPDATE


<trig-upd-exp> ::= UPDATE(<column name>) |
```

```
<trig-upd-exp> AND <trig-upd-exp> |
<trig-upd-exp> OR <trig-upd-exp>
```

In both cases, there is no condition part. However, the SQL statements making up the trigger's action may include control structures, which permits the expression of conditionally executed trigger actions. Several types of statements, including data definition commands and **select** queries, are not permitted in trigger actions. However, commands ROLLBACK TRANSACTION and ROLLBACK TRIGGER are supported. ROLLBACK TRANSACTION rolls back the entire transaction, while ROLLBACK TRIGGER rolls back the triggering operation and any subsequent triggered actions.

Sybase supports two system-defined temporary tables called INSERTED and DELETED. These tables include all tuples that were inserted or deleted by the triggering operation. The tables are computed once, after execution of the triggering statement but before the start of trigger processing. Updates are treated as deletes followed by inserts; that is, for each updated tuple its old value is present in DELETED and its new value is present in INSERTED. In addition, a system-defined variable @@rowcount (which is independent of triggers, but useful in the trigger context) counts the number of tuples affected by each statement.

The following example, taken from [Syb], illustrates how a Sybase trigger can be used to implement the "cascaded delete" form of referential integrity enforcement: The trigger propagates deletions from a **titles** table to tables **title_author** and **sales_detail**. Recall that the special table DELETED contains the tuples of the **titles** table that were deleted by the triggering statement.

```
CREATE TRIGGER del_cascade_trig ON titles
FOR DELETE AS
DELETE title_author
  FROM title_author, DELETED
 WHERE title_author.title_id = DELETED.title_id;
DELETE sales_detail
  FROM sales_detail, DELETED
 WHERE sales_detail.title_id = DELETED.title_id
```

Triggers in Sybase can cascade ("nest" in Sybase's terminology) with a built-in limit of 8 firings. Nesting can be disabled entirely by a configuration command. Normally, triggers cannot fire themselves, but another configuration command can be used to permit self-triggering. No authorization on triggers is specified, and the only user allowed to create a trigger on a given table is the table's owner.

9.3.6   Allbase/SQL

Allbase/SQL supports triggers, referred to as rules, that are triggered before or after the operations INSERT, DELETE, and UPDATE, with a statement-level granularity. Allbase triggers allow a simple condition over the modified tuple, and the action is a procedure invocation. Despite their straightforward syntax, rules in Allbase may be quite complex, since the procedure invoked by a rule action may have parameters, local variables, and control structures, and it may execute DDL or DML statements, including cursor declarations and use. Built-in variables called OLD and NEW may be used in rule conditions to reference the old (for DELETE and UPDATE) and new (for INSERT and UPDATE) values for the modified tuple.

An example Allbase rule, taken from [All92], follows. The rule inserts into the table ListDeletes of the PurchDB database all deleted parts having as initial substring a value different from "XXXX."

```
CREATE RULE PurchDB.RemovePart
AFTER DELETE FROM PurchDB.Parts
WHERE SUBSTRING(PartNumber,1,4) <> "XXXX"
EXECUTE PROCEDURE PurchDB.ListDeletes(OLD.PartNumber);

CREATE PROCEDURE PurchDB.ListDeletes
   (PartNumber CHAR(16) NOT NULL) AS
     BEGIN
       INSERT INTO PurchDB.Deletions
         VALUES (:PartNumber, CURRENT_DATETIME);
     END;
```

There is no limit on the number of rules for a given triggering operation, and the system does not provide any control over the ordering of rules when multiple rules are triggered at the same time. Consequently, it is suggested that rules on the same operation should have mutually exclusive conditions so that at most one rule action actually gets executed. Triggers in Allbase can cascade ("chain" in Allbase's terminology) with a built-in limit of 20 firings. If the limit is exceeded, an error is raised which causes the triggering operation and all subsequent triggered actions to be rolled back. Rules can

be *enabled* and *disabled*, and rule firings can be traced by issuing an explicit
SET PRINTRULES ON statement.

Procedures in rule actions may not include transaction control statements. If such a statement is encountered during rule execution, the procedure fails. (Note that the same procedure invoked by an application can execute successfully.) When a procedure triggered by a rule fails, a special statement RAISE ERROR can be used that will cause the procedure name and an error message to be displayed, then the triggering operation and all subsequent triggered actions will be rolled back.

Some design suggestions for Allbase rules are provided in [All92]. For example, it is suggested to use several rules, each with an independent condition and a simple procedure, rather than one single rule with no condition and a complex conditional procedure.

9.3.7   InterBase

InterBase supports triggers with a syntax that differs in several ways from most other trigger languages:

```
<InterBase trigger> ::= DEFINE TRIGGER <trigger name>
                        FOR <table name>
                        [{ACTIVE | INACTIVE}]
                        {PRE | POST} {STORE | MODIFY | ERASE}
                        [<sequence number>]
                        <trigger action>
                        END TRIGGER
                        <messages>


<message> ::= MESSAGE <abort code> "<message text>"
```

Each trigger monitors one operation, either STORE (insert), MODIFY (update), or ERASE (delete), with statement-level granularity. ACTIVE indicates that the trigger is executed in immediate mode, either PRE (before) or POST (after) the operation. INACTIVE means that the trigger is deferred to the end of the transaction. When multiple triggers are defined for the same operation, the sequence number is used for prioritizing trigger execution. If triggers have the same priority then ordering is random. The trigger action is an arbitrary statement in InterBase's *GDML* language. The action may use OLD and NEW, which reference the modified tuple. The action may also include a special ABORT statement with a message code, which generates a message before rolling back the triggering operation and all subsequent triggered actions.

Finally, the action may include a special statement POST, which notifies an *event manager*, that in turn alerts certain applications.

An example trigger in InterBase is:

```
DEFINE TRIGGER restricting_delete FOR cities
PRE ERASE 0
  BEGIN
    FOR t IN tourism
      WITH t.city = OLD.city AND t.state = OLD.state
      ABORT 1;
    END FOR;
    FOR s IN ski_areas
      WITH s.city = OLD.city AND s.state = OLD.state
      ABORT 2;
    END FOR;
  END;
END_TRIGGER


MESSAGE 1: "This city cannot be deleted because it
            exists in the TOURISM relation"
MESSAGE 2: "This city cannot be deleted because it
            exists in the SKI_AREAS relation"
```

The effect of this trigger is to prevent the deletion of a city from the cities table if that city is present in table tourism or in table ski_areas. Note that the behavior of this trigger is equivalent to two referential integrity specifications with a NO ACTION policy.

9.4
Conclusions

This chapter has surveyed the current status of assertions and triggers in the SQL-92 and SQL3 standards, along with trigger capabilities provided by a number of commercial relational database management systems. Of all the capabilities discussed in this chapter, only the SQL-92 standard can be considered stable at the time of this writing. SQL-92 does not include true active database capabilities, but it does include sophisticated features for table constraints, referential integrity constraints, and general assertions.

Furthermore, the influence of SQL-92 assertions can be seen in the proposed SQL3 standard and in commercial trigger systems.

The proposed SQL3 standard extends the assertion capabilities of SQL-92, and it includes a relatively comprehensive trigger language. Triggers in SQL3 provide options for the time of triggering (BEFORE, AFTER, or INSTEAD OF the triggering operation), the granularity of triggering (tuple-level or statement-level), and for prioritizing (ordering) multiple triggers on the same operation. The permitted sets of triggers are restricted by the construction and checking of a *trigger action graph*, which is intended to eliminate undesirable interactions among triggers. Although many features of the proposed trigger language are clear, the trigger language specification in the SQL3 standard document is very long, it lacks specificity in important aspects, and it can be difficult to understand. It is the sincere hope of the authors that the specification will soon be simplified and clarified, since triggers are an important new feature introduced by the SQL3 standard.

Trigger capabilities in commercial database management systems vary widely in both their syntax and their execution behavior. A rough comparison of features supported by commercial systems and by SQL3 is given in Table 9.1. Many commercial systems were influenced to some extent by the evolving specification for SQL3. However, at the time most commercial trigger systems were designed and implemented, the SQL3 specification was at an earlier stage than the specification reported in this chapter. Consequently, many commercial systems do not support recently added SQL3 features, such as the INSTEAD OF clause, priorities (the ORDER clause), or table-level references.

Currently, the biggest single distinguishing feature among commercial systems is whether they support only tuple-level granularity (Ingres, Rdb, Allbase, InterBase), only statement-level granularity (Sybase), or both granularities (Oracle, Informix). Trigger programmers should be aware that these two granularities introduce different styles of trigger design and very different execution paradigms. In addition, like in the proposed standard, in many commercial trigger systems the exact execution behavior for all possible scenarios is under-specified. For simple trigger applications this lack of specificity usually does not pose a problem. However, for more complex applications it may result in surprising trigger behavior.

Both the proposed standard and the commercial products must cope with the integration of constraint (assertion) checking with trigger processing. Here too a clear specification of the exact execution behavior has not yet emerged, nor has a consensus been reached on which of the many choices for

	SQL3	Oracle	Infor-mix	Ingres	Rdb	Sy-base	All-base	Inter-Base
Multiple events	N	Y	Y	Y	Y	Y	Y	Y
BEFORE clause	Y	Y	Y	Y	Y	Y	Y	Y
AFTER clause	Y	Y	Y	Y	Y	Y	Y	Y
INSTEAD OF clause	Y	N	N	N	N	N	N	N
Condition present	Y	Y	Y	Y	Y	N	Y	N
Tuple-level granularity	Y	Y	Y	Y	Y	N	Y	Y
Old/new tuple references	Y	Y	Y	Y	Y	N	Y	Y
Statement-level granularity	Y	Y	Y	N	N	Y	N	N
Old/new table references	Y	N	N	N	N	Y	N	N
Priorities	Y	N	N	N	N	N	N	Y
Cascaded triggering	Y	Y	Y	Y	Y	Y	Y	Y
Self-triggering	N	Y	Y	Y	N	Y	Y	Y
Max. triggering depth	∞	32	61	20	∞	8	20	?
Explicit authorization	Y	Y	Y	N	N	Y	N	N

TABLE 9.1

Features of SQL3 and commercial trigger systems

integrating constraints and triggers is most appropriate.

The reader may have noticed that we have described trigger facilities for relational systems only. Although most commercial object-oriented database systems do not support triggers at the time of this writing, the usefulness of triggers is not limited to relational systems, and we do expect to see active database features supported by object-oriented systems in the relatively near future.

In conclusion, while the proposed SQL3 standard and a number of commercial products already support relatively powerful active database (trigger) capabilities, there are a number of limitations in both the standard and the products. Some of these limitations appear rather obscure and are likely due to historical reasons. We hope that, in the long term, the limitations of SQL3 will be resolved, and commercial products will introduce some of the features of active database research prototypes described in the previous chapters of this book.

10

Applications of Active Databases

Stefano Ceri and Jennifer Widom

Designing a conventional database application usually consists of two distinct phases: first the database schema is designed, then the application is programmed. When application programs execute, they perform data management, access, and modification functions by interacting with the database management system (DBMS), typically through a programmatic interface. In general, the behavior of the database system is "passive," because it responds only to calls from applications. At most, the database system might prevent certain undesired actions over the data, such as actions that violate system-supported integrity or authorization constraints.

The advent of active databases adds a new ingredient to application design, as illustrated in Figure 10.1. Active rules, positioned between the schema and the applications, now become responsible for monitoring the data and performing some actions automatically. These actions are no longer directly coded into the applications themselves, and they may integrate or even change the programs' semantics. The database management system, which now supports active rules, becomes a "reactive" component instead of simply a "passive" component. As a result, the size of the applications can be reduced, and the design task becomes a three phase process: schema design, active rule design, and application programming.

One significant advantage of using active rules is that the rules impose a unique and consistent behavior on the database, independent of the application or transaction that causes the rules' triggering and execution. In other words, active rules establish and enforce data management policies that no application can violate. Consequently, many of the activities that would normally be coded in each application program to support these data management policies are centralized and "abstracted" using rules. This trend in application design, sometimes called *knowledge independence* [FGVLV94], allows an increasing portion of the applications' semantics to be moved into active rules. One important consequence of achieving full knowledge independence is that data management policies can evolve by modifying one set of rules, instead of by modifying a set of application programs.

The kind of database applications that exploit the behavior of active rules can roughly be classified as *internal*, *extended*, or *external*:

- *Internal* applications use active rules to implement conventional system-supported facilities, where active rules are used as a substitute for a special-purpose mechanism built into the database system. Examples of such facilities are management of integrity constraints, computation of views and derived data, and authorization support.

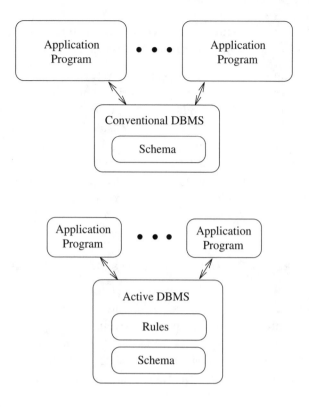

FIGURE 10.1
Application design from conventional to active databases.

- *Extended* applications use active rules as an implementation mechanism to support novel or nonstandard database tasks. For many such applications (along with many internal applications), the appropriate active rules can be generated automatically or semi-automatically from specifications concerning the task. Examples of external applications are workflow management systems, version management (e.g., in the context of engineering databases), and replication management (e.g., in the context of federated databases).

- *External* applications use active rules to obtain automatic reactive behavior in the context of a specific domain or problem. Here, active rules are usually coded in an ad hoc fashion to provide the appropriate behavior. Examples of external applications are manufacturing automation, air traffic control, and power plant management.

The remainder of this chapter considers several active database applications that are representative of these three different types. First, internal applications are discussed by considering active rules for enforcing integrity constraints and for view maintenance. Next, extended applications are discussed in the context of workflow management. Finally, as an example external application, an active database for energy distribution design and management is presented. The chapter concludes with a discussion of general techniques, methodologies, and tools for active rule design and analysis.

10.1
Rules for Integrity Constraint Maintenance

The fact that active rules can be used to support database integrity constraints has long been recognized. Commercial database systems initially motivated the introduction of active rules (triggers) as a mechanism for programming referential integrity between tables. In commercial database system manuals one usually finds the chapters on integrity constraints and active rules close to each other, the latter sometimes being presented as an "implementation technique" for the former. Therefore, it is not surprising that integrity constraint maintenance constitutes one of the primary application areas for active rules.

10.1.1 Features of Constraint Maintenance

Integrity constraints can be classified as either *static* or *dynamic*:

- Static integrity constraints are predicates over database states.

- Dynamic integrity constraints are predicates over transitions from one database state to another.

Each constraint is *valid*, or *consistent*, when it evaluates to an appropriate truth value, either `true` (for constraints in "positive form") or `false` (for constraints in "denial form"). The constraint checking process consists of evaluating the appropriate predicates in order to determine their truth value. Constraint checking can either be *immediate* or *deferred*. Immediate constraint checking takes place immediately after the execution of an operation that may violate the constraint; deferred constraint checking is deferred until the end of the transaction containing the operation that may violate the constraint. Note that checking of certain constraints may inherently need to be deferred: in some cases the intended behavior of a transaction is to produce a final consistent state by passing through a set of intermediate inconsistent states.

When constraint evaluation yields the wrong truth value, the constraint is *violated*. The constraint maintenance system reacts to a violation either by "repairing" the constraint, i.e., performing some suitable database changes that restore the truth value of the constraint, or by rolling back either the specific statement causing the violation or the entire transaction. Rolling back a statement typically is used with immediate checking only; after the deferred detection of a violation, normally the entire transaction must be rolled back.

10.1.2   Active Rules for Constraint Maintenance

Constraint maintenance can be performed by an active database whose rules are generated in an automatic or semi-automatic way. The generated *integrity-preserving* rules perform constraint checking and deal with constraint violations. These rules normally assume that the initial state of each transaction is a consistent state, i.e., a state that satisfies all static constraints. Assuming a standard event-condition-action structure for active rules, each rule is constructed in the following way.

- The triggering event(s) include some or all of the operations that may cause a violation of the constraint predicate.

- The condition checks if the predicate was actually violated.

- The action may either repair the violation, roll back the statement that caused the violation, or roll back the entire transaction.

In order to implement immediate constraint checking, the rules must be executed immediately after the triggering event. If constraint checking is deferred, then the rules must be executed at the end of the transaction in which the rule was triggered.

Several integrity-preserving active rules may correspond to the same integrity constraint. For example, in a relational database if the integrity constraint predicate refers to several tables but active rules monitor only a single table, then there must be at least one integrity-preserving rule per referenced table.

When multiple constraints are violated as the effect of a transaction, several integrity-preserving active rules are executed, possibly according to certain rule priorities. The combined effect of the rules must eventually deal with all constraint violations and produce a final consistent state.

Note that an important practical problem may arise when integrity-preserving rules are first installed, if one cannot assume that the initial database state is consistent. One solution to this problem consists of running the integrity-preserving rules once as if the entire database were just inserted in a single transaction. Of course this mechanism works only when the rules repair constraint violations; a rollback would not be acceptable in this case.

10.1.3   Generation of Active Rules

Integrity-preserving rules can be generated from integrity constraint specifications. Rule generation may involve automated design tools to a varying extent, depending on the decisions that are made automatically by the tools versus those that are left to the designer. The following are possibilities that have been explored in the research literature.

- *Syntactic generation of event(s) and condition.* Triggering events and rule conditions usually can be generated from the integrity constraint specification by means of relatively straightforward syntactic analysis [CW90]. This approach leaves the generation of the action part of rules to the designer.[1]

- *Syntactic generation of event(s) and condition, declarative specification of action.* When multiple repair strategies are possible, the designer may specify, in a declarative style, the integrity constraint together with a repair strategy. Rule generation can then be fully automated [BCP94a, Ger94].

- *Syntactic generation of event(s) and condition, semantic generation of action.* A rule generation tool may exhaustively consider all possible repair actions for a set of constraints and choose an appropriate combination among them, considering the interactions among constraints. Additional information may be gathered from the designer to influence the choice, such as an indication of preferred repair actions for certain constraints [CFPT94, ML91].

---

[1] For restricted constraint types, such as referential integrity constraints or existence and functional dependencies, appropriate repair actions can be generated automatically as well [CW93].

All three approaches are illustrated in the next section using an extended example in a relational database setting.

10.1.4   Example

Consider an accounting application for financial orders that uses the following three tables:

```
Order(OrderNumber,Client,Status,Amount)
Notice(OrderNumber,Bank,State,Date)
Account(Client,Bank)
```

Table `Order` describes orders from clients, table `Notice` indicates that an order is processed by a given bank, and table `Account` indicates that clients have accounts at certain banks.

Consider the following integrity constraint: *There should not be an order with an amount exceeding hundred dollars, processed by a bank in California, such that the client does not have an account at that bank.* The constraint is specified formally using a logical *Datalog*-like language:

```
Order(OrderNumber,Client,Status,Amount),
Amount > 100,
Notice(OrderNumber,Bank,State,Date),
State = "California",
not Account(Client,Bank)
```

Intuitively, the constraint specification is evaluated by looking for assignments of tuples in the database to the tables and variables mentioned in the constraint specification so that all the conditions are satisfied. (For a complete explanation of the evaluation of logical database languages see, e.g., [CGT90, Ull89].) The constraint is in denial form, meaning that the constraint is violated if the specification evaluates to `true`.

Syntactic generation of events and condition

Considering the constraint as specified above, the operations that may violate the constraint are identified as follows.

- Every insert into tables `Order` and `Notice`—the tables mentioned "positively" in the constraint—may produce a new violation (if the new order's amount exceeds 100 and the notice is issued to a bank in California).

- Every deletion from table `Account`—the table mentioned "negatively" in the constraint—may produce a new violation (if the deleted account corresponds to a client and bank with a relevant order and notice).

- Finally, any update to attributes that are used to "join" tables in the constraint specification (i.e., attributes `OrderNumber`, `Client`, and `Bank`) or are used in conditions (i.e., attributes `Amount` and `State`) may produce a new violation, since the updates can turn existing tuples that don't violate the constraint into tuples that violate the constraint.

In summary, the following events may violate the constraint:

```
Order: insert, update OrderNumber, update Client, update Amount
Notice: insert, update OrderNumber, update Bank, update State
Account: delete, update Client, update Bank
```

When the constraint is in denial form, as in the example, the condition part of the active rule is simply the constraint itself. Constraints in positive form must be negated when they are translated to rule conditions.

Combining event generation with condition generation, it is possible to use a relatively straightforward syntactic analysis to automatically generate *rule templates* that include events and conditions but with empty actions. The following three rule templates are generated for the example. Here and in the remainder of the chapter, rules use a simple logic-based syntax that should be self-explanatory. The syntax is closest to that of the *Chimera* rule language, described in Chapter 6.

```
CREATE RULE R1 FOR Order
   ON insert
      update to OrderNumber, Client, Amount
WHEN Order(OrderNumber,Client,Status,Amount), Amount > 100,
     Notice(OrderNumber,Bank,State,Date),
     State = "California", not Account(Client,Bank)
THEN (* Action1 *)


CREATE RULE R2 FOR Notice
   ON insert
      update to OrderNumber, Bank, State
WHEN Order(OrderNumber,Client,Status,Amount), Amount > 100,
     Notice(OrderNumber,Bank,State,Date),
     State = "California", not Account(Client,Bank)
```

```
THEN (* Action2 *)

CREATE RULE R3 FOR Account
  ON delete
     update to Client, Bank
WHEN Order(OrderNumber,Client,Status,Amount), Amount > 100,
     Notice(OrderNumber,Bank,State,Date),
     State = "California", not Account(Client,Bank)
THEN (* Action3 *)
```

In order to complete the rules, a designer must generate the appropriate code for `Action1`, `Action2`, and `Action3`.

Syntactic generation of events and condition, declarative specification of action

A declarative specification of repair strategies for a constraint can be denoted as a collection of *event–repair* pairs. The first element of the pair denotes the event that caused the constraint violation, while the second element denotes the desired repair strategy.[2] Events are indicated as:

- `ON INSERT` *table-name*

- `ON DELETE` *table-name*

- `ON UPDATE` *table-name.attribute-name*

The following repair strategies may be used for any constraint.

- `ALERT(message)`: This strategy signals to the user or application that the constraint has been violated.

- `RESTRICT`: This strategy undoes the operation that caused the constraint's violation. This strategy is possible only when rules are executed in immediate mode.

- `ROLLBACK`: This strategy causes the current transaction to be rolled back.

The following repair strategies may be used when the event is an operation on a table referenced in the constraint.

---

[2]A similar approach for declaring repair strategies in the restricted context of referential integrity is used by the SQL2 standard; see [CO92].

- **ERASE** applies to events on tables with "positive" references in the constraint (e.g., tables **Order** and **Notice** in the example constraint). This strategy deletes from the database all tuples of the event's table that contribute to a constraint violation.

- **CASCADE** applies to **UPDATE** or **DELETE** events on tables with "negative" references in the constraint (e.g., table **Account** in the example constraint). Restrictions on the logical constraint language, omitted here but described in [BCP94a], require that every negative table reference is "linked" by a join with at least one positively referenced table. The positively referenced join table is called the *cascade table*. The repair strategy has two cases:

  1. If the event is **DELETE**, the strategy deletes from cascade tables all tuples that joined with a deleted tuple.

  2. If the event is **UPDATE**, the strategy modifies in cascade tables all attributes that joined with an updated tuple; the cascade tuples are modified to the new join value.

Finally, the following repair strategies may be used when the event is an operation on a table T referenced in the constraint, and the repair action modifies the specified attribute for all tuples in T that contribute to a constraint violation.

- **SET attribute-name NULL** assigns the null value.

- **SET attribute-name DEFAULT** assigns the default value for that attribute (default values are included as part of the schema).

- **SET attribute-name = expression** assigns the result of evaluating the expression; the expression may refer to constants, other attributes, and, in the case of an updated attribute, the old attribute value.

Note that with these last three repair strategies, there is no guarantee that the constraint will be corrected. Hence, it is up to the designer to ensure that the attribute modifications will indeed restore consistency.

Assume that rule events and conditions have been generated automatically as described in the previous section. Once repair strategies have been specified for all triggering events, complete active rules can be generated automatically. Consider the running example, focusing now on constraint violations due to changes to table **Order**. Recall that the triggering events for `Order` are `insert`, `update OrderNumber`, `update Client`, and `update Amount`. Based on the collection of repair actions described above, suppose the following repair strategies are declared.

```
ON INSERT Order ERASE
ON UPDATE Order.OrderNumber CASCADE
ON UPDATE Order.Client ROLLBACK
ON UPDATE Order.Amount ROLLBACK
```

Since there are three different repair strategies (`ERASE`, `CASCADE`, and `ROLLBACK`), three rules are generated as follows. A simplified SQL-like syntax is used for delete and update operations.

```
CREATE RULE R11 FOR Order
  ON insert
WHEN Order(OrderNumber,Client,Status,Amount), Amount > 100,
     Notice(OrderNumber,Bank,State,Date),
     State = "California", not Account(Client,Bank)
THEN delete Order
     where Order(OrderNumber,Client,Status,Amount)


CREATE RULE R12 FOR Order
  ON update to OrderNumber
WHEN Order(OrderNumber,Client,Status,Amount), Amount > 100,
     Notice(OrderNumber,Bank,State,Date),
     State = "California", not Account(Client,Bank)
THEN update Notice
     set OrderNumber = NEW Order.OrderNumber
     where Notice(OrderNumber,Bank,"California",Date)


CREATE RULE R13 FOR Order
  ON update to Client, Amount
WHEN Order(OrderNumber,Client,Status,Amount), Amount > 100,
     Notice(OrderNumber,Bank,State,Date),
     State = "California", not Account(Client,Bank)
THEN Rollback
```

A similar process is used for tables `Notice` and `Account`, generating a complete set of active rules for maintaining the example constraint. Note that if a repair strategy is not specified, a default strategy (such as `ROLLBACK`) could be used so that the designer need only focus on events for which the default action is inappropriate.

Syntactic generation of events and condition, semantic generation of action

Now rules are generated in a fully automatic manner, with few instructions required from the designer beyond the constraint specifications themselves. The approach to this problem described in [CFPT94] is outlined briefly here. (The full details of the algorithm are quite intricate, so the interested reader is referred to [CFPT94].) In addition to constraint specifications, the designer indicates only relative priorities of constraints, and which tables and attributes are permitted to be updated by the integrity-preserving rules. The algorithm explores all possible combinations of repair strategies for the constraints. It produces a set of rules that are guaranteed to establish consistency of all constraints, and that are guaranteed to terminate in any database scenario. (Some constraint violations, however, may not be repaired by rules, but rather will force the transaction to be rolled back.) On the running example, the designer could specify tables `Order` and `Notice` as updatable, while `Account` is specified as read-only. The algorithm might then generate a set of active rules implementing the `ERASE` policy for all events. A related algorithm for generating repair actions is proposed in [ML91], but it is not tailored for generating sets of active rules.

10.2
View Maintenance

Another popular and important internal application of active rules is *view maintenance*. Views are defined by declarations that specify the *name* for the view and a *body* that defines the view. The view body is generally a query in the query language supported by the database system. Once a view has been declared, it may be referenced (by name) in queries, programs, or other view definitions. Views are typically used either to provide a convenient shorthand notation or as a protection mechanism.

Views can be managed in two alternative ways:

- *Virtual views* are not computed or stored. Rather, the view body is combined with queries that reference the view, resulting in modified queries that reference *base* (non-view) data only.

- *Materialized views* are computed from the base data when the view is defined, and the result is stored in the database for use by queries. Materialized views must be kept consistent with the base data over which they are defined. That is, base data changes must be "propagated" to the view.

Both virtual and materialized views can be managed by active rules, as described in the next two sections.

10.2.1   Virtual Views

A description of virtual view management using the POSTGRES rule system was given, along with some examples, in Chapter 2. The ideas are reiterated here, still in a relational context but now using the running example of this chapter and a more generic rule syntax. Recall the example tables from Section 10.1.4:

```
Order(OrderNumber,Client,Status,Amount)
Notice(OrderNumber,Bank,State,Date)
Account(Client,Bank)
```

Consider a view `CriticalOrder` that gives information on orders whose client has no bank account, whose status is not approved, and whose amount is greater than 50. Continuing with the logic-like language used in Section 10.1.4, this view is defined as follows.

```
CREATE VIEW CriticalOrder(OrderNumber,Client,Amount) AS
    Order(OrderNumber,Client,Status,Amount),
    not Account(Client,Bank),
    Status != approved,
    Amount > 50
```

To implement this as a virtual view, an active rule is (automatically) defined for the `select` event on table `CriticalOrder`:

```
CREATE RULE R1 FOR CriticalOrder
  ON select
WHEN true
THEN select OrderNumber,Client,Amount
    from Order
    where Order(OrderNumber,Client,Status,Amount),
          not Account(Client,Bank),
          Status != approved, Amount > 50
```

If updates to a view can be propagated to the underlying base tables without ambiguity, then active rules can be generated automatically to update base tables as a consequence of view updates. For example, the following rule propagates an update to the `Amount` of a `CriticalOrder` to the base table `Order`, provided that the update does not remove the order from the view.

```
CREATE RULE R2 FOR CriticalOrder
  ON update to Amount
WHEN NEW Amount > 50
THEN update Order
     set Amount = NEW CriticalOrder.Amount
     where OrderNumber = NEW CriticalOrder.OrderNumber
```

There are a number of alternatives for handling view updates whose propagation to base tables is ambiguous:

- The designer provides the appropriate active rules for update propagation, as illustrated using POSTGRES in Chapter 2.

- The designer specifies declaratively how updates should be propagated, and the system generates the appropriate active rules.

- The system automatically generates all possible update alternatives, then the choice between alternatives is made by either the system or the designer.

Note that the trade-offs here between designer specification and automatic rule generation are exactly analogous to the trade-offs considered for integrity constraint maintenance in Sections 10.1.3 and 10.1.4.

10.2.2   Materialized Views

Active rules can be used quite naturally to support materialized views. Algorithms for doing so are presented in the context of conventional SQL views in [CW91], and in the context of views defined by deductive database rules (with recursion and stratified negation) in [CW94]. As an example of how these methods work, suppose view `CriticalOrder`, defined in the previous section, is materialized, and consider how changes to the base tables `Orders` and `Client` are propagated to the view.

To propagate changes, the active rules essentially compute and apply *view deltas*: view deltas are the tuples that should be inserted into or deleted from the view. View deltas are computed based on *base table deltas*: the tuples that have been inserted into or deleted from base tables. In general, deltas (also referred to as *delta relations* since they are in fact relations) are much smaller than entire base relations. Therefore, it is usually advantageous to modify materialized views using deltas, rather than recomputing the view from scratch. Modifying views based on deltas is referred to *incremental view maintenance*.

In the example given here, only insertions and deletions are considered; updates are assumed to be modeled as deletions followed by insertions. Delta relations are denoted as the base table prefaced by either `inserted` (for the tuples inserted into the base table) or `deleted` (for the tuples deleted from the base table). For simplicity, assume that the same tuple is not both inserted and deleted by the same transaction (although this case is handled in [CW91, CW94]).

New tuples might be inserted into the view when orders are inserted or when accounts are deleted. The following two active rules handle these cases.

```
CREATE RULE R1 FOR Order
  ON insert
WHEN inserted[Order(OrderNumber,ClientNum,Status,Amount)],
     not Account(Client,Bank),
     Status = approved, Amount > 50
THEN insert into CriticalOrder: (OrderNumber,ClientNum,Amount)


CREATE RULE R2 FOR Account
  ON delete
WHEN Order(OrderNumber,ClientNum,Status,Amount),
     deleted[Account(Client,Bank)],
     Status = approved, Amount > 50
THEN insert into CriticalOrder: (OrderNumber,ClientNum,Amount)
```

Similarly, tuples might be deleted from the view when orders are deleted or when accounts are inserted. The following two active rules handle these cases.

```
CREATE RULE R3 FOR Order
  ON delete
WHEN deleted[Order(OrderNumber,ClientNum,Status,Amount)],
     not Account(Client,Bank),
     Status = approved, Amount > 50
```

```
THEN delete CriticalOrder
    where CriticalOrder(OrderNumber,ClientNum,Amount)


CREATE RULE R4 FOR Account
 ON insert
WHEN Order(OrderNumber,ClientNum,Status,Amount),
    inserted[Account(Client,Bank)],
    Status = approved, Amount > 50
THEN delete CriticalOrder
    where CriticalOrder(OrderNumber,ClientNum,Amount)
```

These examples illustrate the general approach to performing incremental view maintenance using active rules. For this problem, the relevant active rules usually can be generated in a fully automatic way from the view definition. Note that the example view considered here is somewhat more complicated than the simplest possible view, since it includes *negation* in the view definition. (It is negation that causes some base table deletions to be propagated as view insertions, and vice versa.) The rules become more complex when duplicates are present or views are defined recursively; for details see [CW94].

10.3
Rules for Workflow Management

Workflow management systems enable the description and execution of computer-supported, data-intensive activities that involve multiple "steps" of processing. Each step may be processed by a different server and may have a long duration (resulting in what are sometimes referred to as *long-running activities*). Active rules can be a very useful tool for specifying the control and data flow between processing steps in workflow systems. A number of systems have been proposed or developed that use active rules for workflow management, e.g., [BOH+92, BJ94, DHL90].

An example workflow management activity and its handling by active rules is described informally to illustrate the salient points. The example is taken from [DHL90]. Consider a patient information system for a hospital. A patient is first admitted, then examined by a physician. The physician may prescribe a series of procedures (such as laboratory tests, radiology, consultation with a specialist, etc.), he may prescribe medications, and he may require that the patient be hospitalized. After the examination, the various procedures prescribed by the physician must be scheduled and executed within specified deadlines. (Procedures and prescriptions also are recorded, usually for legal and administrative reasons.) If the patient is hospitalized, a room is assigned, and a daily regimen of medication must be followed. As the results of procedures become available, the physician can look at them, reexamine the patient, and prescribe further procedures and medications. At any time, the physician may decide to discharge the patient.

Assume that a patient database, shared by all of the organizations involved, stores patient data in individual "folders." Each activity is modeled as one or more transactions that read or update the database. Clearly there are order and synchronization requirements among the transactions. These requirements can be captured by active rules. Active rules are capable of causing other database updates, of initiating additional transactions, and of communicating with relevant users (possibly through electronic mail or forms). As one example, an active rule could be defined that checks prescriptions against known patient allergies—stored in the patient's folder in the database—and notifies the physician about relevant allergies.

To better handle synchronization requirements between activities, active rules may use extended transaction models, such as *nested transactions* [Mos82], *sagas* [GMS87], or *contracts* [Reu89]. The active rules specified for the hospital workflow example in [DHL90] make use of the *coupling modes* of the HiPAC system (Chapter 7). Recall that rule actions in HiPAC may run as *detached* transactions, which are either *independent* from or *dependent* on the original transaction. In the former case, the spawned transaction runs independently; in the latter case, the spawned transaction is serialized after the original transaction, and it commits only if the original transaction commits.

The following scenario illustrates the use of coupling modes for the hospital workflow example. Initially, the patient's admission is handled by a transaction called *admission* that creates an admission record in the patient's folder. If there is no folder, a dependent transaction, *new-patient*, is generated by a suitable active rule; transaction *new-patient* creates a new folder by eliciting information from the patient. After admission, an independent transaction *examine* is created, where the physician enters his initial diagnosis and may insert requests for procedures or prescribe medications. On commit of the *examine* transaction, medications are checked (e.g., against patient's allergies). Then several parallel, independent *scheduling* transactions are initiated for laboratory procedures that were requested during the examination.

If procedure results are due within a given deadline, suitable events may be set using a timer process.

The model of [DHL90] also supports a special kind of active rule called a *compensating rule*. Suppose the physician decides to hospitalize the patient. As a result, several independent transactions are triggered (such as assigning a room, scheduling daily medications, etc.). Now suppose the physician quickly decides to discharge the patient. If the above transactions have already committed, then they need to be compensated by other transactions (such as freeing the room, canceling the medications, etc.). In the proposed model, when the physician decides to discharge the patient a special event is raised that triggers appropriate compensating rules.

The above examples indicate that active rules can be very useful for workflow management. It is not expected that the appropriate rules will be programmed "by hand." Rather, as with the applications described earlier, a higher level workflow description language can be used, and the active rules can be generated in an automatic or semi-automatic way. Unlike the constraint and view applications described earlier, it is expected that workflow management will require additional special-purpose machinery in addition to the active database system used as a core.

10.4
Rules for Energy Management

A number of external (i.e., ad hoc) applications of active rules have been reported. Examples include software engineering and testing, container packing and loading, order processing, stock market and financial activities [CS94], production control, and even air traffic management. Many of these applications have been designed and prototyped, but only a few have been deployed so far. This section describes an active database prototype for an *Energy Management System*, referred to as *EMS*.

The EMS application has been designed under the auspices of the Italian Energy Board (*ENEL*) for managing the evolution of the Italian electrical power distribution network. Further details of the project can be found in [BCMP94, CW90]. The EMS database provides both:

1. A description of the network's static structure, i.e., the network topology.

2. A description of the network's dynamic operation, i.e., the way power is distributed through the network at a given time.

The power network is composed of *sites* together with *branches* connecting site pairs. Sites can be power stations, where power is generated; intermediate nodes, used for power redistribution; and final users, which make use of the power. Power stations are said to be *distributors*, since they distribute power, while users are said to be *receivers*, since they receive power. Intermediate nodes are both distributors and receivers. Branches have two *switch gears* located at their ends. The open or closed state of each branch is determined by the state of its two switch gears: The branch is open if both switch gears are closed. The network's dynamic operation is described by the state of all of its switch gears and the direction of the current flow associated with all open branches. Operating conditions of the network are monitored daily, with frequent reconfigurations. The topology is modified approximately once per month. The actual network consists of approximately 1600 power stations, 500,000 other sites, and 550,000 branches.

The EMS database schema is object-oriented. The most important classes are *site*, *branch*, and *switch*. The various sites of the network are described by a class hierarchy, rooted in the class *site*. Each site has as attributes a *name* and a *description*. Additional attributes of *distributor* sites describe branches exiting from distributors as well as output power (actual and maximum). Additional attributes of *receiver* sites describe branches entering the site, input power, and power absorbed by the site. Subclasses *distributor* and *receiver* inherit from *site*. Subclass *powerStation* inherits from *distributor*, *user* inherits from *receiver*, and *node* inherits from both *distributor* and *receiver*. Hence, the schema for this class hierarchy is declared as:

```
define object class site
   attributes name: string(20),
              description: string(40)

define object class distributor
   inherits from site
   attributes branchOut: set_of(branch),
              powerOut: real,
              maxPower: real
```

```
define object class receiver
   inherits from site
   attributes branchIn: branch,
              powerIn: real,
              absorbedPower: real

define object class powerStation
   inherits from distributor

define object class node
   inherits from distributor, receiver

define object class user
   inherits from receiver
```

Classes *branch* and *switch* describe connections between sites. The network topology is described by the class *branch*, whose attributes indicate the sites connected, along with the actual and maximum power passed by the branch. The class *switch* describes switches, located at both ends of branches, which have a status set to either "open" or "closed."

```
define object class branch
   attributes name: string(20),
              site1: site,
              site2: site,
              orientation: record(from:distributor, to:receiver),
              maxPower: real,
              passingPower: real

define object class switch
   attributes site: site,
              branch: branch,
              status: (open,closed)
```

Active rules are used in EMS for several different purposes:

- *Topology rules* assist designers in completing or assessing the design of a network whose topology may be incompletely specified.

- *Power distribution rules* redistribute power due to a change in user needs. These rules do not perform changes to the network's topology.

- *Wiring rules* check the wiring design. Each branch carries a collection of *wires*, and each wire has an associated voltage and power. The voltage and power of a wire must not exceed the maximum voltage and power for the *wire type*. The wires associated with a branch must be enclosed in an appropriate *tube*.

In the remainder of this section, some of the topology and power distribution rules are presented. (A few simplifications are introduced to keep the example to a manageable size.) The simple rule language used earlier in the chapter is used here as well, although now with a more object-oriented style. Note in particular that variables representing object identity are used to bind objects in a rule's condition and pass them to the rule's action. Conditions and actions are pseudo-coded in some cases for convenience and readability. A complete set of active rules for this example written using the rule language of *Chimera* (Chapter 6) can be found in [BCMP94]. Wiring rules written in the *Starburst* rule language (Chapter 4) can be found in [CW90].

10.4.1 Topology Rules

The following rules automatically insert and delete appropriate switches when branches are inserted or deleted. They also automatically delete switches when sites are deleted. With these rules, network designers need only manually insert or delete sites and insert branches. Handling of switches and of branch deletions is taken care of by the rules.

```
CREATE RULE R11 FOR branch
  ON insert
WHEN inserted(branch(B))
THEN insert switch(site:B.site1, branch:B, status:open)
     insert switch(site:B.site2, branch:B, status:open)

CREATE RULE R12 FOR branch
  ON delete
WHEN deleted(branch(B))
THEN delete switch S
     where S.branch = B

CREATE RULE R13 FOR site
  ON delete
WHEN deleted(site(S))
```

```
THEN delete branch B
     where B.site1 = S or B.site2 = S
```

The following rules control and monitor the current flow within branches. When switches are opened or closed (by network designers), the current flow must be updated or checked accordingly. Recall that current passes through a branch only when both switches are closed. Hence, when a switch is opened, the passing power is set to zero. When a switch is closed, only one end of the corresponding branch should have a positive (non-zero) input power; if this condition is violated, an error is reported (rules R17 and R18). Otherwise (rule R15), the orientation of the branch is set to reflect the current flow.

```
CREATE RULE R14 FOR switch
   ON update to status
WHEN updated(switch(S)), NEW S.status = open
THEN update branch B
     set B.passingPower = 0
     where S.branch = B


CREATE RULE R15 FOR switch
   ON update to status
WHEN updated(switch(S)), NEW S.status = closed
     and (the other switch of the branch has status = closed)
     and (exactly one site S1 of the two end sites S1,S2
          has powerIn > 0)
THEN update branch B
     set B.orientation.from = S1,
         B.orientation.to = S2
     where S.branch = B


CREATE RULE R16 FOR switch
   ON update to status
WHEN updated(switch(S)), NEW S.status = closed
     and (the other switch of the branch has status = closed)
     and (powerIn = 0 for both end sites S1,S2)
THEN report-error("branch S1-S2 has no current flow")


CREATE RULE R17 FOR switch
   ON update to status
```

```
WHEN updated(switch(S)), NEW S.status = closed
     and (the other switch of the branch has status = closed)
     and (powerIn > 0 for both end sites S1,S2)
THEN report-error("branch S1-S2 has double incoming flow")
```

10.4.2 Power Distribution Rules

The next three rules primarily react to changes in power requests from users. The rules redistribute power by propagating the change along the tree connecting the relevant user to its power station. Rule R21 reacts to changes in user requirements by propagating the changes to the relevant input branch. Rule R22 reacts similarly to changes of requirements at intermediate nodes. Rule R23 reacts to a change in passing power at a branch. It considers the input site to the branch, recalculates the total passing power of branches from that input site, and assigns the new value as the outgoing power of that site. Note that these rules can also handle new users, branch insertions, and changes to absorbed power at intermediate nodes.

```
CREATE RULE R22 FOR user
   ON insert, update to absorbedPower
  WHEN updated(user(U)), NEW U.absorbedPower != U.powerIn
  THEN update U
          set U.powerIn = U.absorbedPower;
       update branch B
          set B.passingPower = U.powerIn
          where U.branchIn = B


CREATE RULE R22 FOR node
   ON insert, update to powerOut, absorbedPower
  WHEN updated(node(N)),
       NEW N.absorbedPower + NEW N.powerOut != powerIn
  THEN update N
          set N.powerIn = N.absorbedPower + N.powerOut;
       update branch B
          set B.passingPower = N.powerIn
          where N.branchIn = B


CREATE RULE R23 FOR branch
   ON insert, update to passingPower
  WHEN inserted(B) or updated(B),
```

```
        S = B.orientation.from,
        T = (total of passingPowers of branches output from S),
        T != S.powerOut
   THEN update S
        set S.powerOut = T
```

The next two rules, R24 and R25, react to violations of the maximum power supported by power plants, nodes, or branches by rolling back the current transaction. Here rule priorities are introduced. Rules R24 and R25 are specified to run "before" (with higher priority than) rules R22 and R23, respectively. This is for efficiency: Since rules R24 and R25 are triggered by the same updates as rules R22 and R23, respectively, then if the transaction is to be rolled back there is no reason for executing R22 or R23 first.

```
CREATE RULE R24 FOR distributor
   ON insert, update to powerOut
 WHEN inserted(D) or updated(D),
        NEW D.powerOut > D.maxPower
 THEN Rollback
 BEFORE R22


CREATE RULE R25 FOR branch
   ON insert, update to passingPower
 WHEN inserted(B) or updated(B),
        NEW B.passingPower > B.maxPower
 THEN Rollback
 BEFORE R23
```

10.4.3   Discussion

Although still relatively modest in size, the EMS case study, particularly the power distribution rules, generate some interesting observations:

- The exact semantics of the active rules has not been specified, although their intuitive meaning is clear. Note that the power distribution rules are correct with either tuple-oriented or with set-oriented rule execution. Tuple-oriented execution propagates each individual change from users to power stations, while set-oriented execution can effectively cluster together changes that are at the same distance from a power station.

- Increases and decreases of power may be propagated simultaneously through the network (through interleaving of rule executions). Consequently, it is possible for rule R24 or R25 to generate a rollback as a result of excess power at a site or branch, even when there are pending decreases for that same site or branch. This problem can be circumvented by modifying the rules as follows. Each rule R21, R22, and R23 is rewritten as a pair of rules, one of which is activated by insertions and power increases, the other by power decreases. (Increases versus decreases must be checked as part of the rule's condition.) Then the decrease rules are specified to have priority over the increase rules.

- Rules R22 and R23 are mutually triggering: one of them is triggered by changes to `passingPower` and performs changes to `powerOut`, while the other is triggered by changes to `powerOut` and performs changes to `passingPower`. Despite the mutual triggering, there is no problem with termination, assuming that the power network itself does not have cycles. Rule termination is discussed further in Section 10.5.2.

10.5
Approaches to Active Rule Design

Even small numbers of active rules can be quite complex to understand and manage: They may react to arbitrary database modifications and event sequences, they may trigger each other, and sometimes the outcome of rule processing may depend on the order in which events occur or rules are scheduled. In addition, most of the commercially available active rule systems (and many research prototypes) operate at a relatively low level of abstraction and are heavily influenced by implementation-dependent procedural features.

Understanding the meaning of a collection of rules is especially difficult as rules are added or deleted. Predicting rule behavior after the set of rules has changed is often much harder than one would expect, due to subtle interactions between rules. The interactions, and indeed the rules themselves, are not always well understood just by looking at their specifications. Furthermore, even when the outcome of rule processing is clear, database designers are sometimes worried that the use of active rules may reduce the overall performance of their applications. For these reasons, active rules so far have been approached with a great deal of care (and some degree of skepticism), even in the context of commercial relational systems that have supported simple triggers for some time. A number of steps are envisioned to improve the situation:

- With complex databases involving several application developers, rule programming can be considered as a *privileged task* assigned to the database administrator, rather than being delegated to application programmers. One can consider rule programming as a schema design activity, handled by experts. In this way, although preventing unexpected behavior is still difficult, rules affecting all users are placed within a clear centralized control, and rule behavior can be more closely monitored.

- The *level of abstraction* of many popular applications of active rule systems can be raised. As described earlier in this chapter, for applications such as integrity constraints, views, and workflow, it is possible to specify the application at a higher level of abstraction and then generate the appropriate active rules in an automatic or semi-automatic way.

- *Design tools* can be provided, offering assistance to the rule designer in specifying, installing, and debugging rules. Facilities for off-line analysis of sets of active rules can help predict undesirable rule behavior. Trace facilities can help users understand the behavior and performance of rule execution. Dynamic controls can be provided for debugging rules by allowing their on-line modification without recompilation.

- Designers can be offered *methodological guidance* in designing the appropriate set of rules for a particular application. In particular, *modularization mechanisms* can be provided for active rules, enabling the designer to focus on internal module design separate from module interaction; see, e.g., [BCP94b]. Such mechanisms introduce for active rules a notion of programming "in the small" and "in the large," which is typical of programming languages but is currently lacking for most active rule languages.

The remainder of this section discusses some of these issues in more depth. The first subsection addresses automatic generation of active rules. A framework is described that unifies the rule generation approaches illustrated earlier in the chapter for integrity constraints and views. In the next subsection, the topic of automatic rule analysis is addressed. The last subsection discusses rule debugging.

10.5.1   Rule Generation

It appears that many *internal* and *extended* applications[3] of active databases can be specified at a higher level than the active rules themselves. The higher level specifications are then compiled into a set of appropriate rules in an automatic or semi-automatic way. This approach was illustrated for the integrity constraints application in Section 10.1 and for the view maintenance application in Section 10.2. Section 10.3 indicated that rules for the workflow application could also be generated from higher level specifications. There are a number of advantages to generating rules automatically in addition to ease of programming: Generated rules have a known structure, they may automatically be analyzed and optimized, and it is possible to guarantee through the compilation process that the generated rules will behave correctly.

Figure 10.2 shows a "reference architecture" for the semi-automatic generation of active rules starting from a high level specification. Initial declarative specifications are provided by the designer, possibly through an interactive analysis and feedback process. Then, specifications are translated into a preliminary set of active rules or rule templates. For some applications, the user may need to fill in the rule templates (as was illustrated by examples in Section 10.1.4), or the user may need to make some choices among different possible sets of active rules. Once the rules are fully constructed, they are processed by a rule analyzer in order to detect potential problems in rule interaction. (Rule analysis is discussed further in Section 10.5.2.) The rules are finally processed by a rule optimizer. A variety of techniques are possible in the rule optimization step, such as replacing several related rules with a single rule, and substituting references to entire tables with references to smaller "delta" tables containing relevant changes (recall Section 10.2.2).[4]

A number of the steps illustrated in Figure 10.2 may be skipped. For example, if specification is a one-step process, if rule generation is fully automatic, if no rule analysis is necessary, and if no optimization is possible, then the *preliminary specifications* are fed directly to the *rule generator,* and the rules produced by the *rule generator* are the final rules installed in the active database system.

---

[3]Recall that these terms were defined in the introduction to this chapter.
[4]Further discussion of active rule optimization in the context of rules for integrity constraints can be found in [CW90].

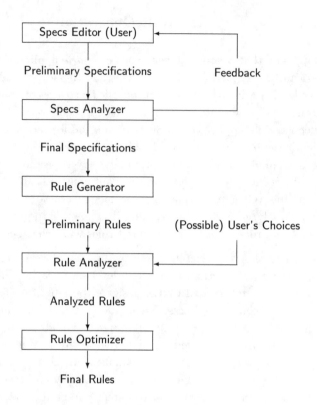

FIGURE 10.2

Generating active rules from declarative specifications.

10.5.2   Rule Analysis

Formal properties of rules, detectable by static analysis, can be very useful in predicting and debugging the run-time behavior of a set of rules. For example, it is very useful to know in advance that rule processing is guaranteed to terminate under all circumstances (i.e., regardless of the triggering transaction and the database state). In addition, it can be useful to know that a set of rules that are not fully prioritized will always have the same outcome, independent of choices among non-prioritized rules. Of course in addition to satisfying the above properties, rules should be "correct," meaning that they perform exactly the activity that is required by the application. In many cases the correctness of each individual rule is evident, so the primary issue is predicting and understanding the interaction between rules. Analyzing formal properties such as those described above is generally a good first step (if not a sufficient step) to guaranteeing that rule interactions are correct.

Hence, *rule analysis* is a static, compile-time analysis performed on a given collection of rules. The goal of rule analysis is to establish formal properties of rules that hold for arbitrary transactions and database states. Three such properties of interest are:

- *Termination*—ensuring that rule processing is guaranteed to terminate, i.e., rules do not trigger each other forever.

- *Confluence*—ensuring that rule processing will produce the same final database state, independent of the execution order of non-prioritized, simultaneously triggered rules.

- *Observable determinism*—ensuring that all visible actions performed by rules (such as screen output, messages transmitted, errors raised, transaction rollbacks, etc.) are the same, independent of the execution order of non-prioritized, simultaneously triggered rules.

Termination and confluence analysis are discussed briefly in the next two subsections. A fair amount of technical work has been done in the area of rule analysis; for details see, e.g., [AWH92, BW94, KU94, vdVS93, ZH90].

Termination

The typical way to analyze a set of active rules for the termination property is to construct a *triggering graph*. The nodes of the graph correspond to the rules in the set. There is a directed edge from node R_i to node R_j if and only if execution of rule R_i's action can trigger rule R_j. If there is a cycle in the graph, such as that illustrated in Figure 10.3, then rules may trigger each other indefinitely and the termination property does not hold.

Termination analysis is generally *conservative*. This means that if the analysis determines that the rules are guaranteed to terminate, then indeed the property holds. However, the analysis could determine that the rules "may not" terminate, even when the property does hold. Hence, in practice, cycles in triggering graphs simply indicate all possible causes of nontermination. The designer can then analyze each of the "dangerous" cases, and either determine that rule processing is in fact guaranteed to terminate (due to additional semantics of rules, or known properties of the underlying database), or the designer can modify the rules and run the analysis again.

The accuracy of the analysis—how conservative it is— depends in large part on the accuracy of the procedure used to place the triggering edges in

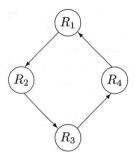

FIGURE 10.3
Cyclic triggering graph.

the graph. Using a simple syntactic analysis (as performed in, e.g., [AWH92, CW90]) there is an edge from R_i to R_j whenever any of rule R_i's actions corresponds to a triggering event of rule R_j. Using a more sophisticated and accurate analysis (as performed in, e.g., [BW94]), in some cases it is possible to determine that, even though R_i's action contains an event of R_j, after execution of R_i the condition of R_j will always be false. In such cases, there is no edge from R_i to R_j.

Even with accurate edge analysis, there are some cases where cycles are produced in the graph but termination is still guaranteed. For example, termination is guaranteed if cyclic rules perform monotonic operations with a finite bound, such as deleting from but never inserting into a given table, or if rules "traverse" a database representing an acyclic graph. A scenario illustrating the latter case was discussed in Section 10.4.3.

Confluence

If all rules in the rule set of interest are prioritized, that is, there is a total ordering on the set of rules, then rule processing is fully deterministic and confluence is guaranteed. Confluence also is guaranteed if it is certain that no two rules will ever be triggered at the same time (as prescribed by some commercial trigger systems). However, if multiple rules may be triggered at the same time, and if rules are not fully prioritized, then confluence is not guaranteed. In general, analyzing rules for the confluence property is considerably more complex than analyzing termination.

In order to analyze confluence, it is first necessary to determine whether two rules are *commutative*. Two rules R_i and R_j commute if, given any

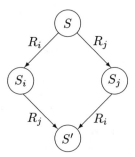

FIGURE 10.4
Commutative rules.

database state S in which R_i and R_j are both triggered, processing rule R_i and then rule R_j from state S produces the same state S' as processing rule R_j and then rule R_i. Commutativity is illustrated in Figure 10.4.

One way to analyze confluence is to test if all pairs of rules in the rule set commute; if so, then confluence holds. However, in many cases this condition is too restrictive. For example, there may be priorities between certain pairs of rules, and it may be known that certain pairs of rules cannot be triggered at the same time. Such rules need not necessarily be commutative. Hence, taking these factors into account, a more complicated but less conservative method for analyzing confluence has been developed in [AWH92] in the context of the *Starburst* rule system (Chapter 4). Let S be the set of rules, let P be a partial order on S indicating priorities (i.e., $R_1 > R_2 \in P$ denotes that R_1 has precedence over R_2), and let $T(R)$ be a function returning all rules that may be triggered by R (possibly including R itself). Let R_i and R_j be any pair of non-prioritized rules in S. Let $S_1 \subseteq S$ and $S_2 \subseteq S$ be constructed by the following algorithm.

$$S_1 \leftarrow \{R_i\}$$
$$S_2 \leftarrow \{R_j\}$$

repeat until unchanged:

$$S_1 \leftarrow S_1 \cup \{R \in S \mid R \in T(R_1) \text{ for some } R_1 \in S_1$$
$$\text{and } R > R_2 \in P \text{ for some } R_2 \in S_2$$
$$\text{and } R \neq R_j\}$$

$$S_2 \leftarrow S_2 \cup \{R \in S \mid R \in T(R_2) \text{ for some } R_2 \in S_2$$
$$\text{and } R > R_1 \in P \text{ for some } R_1 \in S_1$$
$$\text{and } R \neq R_i\}$$

Confluence is guaranteed if, for every pair of non-prioritized rules R_i and R_j in S, when the algorithm above is applied, every pair of rules $R_1 \in S_1$ and $R_2 \in S_2$ commute. The intuition behind this analysis technique—and the proof that it is correct—is quite intricate and can be found in [AWH92].

10.5.3   Rule Debugging

Rule generation and rule analysis are very useful techniques for designing and performing compile-time tests on sets of rules. However, even with such techniques, a run-time debugger is a crucial component of a rule development environment, especially for rules that are coded "by hand." To learn about features that a rule debugger might provide, the reader is referred to Chapter 6, which describes a comprehensive debugger for the *Chimera* rule language. Another debugger, with somewhat fewer features but providing an interesting graphical interface for observing rule execution, is supplied with the *EXACT* active database system; see [DJP93] for details. An alternative approach to active rule debugging based on simulation is described in [Beh94]. To date, most active database systems do not provide a useful rule debugger.

Using the facilities provided by a rule debugger, it is generally possible for the designer to step through rule execution, either at a built-in or a specified level of granularity. The designer can then follow rule behavior and database state closely, and may be able to modify certain aspects of rule execution dynamically to correct errors. For large ad hoc active database applications, such as the EMS case study described in Section 10.4, a powerful debugger is an essential tool for developing and fine-tuning the appropriate set of active rules.

10.6
Conclusions

This chapter has illustrated, primarily through a number of examples, that active databases can be used for a wide variety of applications. In addition, several issues related to the task of designing active rules have been discussed. The chapter has advocated a "declarative approach" for certain rule applications, where an appropriate set of active rules can be generated from a higher level, more declarative application specification. Techniques for static analysis of active rules have been presented, along with a discussion of run-time rule debugging.

Through the examples and discussion in this chapter it is evident that active rules can form a fundamental implementation mechanism for many database applications (both *internal* and *extended*), and active rules can be an important ingredient of more complex *external* facilities. It is expected that further development and deployment of rule analysis techniques and design tools, as well as modularization mechanisms and better understanding of rule interactions, will increase the use (and ease of use) of active rules at all levels.

11

Conclusions and Future Directions

Jennifer Widom and Stefano Ceri

Rather than summarizing the preceding chapters of the book, this short concluding chapter serves instead to highlight general trends in the area of active database systems (Section 11.1), to point out significant areas of consensus in the field, or lack thereof (Sections 11.1 and 11.2), to assess commercial standardization and its relationship to research prototypes (Section 11.3), and to both predict and suggest directions for future progress in the field (Section 11.4).

11.1
Trends and Consensus

Chapter 1 introduced the basic concepts of active database systems, including issues regarding active rule languages, rule execution semantics, system architecture, and implementation issues. Chapters 2–8 then explained how these issues have been addressed in seven different active database research projects. Although there are significant differences across the projects (see Section 11.2 below), there appears to be general consensus on a number of issues, including both strengths and weaknesses of current systems.

Rule paradigm

The *Event-Condition-Action* (ECA) rule paradigm is widely accepted for active database systems, and it provides the flexibility required by most applications. The alternative *Condition-Action* (CA) rule paradigm—bearing a closer resemblance to AI rule languages and to deductive databases—is not as flexible but tends to be easier to use from the rule programmer's perspective. Most active database systems provide only ECA rules, although some systems provide both ECA rules and CA rules. An alternative approach is to provide only ECA rules in the kernel rule language and system, but then to provide the additional capability to translate CA rules into an appropriate set of ECA rules.

Events, conditions, and actions

All active database systems that support ECA rules provide, as basic features, *events* that correspond to data modification operations, *conditions* that correspond to (sometimes limited) queries or predicates over the database, and *actions* that are database operations. Extensions to these basic features, however, vary widely from system to system.

Condition evaluation

Crucial to the performance of active database systems is efficient evaluation of rule conditions. Techniques such as *discrimination networks* and *incremental evaluation* (introduced in Chapter 1) have been incorporated into some systems, but many systems still evaluate rule conditions using a "brute force" query execution method. For scalability of rule processing—scalability in both the number of rules and the size of the database—sophisticated mechanisms for efficient condition evaluation may become necessary.

Application interaction

Most active database systems are relatively "internal" to the database system itself, with limited capabilities for interacting with applications. Although some of the more ambitious systems have integrated external application events and procedure calls within their active rule language (e.g., HiPAC; see Chapter 7), these systems have not been fully implemented. Most systems have not addressed how rule processing might interact spontaneously with users and applications, such as when data is retrieved automatically by rules, or when errors or exceptions occur.

Coupling modes

The notion of *coupling modes*, used to specify the relationship between the execution of rule components and transactions (recall Chapter 1), appears in a number of active database systems, although not all. As with application interaction, most systems that suggest supporting a full complement of coupling modes have not been fully implemented. However, it is recognized that coupling modes are very useful for many applications, for both functionality and performance. An alternative approach is to not provide coupling modes as part of the active rule system itself, but rather to enable rule conditions and actions to invoke existing database facilities that provide the desired transactional behavior.

Relational versus object-oriented

Relational and object-oriented active database systems have a number of natural differences due to their fundamentally different data models, and due to the richer structural and behavioral aspects of object-oriented systems. However, many of the issues associated with active database systems—issues discussed in this chapter and in Chapter 1—are common to both relational and object-oriented systems.

One distinct advantage of object-oriented databases, exploited in several active database systems, is that often rules can be treated as first-class objects within the system. Treating rules as first-class objects means that certain capabilities for rules are obtained automatically, e.g., rule creation and deletion, concurrency control, and authorization. The same capabilities usually must be "hard coded" for active rules in a relational system. Furthermore, object-oriented systems usually provide features that can be used for structuring or modularizing rule sets, such as classes, collections, and inheritance.

System architecture

There are several alternatives for the system architecture of an active database system, discussed in detail in Chapter 1. Although many architectures are represented in the research projects discussed in this book, it is generally accepted that a *built-in* architecture—active database capabilities incorporated directly into the core database system itself—is most advantageous in terms of performance and scalability. In addition, a built-in architecture usually is necessary to fully integrate active database functionality with database facilities such as authorization, concurrency control, and recovery.

Unfortunately, as discussed in Chapter 1, built-in architectures may inhibit portability of active rule facilities, and they may inhibit interoperability among different active database systems. Using a *toolkit* architecture—where basic database facilities are developed separately and then configured into a full system—may provide good performance and system integration without compromising portability and interoperability. Except for the Ariel system (Chapter 3), the toolkit approach for active database systems has not been explored in depth.

Other architectures discussed (e.g., *layered*, *compiled*) usually result in inferior performance and/or functionality as compared with a built-in or toolkit architecture. However, these architectures do generally provide a shorter path to a prototype system; hence they can be very useful for experimentation.

11.2
Significant Differences

Despite the areas of relative agreement described in the preceding section, in a number of other areas there is still little consensus among systems. Broadly speaking, the disagreements usually can be attributed to the fact that a choice must be made between a number of reasonable alternatives, and each alternative seems to be appropriate for certain scenarios. Some of the significant differences across the systems covered in this book are in the following areas.

Rule processing semantics

The semantics of rule processing varies widely from system to system. Some of the semantic differences are large and obvious, such as whether multiply triggered rules execute sequentially or concurrently, while other differences are more subtle, such as instance-oriented versus set-oriented rule execution in relational systems. Additional differences include the conflict resolution strategy (if there is one at all), recursive versus iterative rule processing, the granularity of rule execution with respect to user commands or transactions, and many other differences that are particular to given systems. A strong disadvantage of this variety in execution semantics is that rules appearing syntactically similar (or even identical) may behave in quite different ways in different systems. Historically, the differences can be justified by the fact that each semantics is useful for certain applications; however, some degree of standardization clearly is needed.

Transition values

Related to the differences in execution semantics are differences in how rules reference *transition values* and prior database states (recall Chapter 1). As an example of the discrepancies, in one system the keyword **inserted** refers to a set of tuples or objects that have been inserted, while in another system the same keyword refers to a single value. Keyword **old** in one system refers to the prior value of an updated tuple, in another system it refers to the database state preceding the most recent command, while in yet another system it refers to the state at the start of the current transaction. As a final example, in some systems a reference to a relation (or class) name refers not to the current or even past value of that relation, but rather to one or more elements of the relation whose modification triggered the rule. Discrepancies in transition value and past state references, as with execution semantics, can make rules that appear similar behave very differently. Again, the differences are due historically to a variety of application needs, but the differences can be very confusing, and some level of agreement is needed.

Value passing

Different mechanisms are used, and different levels of capability are supported, for passing values from rule events to conditions, and for passing values from conditions to actions. In some systems values are passed explicitly, while in other systems an implicit mechanism is used. Some systems simply do not let values be passed among rule components at all. (However, it is generally accepted that at least some mechanism for value passing is useful if not necessary for many of the more interesting active database applications.)

Rule ordering

Approaches to ordering or prioritizing rules vary considerably across systems. Almost all systems permit some degree of nondeterminism in rule execution behavior (although commercial systems and forthcoming standards impose considerable restrictions to avoid nondeterminism). Approaches that allow the user or system administrator to "control" nondeterminism vary from relative priorities between pairs of rules to numerical priority assignments to complex and configurable conflict resolution strategies.

11.3
Standardization

Needless to say, it would be useful if a consensus could be reached on the confusing and sometimes conflicting issues discussed in the previous section. Unfortunately, as mentioned above, for each alternative there seems to be a convincing argument or motivating application where that particular alternative is appropriate.

One place where a consensus is hoped to be reached is within the forthcoming SQL3 standard [ISO94]. It is interesting to note that even among commercial vendors, currently there are significant and subtle differences across trigger systems (recall Chapter 9), similar in spirit to many of the differences discussed in Section 11.2 with respect to research prototypes. It is expected that the consolidation of the standard will go a long way towards resolving these discrepancies. However, it must be noted that the current SQL3 standard document does little to clarify the important choices and distinctions, and the document is very long and quite difficult to understand and interpret. Hence, there is certainly a danger that even different commercial active database systems, all apparently conforming (syntactically) to a single standard, will behave differently in subtle ways.[1]

Another important point to note is that the proposed SQL3 standard, along with most current products, imposes considerable restrictions on the features of the rule language, particularly on the sets of rules allowable in the system. These limitations are designed primarily to avoid complicated and unexpected rule interactions, a laudable goal. However, the restrictions themselves can be complex to understand (recall again Chapter 9), and many active database applications simply are not possible given the restrictions of commercial trigger systems.

The consolidation and associated restrictions of commercial trigger systems leads to the question of what the future of active database technology brings, in light of the SQL3 standard. It is generally felt that similar to, e.g., query languages or transaction management, research in the field will remain several steps ahead of commercialization, with research projects and prototypes providing richer and more flexible capabilities than commercially available systems. From a system architecture standpoint, however, it may be discovered that a traditional database system incorporating SQL3 triggers can provide an appropriate basis for implementing richer active database capabilities. The expressive rule languages and other features suggested by research prototypes may become "add on" capabilities of traditional database systems.

11.4
Future Directions

The projects described in this book may be considered as representative of a "first generation" of active database systems. Even these systems vary considerably in their power (as discussed in Section 11.2 above). There is a relatively clear division, however, between less powerful systems that have been fully implemented and tested, and more powerful systems that have been designed but only partially implemented. As a first step in the "next generation," it is expected that many of the more complex features will be implemented, with a considerable focus on efficient mechanisms for all aspects of implementation. In addition, the following features have been suggested

---

[1]The cynical reader may note that if this does happen, it will not be the first time in the history of SQL.

either by the active database researchers themselves, or by the application developers who wish to exploit active database technology.

Event languages

There is a clear trend towards more expressive and complex triggering events for rules, usually specified using a special-purpose *event language*. Of the projects represented in this book, the HiPAC system (Chapter 7) provides relatively complex events, while the Ode system (Chapter 8) incorporates a very rich event language. Other research projects focusing on expressive rule events include SAMOS [GD94] and Sentinel [CKAK94], described briefly in Chapter 1.

Event languages may include a number of special operators in addition to standard Boolean operators, and they may incorporate time-related events, transactional operations, and application interaction. Such languages permit very complex behavior to be programmed within active rules, hence they further complicate rule execution semantics and interaction among rules and should be used with care.

Rules and transactions

Although there is some discrepancy among current systems in how rules may interact with transactions (as discussed in Section 11.2), there is certainly a general trend towards providing more flexibility in the rule-transaction relationship. Flexibility can be achieved partially through coupling modes; combining rules with nontraditional transaction models (such as sagas [GMS87], contracts [Reu89], and their successors [Elm92]) might prove useful as well. Most important is that rules should be able to exploit the characteristics of and guarantees provided by transactions when they are appropriate, but rules should not be "burdened" by transaction mechanisms when they are inappropriate.

Application interaction

As described earlier, most current active database systems provide limited support for interacting with applications. Clearly the next generation of systems must provide such support. Initial experience with active database applications—those built using commercial trigger systems as well as those built using research prototypes—has indicated a strong need for closer interaction between applications and rules. Although ideally it may seem that "correct" rule behavior should be invisible to applications, and indeed this may be so when rules are used for simple integrity constraints or view maintenance, triggering events and triggered actions often involve applications, and some form of interaction becomes imperative in the presence of errors and exceptions.

Configurable and extensible systems

It has been observed in Section 11.2 that one reason no single active database paradigm has emerged is because, among the alternatives proposed, there are motivating uses for each. One solution to this problem, of course, is to provide all of the alternatives; that is, provide an active database *toolkit*, or a *configurable* or *extensible* active database system. Some alternatives are provided in the Chimera system, discussed in Chapter 6, while the recent EXACT system is designed specifically for extensibility.

Although configurability can be very attractive, it also can introduce considerable complexity. If different alternatives are permitted to coexist, then instead of understanding how a set of rules with a fixed functionality behaves—already often a difficult task—it becomes necessary to understand how sets of rules with very different features interact. Still, with the appropriate restrictions and tools, or by configuring the system for a particular application, this approach may prove to be very useful.

Temporal and real-time active databases

Recent trends in the database field have led to *temporal databases*, in which queries may be posed over the history of the database rather than only its current state, and *real-time databases*, in which operations or transactions are executed with specific deadlines. Active rules inherently operate over at least a limited history of the database (since rules are triggered by database changes), and active databases often are useful for time-related activities. Consequently, there appears to be a natural connection between active, temporal, and real-time databases. Surprisingly, there has been only limited work so far in integrating these areas: temporal active databases are discussed in [CSS94, EGS93, EGS94, SC93], while HiPAC (Chapter 7) and REACH [BBKZ93] address real-time activities to some extent. Considerable further work is anticipated.

Relationship to expert systems

Active database systems bear a strong resemblance to *expert systems* in the artificial intelligence field, although the Event-Condition-Action paradigm of active database systems contrasts somewhat with the Condition-

Action paradigm of expert systems, and the general mode of rule processing differs slightly as well (recall Chapter 1). Still, there is no question that active database systems can provide a useful basis for building expert systems that operate on very large databases, and only limited work has been done in exploiting the relationship between the fields, e.g., [DE89, DOS$^+$92, GP91, SLR88]. Although the next generation of active database systems seems to be moving even more towards database- and application-specific features (such as complex events and interaction with applications and transactions), it is hoped that integration with AI rule systems will find its way onto the agenda as well.

Formal foundations and usability

Finally, two largely neglected and crucially important areas within the field of active database systems are *formal foundations* and *usability*. Although some very preliminary work has been done in the area of formal foundations [FMT94, Wid92, Zan93], there is no unifying theory underlying active database systems comparable to the theory underlying deductive database systems, or even comparable to the theory underlying more systems-oriented database areas such as query optimization and transaction management. A formal foundation for active database rule languages would provide a very important step in understanding and characterizing the commonalities and differences across systems.

Usability issues in active database systems have been discussed at some length, particularly in Chapters 1 and 10. Usability, or lack thereof, is currently one of the biggest complaints among those who have built active database applications. Hence, the next generation of systems almost certainly will include features developed especially for usability: features such as active rule design methodologies, structuring mechanisms, and tracing and debugging tools.

Bibliography

[ABC+76] M.M. Astrahan, M.W. Blasgen, D.D. Chamberlin, K.P. Eswaran, J.N. Gray, P.P. Griffiths, W.F. King, R.A. Lorie, P.R. McJones, J.W. Mehl, G.R. Putzolu, I.L. Traiger, B.W. Wade, and V. Watson. System R: Relational approach to database management. *ACM Transactions on Database Systems*, 1(2):97–137, June 1976.

[ACL91] R. Agrawal, R.J. Cochrane, and B. Lindsay. On maintaining priorities in a production rule system. In *Proceedings of the Seventeenth International Conference on Very Large Data Bases*, pages 479–487, Barcelona, Spain, September 1991.

[AG89a] R. Agrawal and N. Gehani. Ode (Object database and environment): The language and the data model. In *Proceedings of the ACM SIGMOD International Conference on Management of Data*, pages 36–45, Portland, Oregon, May 1989.

[AG89b] R. Agrawal and N. Gehani. Rationale for the design of persistence and query processing facilities in the database programming language O++. In *Proceedings of the Second International Workshop on Database Programming Languages*, pages 1–6, Portland, Oregon, June 1989.

[All92] Allbase manuals, June 1992.

[AMC93] E. Anwar, L. Maugis, and S. Chakravarthy. A new perspective on rule support for object-oriented databases. In *Proceedings of the ACM SIGMOD International Conference on Management of Data*, pages 99–108, Washington, D.C., May 1993.

303

[AS91]   S. Abiteboul and E. Simon. Fundamental properties of deter-
            ministic and nondeterministic extensions of datalog. *Theoretical
            Computer Science*, 78:137–158, 1991.

[ASK92]   ASK Computer Systems. *INGRES/SQL Reference Manual, Ver-
            sion 6.4*, 1992.

[ASL90]   A.M. Alasqur, S.Y.W. Su, and H. Lam. A rule based language for
            deductive object-oriented databases. In *Proceedings of the Sixth
            International Conference on Data Engineering*, pages 58–67, Los
            Angeles, California, February 1990.

[AWH92]   A. Aiken, J. Widom, and J.M. Hellerstein. Behavior of database
            production rules: Termination, confluence, and observable de-
            terminism. In *Proceedings of the ACM SIGMOD International
            Conference on Management of Data*, pages 59–68, San Diego,
            California, June 1992.

[BBC80]   P.A. Bernstein, B.T. Blaustein, and E.M. Clarke. Fast mainte-
            nance of semantic integrity assertions using redundant aggregate
            data. In *Proceedings of the Sixth International Conference on
            Very Large Data Bases*, pages 126–136, Montreal, Canada, Oc-
            tober 1980.

[BBKZ92]   A.P. Buchmann, H. Branding, T. Kudrass, and J. Zimmerman.
            REACH: A REal-time, ACtive, and Heterogeneous mediator sys-
            tem. *IEEE Data Engineering Bulletin, Special Issue on Active
            Databases*, 15(4):44–47, December 1992.

[BBKZ93]   H. Branding, A. Buchmann, T. Kudrass, and J. Zimmerman.
            Rules in an open system: The REACH rule system. In *Proceed-
            ings of the First International Workshop on Rules in Database
            Systems*, pages 111–126, Edinburgh, Scotland, August 1993.

[BC79]   O.P. Buneman and E.K. Clemons. Efficiently monitoring re-
            lational databases. *ACM Transactions on Database Systems*,
            4(3):368–382, September 1979.

[BCMP94]   E. Baralis, S. Ceri, G. Monteleone, and S. Paraboschi. An intel-
            ligent database system application: The design of EMS. In *Pro-
            ceedings of the First International Conference on Applications of*

Databases, number 851 in LNCS, Vadstena, Sweden, June 1994. Springer-Verlag.

[BCN92]   C. Batini, S. Ceri, and S.B. Navathe. *Conceptual Database Design: an Entity-Relationship Approach.* Benjamin/Cummings, Redwood City, California, 1992.

[BCP94a]   E. Baralis, S. Ceri, and S. Paraboschi. Declarative specification of constraint maintenance. In *Proceedings of the International Conference on the Entity-Relationship Approach*, Manchester, UK, December 1994.

[BCP94b]   E. Baralis, S. Ceri, and S. Paraboschi. Modularization techniques in active rules design. Technical Report IDEA.WP.22P.003.01, Politecnico di Milano, Milano, Italy, December 1994.

[BD88]   A. Buchmann and U. Dayal. Constraint and exception handling for design, reliability, and maintainability. In *Proceedings of the ASME Symposium on Engineering Database Management: Emerging Issues*, August 1988.

[Beh94]   H. Behrends. Simulation-based debugging of active databases. In *Proceedings of the Fourth International Workshop on Research Issues in Data Engineering (RIDE-ADS '94)*, pages 172–180, Houston, Texas, February 1994.

[BFKM85]   L. Brownston, R. Farrell, E. Kant, and N. Martin. *Programming Expert Systems in OPS5: An Introduction to Rule-Based Programming.* Addison-Wesley, Reading, Massachusetts, 1985.

[BJ93]   P. Bayer and W. Jonker. A framework for supporting triggers in deductive databases. In *Proceedings of the First International Workshop on Rules in Database Systems*, pages 316–330, Edinburgh, Scotland, August 1993.

[BJ94]   C. Bussler and S. Jablonski. Implementing agent coordination for workflow management systems using active database systems. In *Proceedings of the Fourth International Workshop on Research Issues in Data Engineering (RIDE-ADS '94)*, pages 53–59, Houston, Texas, February 1994.

[BL85]   R.J. Brachman and H.J. Levesque, editors. *Readings in Knowledge Representation.* Morgan Kaufmann, San Francisco, California, 1985.

[BL92]   M. Berndtsson and B. Lings. On developing reactive object-oriented databases. *IEEE Data Engineering Bulletin, Special Issue on Active Databases,* 15(4):31–34, December 1992.

[BM91]   C. Beeri and T. Milo. A model for active object oriented database. In *Proceedings of the Seventeenth International Conference on Very Large Data Bases,* pages 337–349, Barcelona, Spain, September 1991.

[BM93]   D.A. Brant and D.P. Miranker. Index support for rule activation. In *Proceedings of the ACM SIGMOD International Conference on Management of Data,* pages 42–48, Washington, D.C., May 1993.

[BMHD89]   A. Buchmann, D. McCarthy, M. Hsu, and U. Dayal. Time-critical database scheduling: A framework for integrating real-time scheduling and concurrency control. In *Proceedings of the Fifth International Conference on Data Engineering,* February 1989.

[BOH+92]   A.P. Buchmann, M.T. Ozsu, M. Hornick, D. Georgakopoulos, and F. Manola. A transaction model for active, distributed object systems. In A.K. Elmagarmid, editor, *Database Transaction Models for Advanced Applications.* Morgan Kaufmann, San Francisco, California, 1992.

[BS94]   P. Bichler and M. Schrefl. Active object-oriented database design using active object/behavior diagrams. In *Proceedings of the Fourth International Workshop on Research Issues in Data Engineering (RIDE-ADS '94),* pages 163–171, Houston, Texas, February 1994.

[Buc91]   A.P. Buchmann. Modeling heterogeneous systems as an active object space. In A. Dearle, G.M. Shaw, and S.B. Zdonik, editors, *Implementing Persistent Object Bases, Principles and Practice.* Morgan Kaufmann, San Francisco, California, 1991.

[BW94]   E. Baralis and J. Widom. An algebraic approach to rule analysis in expert database systems. In *Proceedings of the Twentieth International Conference on Very Large Data Bases*, Santiago, Chile, September 1994.

[BZ87]   T. Bloom and S.B. Zdonik. Issues in the design of object-oriented database programming languages. In *Proceedings of the ACM Conference on Object-Oriented Programming Systems, Languages, and Applications*, pages 441–451, Orlando, Florida, October 1987.

[CBB+89]   S. Chakravarthy, B. Blaustein, A.P. Buchmann, M. Carey, U. Dayal, D. Goldhirsch, M. Hsu, R. Jauhari, R. Ladin, M. Livny, D. McCarthy, R. McKee, and A. Rosenthal. HiPAC: A research project in active, time-constrained database management. Technical Report XAIT-89-02, Xerox Advanced Information Technology, Cambridge, Massachusetts, July 1989.

[CCCR+90]   F. Cacace, S. Ceri, S. Crespi-Reghizzi, L. Tanca, and R. Zicari. Integrating object-oriented data modeling with a rule-based programming paradigm. In *Proceedings of the ACM SIGMOD International Conference on Management of Data*, pages 225–236, Atlantic City, New Jersey, May 1990.

[CCL+90]   S. Ceri, S. Crespi Reghizzi, G. Lamperti, L. Lavazza, and R. Zicari. Algres: An advanced database for complex applications. *IEEE Software*, 7(4):68–78, July 1990.

[CCS94]   C. Collet, T. Coupaye, and T. Svensen. NAOS—efficient and modular reactive capabilities in an object-oriented database system. In *Proceedings of the Twentieth International Conference on Very Large Data Bases*, pages 132–143, Santiago, Chile, September 1994.

[CDF+86]   M. Carey, D. DeWitt, D. Frank, G. Graefe, J. Richardson, E. Shekita, and M. Muralikrishna. The architecture of the EXODUS extensible DBMS. In *Proceedings of the International Workshop on Object-Oriented Database Systems*, pages 52–65, September 1986.

[Cer92]   S. Ceri. A declarative approach to active databases. In *Proceedings of the Eighth International Conference on Data Engineering* (invited paper), pages 452–456, Tempe, Arizona, February 1992.

[CFPT94]   S. Ceri, P. Fraternali, S. Paraboschi, and L. Tanca. Automatic generation of production rules for integrity maintenance. *ACM Transactions on Database Systems*, 19(3):367–422, September 1994.

[CGT90]   S. Ceri, G. Gottlob, and L. Tanca. *Logic Programming and Databases*. Springer-Verlag, Berlin, 1990.

[Cho92a]   J. Chomicki. History-less checking of dynamic integrity constraints. In *Proceedings of the Eighth International Conference on Data Engineering*, pages 557–564, Phoenix, Arizona, February 1992.

[Cho92b]   J. Chomicki. Real-time integrity constraints. In *Proceedings of the Eleventh ACM SIGACT-SIGMOD-SIGART Symposium on Principles of Database Systems*, pages 274–282, San Diego, California, June 1992.

[CHS92]   S. Chakravarthy, E. Hanson, and S.Y.W. Su. Active data/ knowledge base research at the University of Florida. *IEEE Data Engineering Bulletin, Special Issue on Active Databases*, 15(4):35–39, December 1992.

[CJL91]   M.J. Carey, R. Jauhari, and M. Livny. On transaction boundaries in active databases: A performance perspective. *IEEE Transactions on Knowledge and Data Engineering*, 3(3), September 1991.

[CKAK94]   S. Chakravarthy, V. Krishnaprasad, E. Anwar, and S.-K. Kim. Composite events for active databases: Semantics, contexts, and detection. In *Proceedings of the Twentieth International Conference on Very Large Data Bases*, pages 606–617, Santiago, Chile, September 1994.

[CL92]   S. Chakravarthy and D. Lomet, editors. *Special Issue on Active Databases*, IEEE Data Engineering Bulletin 15(4), December 1992.

[CM93]   S. Ceri and R. Manthey.   Consolidated specification of Chimera, the conceptual interface of Idea. Technical Report IDEA.DD.2P.004, Politecnico di Milano, Milan, Italy, June 1993.

[CN90]   S. Chakravarthy and S. Nesson.   Making an object-oriented DBMS active: Design, implementation, and evaluation of a prototype. In *Advances in Database Technology—EDBT '90, Lecture Notes in Computer Science 416*. Springer-Verlag, Berlin, March 1990.

[CO92]   S.J. Cannan and G.A.M. Otten. *SQL—The Standard Handbook*. McGraw-Hill, London, 1992.

[Coc92]   R.J. Cochrane. *Issues in Integrating Active Rules into Database Systems*. Ph.D. thesis, University of Maryland, College Park, January 1992.

[COD73]   CODASYL data description language committee, June 1973. CODASYL Data Description Language Journal of Development.

[Coh89]   D. Cohen. Compiling complex database transition triggers. In *Proceedings of the ACM SIGMOD International Conference on Management of Data*, pages 225–234, Portland, Oregon, May 1989.

[Cor88]   Symbolics Corporation.   Symbolics Common Lisp Reference Manual, February 1988.

[CS94]   R. Chandra and A. Segev.   Active databases for financial applications. In *Proceedings of the Fourth International Workshop on Research Issues in Data Engineering (RIDE-ADS '94)*, pages 46–52, Houston, Texas, February 1994.

[CSS94]   R. Chandra, A. Segev, and M. Stonebraker. Implementing calendars and temporal rules in next generation databases. In *Proceedings of the Tenth International Conference on Data Engineering*, pages 264–273, Houston, Texas, February 1994.

[CW90]   S. Ceri and J. Widom. Deriving production rules for constraint maintenance. In *Proceedings of the Sixteenth International Conference on Very Large Data Bases*, pages 566–577, Brisbane, Australia, August 1990.

[CW91]   S. Ceri and J. Widom. Deriving production rules for incremental view maintenance. In *Proceedings of the Seventeenth International Conference on Very Large Data Bases*, pages 577–589, Barcelona, Spain, September 1991.

[CW92]   S. Ceri and J. Widom. Production rules in parallel and distributed database environments. In *Proceedings of the Eighteenth International Conference on Very Large Data Bases*, pages 339–351, Vancouver, British Columbia, August 1992.

[CW93]   S. Ceri and J. Widom. Managing semantic heterogeneity with production rules and persistent queues. In *Proceedings of the Nineteenth International Conference on Very Large Data Bases*, pages 108–119, Dublin, Ireland, August 1993.

[CW94]   S. Ceri and J. Widom. Deriving incremental production rules for deductive data. *Information Systems*, 19(6):467–490, 1994.

[D+87]   U. Dayal, et al. PROBE—a research project in knowledge-oriented database systems: Final report. Technical report, Computer Corporation of America, Boston, Massachusetts, November 1987.

[Dat81]   C. Date. Referential integrity. In *Proceedings of the Seventh International Conference on Very Large Data Bases*, Cannes, France, September 1981.

[Day89]   U. Dayal. Queries and views in an object-oriented data model. In *Proceedings of the Second International Workshop on Database Programming Languages*, pages 80–102, June 1989.

[DE88]   L.M.L. Delcambre and J.N. Etheredge. A self-controlling interpreter for the Relational Production Language. In *Proceedings of the ACM SIGMOD International Conference on Management of Data*, pages 396–403, Chicago, Illinois, June 1988.

[DE89]   L.M.L. Delcambre and J.N. Etheredge. The Relational Production Language: A production language for relational databases. In L. Kerschberg, editor, *Expert Database Systems—Proceedings from the Second International Conference*, pages 333–351. Benjamin/Cummings, Redwood City, California, 1989.

[DHL90]   U. Dayal, M. Hsu, and R. Ladin. Organizing long-running activities with triggers and transactions. In *Proceedings of the ACM SIGMOD International Conference on Management of Data*, pages 204–214, Atlantic City, New Jersey, May 1990.

[DHL91]   U. Dayal, M. Hsu, and R. Ladin. A transactional model for long-running activities. In *Proceedings of the Seventeenth International Conference on Very Large Data Bases*, pages 113–122, Barcelona, Spain, September 1991.

[DJP93]   O. Diaz, A. Jaime, and N.W. Paton. DEAR: A debugger for active rules in an object-oriented context. In *Proceedings of the First International Workshop on Rules in Database Systems*, pages 180–193, Edinburgh, Scotland, August 1993.

[dMS88a]   C. de Maindreville and E. Simon. Modeling non-deterministic queries and updates in a deductive database. In *Proceedings of the Fourteenth International Conference on Very Large Data Bases*, Los Angeles, California, August 1988.

[dMS88b]   C. de Maindreville and E. Simon. A production rule based approach to deductive databases. In *Proceedings of the Fourth International Conference on Data Engineering*, pages 234–241, Los Angeles, California, February 1988.

[DOS⁺92]   H.M. Dewan, D. Ohsie, S.J. Stolfo, O. Wolfson, and S. Da Silva. Incremental database rule processing in PARADISER. *Journal of Intelligent Information Systems*, 1992.

[DPG91]   O. Diaz, N. Paton, and P. Gray. Rule management in object-oriented databases: A uniform approach. In *Proceedings of the Seventeenth International Conference on Very Large Data Bases*, pages 317–326, Barcelona, Spain, September 1991.

[DS94a]   H.M. Dewan and S.J. Stolfo. Meta-level control of rule execution in a parallel and distributed expert database system. In *Proceedings of the Fourth International Workshop on Research Issues in Data Engineering (RIDE-ADS '94)*, pages 105–114, Houston, Texas, February 1994.

[DS94b]   H.M. Dewan and S.J. Stolfo. Predictive dynamic load balancing of parallel and distributed rule and query processing. In

Proceedings of the ACM SIGMOD International Conference on Management of Data, pages 277–288, Minneapolis, Minnesota, May 1994.

[DUHK92]   S. Dietrich, S.D. Urban, J.V. Harrison, and A.P. Karamdice. A DOOD RANCH at ASU: Integrating active, deductive, and object-oriented databases. *IEEE Data Engineering Bulletin, Special Issue on Active Databases*, 15(4):40–43, December 1992.

[DWE89]   L.M.L. Delcambre, J. Waramahaputi, and J.N. Etheredge. Pattern match reduction for the Relational Production Language in the USL MMDBS. *SIGMOD Record, Special Issue on Rule Management and Processing in Expert Database Systems*, 18(3):59–67, September 1989.

[EC75]   K.P. Eswaran and D.D. Chamberlin. Functional specifications of a subsystem for data base integrity. In *Proceedings of the First International Conference on Very Large Data Bases*, pages 48–67, Framingham, Massachusetts, September 1975.

[EGS93]   O. Etzion, A. Gal, and A. Segev. Data driven and temporal rules in PARDES. In *Proceedings of the First International Workshop on Rules in Database Systems*, pages 92–108, Edinburgh, Scotland, August 1993.

[EGS94]   O. Etzion, A. Gal, and A. Segev. Retroactie and proactive database processing. In *Proceedings of the Fourth International Workshop on Research Issues in Data Engineering (RIDE-ADS '94)*, pages 126–131, Houston, Texas, February 1994.

[Elm92]   A.K. Elmagarmid, editor. *Database Transaction Models for Advanced Applications*. Morgan Kaufmann, San Francisco, California, 1992.

[EN94]   R. Elmasri and S.B. Navathe. *Fundamentals of Database Systems*. Benjamin/Cimmings, Redwood City, California, 1994.

[Esw76]   K.P. Eswaran. Specifications, implementations and interactions of a trigger subsystem in an integrated database system. IBM Research Report RJ 1820, IBM San Jose Research Laboratory, San Jose, California, August 1976.

[FGVLV94] O. Friesen, G. Gauthiers-Villars, A. Lefebvre, and L. Vieille. Applications of deductive object-oriented databases (DOOD) using datalog extended language (DEL). In R. Ramakrishnan, editor, *Applications of Logic Databases*. Kluwer Academic Publishers, Norwell, Massachusetts, 1994.

[FMT94]   P. Fraternali, D. Montesi, and L. Tanca. Active database semantics. In *Proceedings of the Fifth Australasian Database Conference*, Canterbury, New Zealand, January 1994.

[For82]   C.L. Forgy. Rete: A fast algorithm for the many pattern/many object pattern match problem. *Artificial Intelligence*, 19:17–37, 1982.

[FRS93]   F. Fabret, M. Regnier, and E. Simon. An adaptive algorithm for incremental evaluation of production rules in databases. In *Proceedings of the Nineteenth International Conference on Very Large Data Bases*, pages 455–467, Dublin, Ireland, August 1993.

[GD92]   S. Gatziu and K.R. Dittrich. SAMOS: An active object-oriented database system. *IEEE Data Engineering Bulletin, Special Issue on Active Databases*, 15(4):23–26, December 1992.

[GD94]   S. Gatziu and K.R. Dittrich. Detecting composite events in active database systems using petri nets. In *Proceedings of the Fourth International Workshop on Research Issues in Data Engineering (RIDE-ADS '94)*, pages 2–9, Houston, Texas, February 1994.

[Ger94]   M. Gertz. Specifying reactive integrity control for active databases. In *Proceedings of the Fourth International Workshop on Research Issues in Data Engineering (RIDE-ADS '94)*, pages 62–70, Houston, Texas, February 1994.

[GGD91]   S. Gatziu, A. Geppert, and K.R. Dittrich. Integrating active concepts into an object-oriented database system. In *Proceedings of the Third International Workshop on Database Programming Languages*, Nafplion, Greece, August 1991.

[GHJ92]   S. Ghandeharizadeh, R. Hull, and D. Jacobs. Implementation of delayed updates in Heraclitus. In *Advances in Database*

Technology—EDBT '92, Lecture Notes in Computer Science 580, pages 261–276, Springer-Verlag, Berlin, March 1992.

[GHJ⁺93]   S. Ghandeharizadeh, R. Hull, D. Jacobs, et al. On implementing a language for specifying active database execution models. In *Proceedings of the Nineteenth International Conference on Very Large Data Bases*, Dublin, Ireland, August 1993.

[GJ91]   N. Gehani and H.V. Jagadish. Ode as an active database: Constraints and triggers. In *Proceedings of the Seventeenth International Conference on Very Large Data Bases*, pages 327–336, Barcelona, Spain, September 1991.

[GJS92a]   N. Gehani, H.V. Jagadish, and O. Shmueli. Compose: A system for composite event specification and detection. In N.R. Adam and B. Bhargava, editors, *Advanced Database Concepts and Research Issues, Lecture Notes in Computer Science.* Springer-Verlag, Berlin, 1992.

[GJS92b]   N. Gehani, H.V. Jagadish, and O. Shmueli. Composite event specification in active databases: Model & implementation. In *Proceedings of the Eighteenth International Conference on Very Large Data Bases*, pages 327–338, Vancouver, British Columbia, August 1992.

[GJS92c]   N. Gehani, H.V. Jagadish, and O. Shmueli. Event specification in an active object-oriented database. In *Proceedings of the ACM SIGMOD International Conference on Management of Data*, pages 81–90, San Diego, California, June 1992.

[GL93]   M. Gertz and U.W. Lipeck. Deriving integrity maintaining triggers from transition graphs. In *Proceedings of the Ninth International Conference on Data Engineering*, pages 22–29, Vienna, Austria, April 1993.

[GMS87]   H. Garcia-Molina and K. Salem. Sagas. In *Proceedings of the ACM SIGMOD International Conference on Management of Data*, San Francisco, California, May 1987.

[Goh91]   J. Goh. Rule processing with query rewrite. Master's thesis, University of California, Berkeley, June 1991.

[GP91]   D.N. Gordin and A.J. Pasik. Set-oriented constructs: From Rete rule bases to database systems. In *Proceedings of the ACM SIG-MOD International Conference on Management of Data*, pages 60–67, Denver, Colorado, May 1991.

[Han89]   E.N. Hanson. An initial report on the design of Ariel: A DBMS with an integrated production rule system. *SIGMOD Record, Special Issue on Rule Management and Processing in Expert Database Systems*, 18(3):12–19, September 1989.

[Han92]   E.N. Hanson. Rule condition testing and action execution in Ariel. In *Proceedings of the ACM SIGMOD International Conference on Management of Data*, pages 49–58, San Diego, California, June 1992.

[Han93]   E.N. Hanson. Gator: A generalized discrimination network for production rule matching. In *Proceedings of the IJCAI Workshop on Production Systems and Their Innovative Applications*, August 1993.

[HC90]   E.N. Hanson and M. Chaabouni. The IBS tree: A data structure for finding all intervals that overlap a point. Technical Report WSU-CS-90-11, Wright State University, Dayton, Ohio, April 1990.

[HCKW90]   E.N. Hanson, M. Chaabouni, C.-H. Kim, and Y.-W. Wang. A predicate matching algorithm for database rule systems. In *Proceedings of the ACM SIGMOD International Conference on Management of Data*, pages 271–280, Atlantic City, New Jersey, May 1990.

[HCL+90]   L.M. Haas, W. Chang, G.M. Lohman, J. McPherson, P.F. Wilms, G. Lapis, B. Lindsay, H. Pirahesh, M. Carey, and E. Shekita. Starburst mid-flight: As the dust clears. *IEEE Transactions on Knowledge and Data Engineering*, 2(1):143–160, March 1990.

[HD93]   J.V. Harrison and S.W. Dietrich. Integrating active and deductive rules. In *Proceedings of the First International Workshop on Rules in Database Systems*, pages 288–305, Edinburgh, Scotland, August 1993.

[HDR93]   E.N. Hanson, R. Dastur, and V. Ramaswamy. An architecture for recoverable interaction between applications and active databases. Technical Report CIS-TR-93-024, University of Florida, July 1993.

[HJ91]   R. Hull and D. Jacobs. Language constructs for programming active databases. In *Proceedings of the Seventeenth International Conference on Very Large Data Bases*, pages 455–468, Barcelona, Spain, September 1991.

[HJ92]   E.N. Hanson and T. Johnson. The interval skip list: A data structure for finding all intervals that overlap a point. Technical Report TR92-016, University of Florida, Gainesville, June 1992.

[HLM88]   M. Hsu, R. Ladin, and D. McCarthy. An execution model for active database management systems. In *Proceedings of the Third International Conference on Data and Knowledge Bases*, Jerusalem, Israel, June 1988.

[HS78]   M.M. Hammer and S. Sarin. Efficient monitoring of database assertions. In *Proceedings of the ACM SIGMOD International Conference on Management of Data*, June 1978.

[HSL92]   I.-M. Hsu, M. Singhal, and M.T. Liu. Distributed rule processing in active databases. In *Proceedings of the Eighth International Conference on Data Engineering*, Tempe, Arizona, February 1992.

[Inf94a]   Informix guide to SQL, Syntax, Version 6, March 1994. Number 000-7597.

[Inf94b]   Informix guide to SQL, Tutorial, Version 6, March 1994. Number 000-7598.

[ISO94]   ISO-ANSI working draft: Database language SQL3, 1994. X3H2/94/080 and SOU/003.

[JQ92]   H.V. Jagadish and X. Qian. Integrity maintenance in an object-oriented database. In *Proceedings of the Eighteenth International Conference on Very Large Data Bases*, pages 469–480, Vancouver, British Columbia, August 1992.

[JS92]   H.V. Jagadish and O. Shmueli. Synchronizing trigger events in a distributed object-oriented database. In *Proceedings of the International Workshop on Distributed Object Management*, Edmonton, Alberta, August 1992.

[KC86]   S.N. Khoshafian and G.P. Copeland. Object identity. In *Proceedings of the ACM Conference on Object-Oriented Programming Systems, Languages, and Applications*, pages 406–416, Portland, Oregon, September 1986.

[KDM88]   A.M. Kotz, K.R. Dittrich, and J.A. Mulle. Supporting semantic rules by a generalized event/trigger mechanism. In *Advances in Database Technology—EDBT '88, Lecture Notes in Computer Science 303*, pages 76–91. Springer-Verlag, Berlin, March 1988.

[KdMS89]   J. Kiernan, C. de Maindreville, and E. Simon. The design and implementation of an extendible deductive database system. *SIGMOD Record, Special Issue on Rule Management and Processing in Expert Database Systems*, 18(3):68–78, September 1989.

[KdMS90]   J. Kiernan, C. de Maindreville, and E. Simon. Making deductive databases a practical technology: A step forward. In *Proceedings of the ACM SIGMOD International Conference on Management of Data*, pages 237–246, Atlantic City, New Jersey, May 1990.

[KS86]   H.F. Korth and A. Silberschatz. *Database System Concepts*. McGraw-Hill, New York, 1986.

[KU94]   A.P. Karadimce and S.D. Urban. Conditional term rewriting as a formal basis for analysis of active database rules. In *Fourth International Workshop on Research Issues in Data Engineering (RIDE-ADS '94)*, pages 156–162, Houston, Texas, February 1994.

[Lis85]   B.H. Liskov. The Argus language and system. In *Distributed Systems: Methods and Tools for Specification*, pages 343–430, Springer-Verlag, Berlin, 1985.

[MD87]   F. Manola and U. Dayal. An overview of PDM: An object-oriented data model. In K. Dittrich, U. Dayal, and A. Buchmann, editors, *Object-Oriented Database Systems*. Springer-Verlag, Berlin, 1987.

[MD89]   D.R. McCarthy and U. Dayal. The architecture of an active database management system. In *Proceedings of the ACM SIGMOD International Conference on Management of Data*, pages 215–224, Portland, Oregon, May 1989.

[Min88]   J. Minker. *Foundations of Deductive Databases and Logic Programming*. Morgan Kaufmann, San Francisco, California, 1988.

[Mir87]   D.P. Miranker. TREAT: A better match algorithm for AI production systems. In *Proceedings of the AAAI Conference on Artificial Intelligence*, pages 42–47, August 1987.

[ML91]   G. Moerkotte and P.C. Lockemann. Reactive consistency control in deductive databases. *ACM Transactions on Database Systems*, 16(4):670–702, December 1991.

[Mor83]   M. Morgenstern. Active databases as a paradigm for enhanced computing environments. In *Proceedings of the Ninth International Conference on Very Large Data Bases*, pages 34–42, Florence, Italy, October 1983.

[Mos82]   J.E.B. Moss. Nested transactions and reliable distributed computing. In *Proceedings of the Second Symposium on Reliability in Distributed Software and Database Systems*, 1982.

[MP91]   C. Medeiros and P. Pfeffer. Object integrity using rules. In *Proceedings of the European Conference on Object-Oriented Programming, Lecture Notes in Computer Science 512*. Springer-Verlag, Berlin, July 1991.

[MS93]   J. Melton and A.R. Simon. *Understanding the New SQL: A Complete Guide*. Morgan Kaufmann, San Francisco, California, 1993.

[NI93]   W. Naqvi and M.T. Ibrahim. Rule and knowledge management in an active database system. In *Proceedings of the First International Workshop on Rules in Database Systems*, pages 58–69, Edinburgh, Scotland, August 1993.

[NTC92]   S.B. Navathe, A.K. Tanaka, and S. Chakravarthy. Active database modeling and design tools: Issues, approach, and architecture. *IEEE Data Engineering Bulletin, Special Issue on Active Databases*, 15(4):6–9, December 1992.

[ODSS94]   D. Ohsie, H.M. Dewan, S.J. Stolfo, and S. Da Silva. Performance of incremental update in database rule processing. In *Proceedings of the Fourth International Workshop on Research Issues in Data Engineering (RIDE-ADS '94)*, pages 10–18, Houston, Texas, February 1994.

[Ong91]   L.P. Ong. Version modeling using production rules in the POSTGRES DBMS. Master's thesis, University of California, Berkeley, June 1991.

[ORA92a]   ORACLE 7 server application developer's guide, December 1992. Number 6695-70.

[ORA92b]   ORACLE 7 server concepts manual, December 1992. Number 6693-70.

[Pot91]   S. Potamianos. *Semantics and Performance of Integrated DBMS Rule Systems*. Ph.D. thesis, University of California, Berkeley, 1991.

[PP93]   S. Paraboschi and G. Psaila. Specification of UFI and triggers compilers for Chimera (Algres testbed). Technical Report IDEA.DE.3P.004, Politecnico di Milano, Milan, Italy, December 1993.

[PT94]   L. Palopoli and R. Torlone. Modeling database applications using generalized production rules. In *Proceedings of the Fourth International Workshop on Research Issues in Data Engineering (RIDE-ADS '94)*, pages 30–38, Houston, Texas, February 1994.

[PW93]   N.W. Paton and M.H. Williams, editors. *Rules in Database Systems*, Edinburgh, Scotland, 1993. Springer-Verlag, Berlin.

[QW91]   X. Qian and G. Wiederhold. Incremental recomputation of active relational expressions. *IEEE Transactions on Knowledge and Data Engineering*, 3(3):337–341, September 1991.

[RC88]   A. Rosenthal and S. Chakravarthy. Anatomy of a modular multiple query optimizer. In *Proceedings of the Fourteenth International Conference on Very Large Data Bases*, pages 230–239, Los Angeles, California, September 1988.

[RCBB89] A. Rosenthal, S. Chakravarthy, B. Blaustein, and J. Blakeley. Situation monitoring for active databases. In *Proceedings of the Fifteenth International Conference on Very Large Data Bases*, pages 455–464, Amsterdam, The Netherlands, August 1989.

[RCS89]   J.E. Richardson, M.J. Carey, and D.T. Schuh. The design of the E programming language. Technical Report 824, University of Wisconsin, Madison, January 1989.

[Rdb91]   Rdb/VMS—SQL reference manual. Digital Equipment Corporation, Maynard, Massachusetts, 1991.

[Reu89]   A. Reuter. Contracts: A means for extending control beyond transaction boundaries. In *Proceedings of the Third Workshop on High Performance Transaction Systems*, Pacific Grove, California, September 1989.

[Ris89]   T. Risch. Monitoring database objects. In *Proceedings of the Fifteenth International Conference on Very Large Data Bases*, Amsterdam, The Netherlands, August 1989.

[RS92]   T. Risch and M. Sköld. Active rules based on object-oriented queries. *IEEE Data Engineering Bulletin, Special Issue on Active Databases*, 15(4):27–30, December 1992.

[SC93]   S.Y.W. Su and H.-H.M. Chen. Temporal rule specification and management in object-oriented knowledge bases. In *Proceedings of the First International Workshop on Rules in Database Systems*, pages 73–91, Edinburgh, Scotland, August 1993.

[SDLT86] M.I. Schor, T.P. Daly, H.S. Lee, and B.R. Tibbitts. Advances in RETE pattern matching. In *Proceedings of the Fifth National Conference on Artificial Intelligence*, pages 226–232, Philadelphia, Pennsylvania, August 1986.

[SdM88]   E. Simon and C. de Maindreville. Deciding whether a production rule is relational computable. In *Proceedings of the Second International Conference on Database Theory*, Bruges, Belgium, September 1988.

[Sel89]   T. Sellis, editor. *Special Issue on Rule Management and Processing in Expert Database Systems*, SIGMOD Record 18(3), September 1989.

[Shi81]   D. Shipman. The functional data model and the data language DAPLEX. *ACM Transactions on Database Systems*, 6(1), March 1981.

[SHP88]   M. Stonebraker, E.N. Hanson, and S. Potamianos. The POST-GRES rule manager. *IEEE Transactions on Software Engineering*, 14(7):897–907, July 1988.

[SHP89]   M. Stonebraker, M. Hearst, and S. Potamianos. A commentary on the POSTGRES rules system. *SIGMOD Record, Special Issue on Rule Management and Processing in Expert Database Systems*, 18(3):5–11, September 1989.

[SJGP90]   M. Stonebraker, A. Jhingran, J. Goh, and S. Potamianos. On rules, procedures, caching and views in data base systems. In *Proceedings of the ACM SIGMOD International Conference on Management of Data*, pages 281–290, Atlantic City, New Jersey, May 1990.

[SKdM92]   E. Simon, J. Kiernan, and C. de Maindreville. Implementing high level active rules on top of a relational DBMS. In *Proceedings of the Eighteenth International Conference on Very Large Data Bases*, pages 315–326, Vancouver, British Columbia, August 1992.

[SLR88]   T. Sellis, C.-C. Lin, and L. Raschid. Implementing large production systems in a DBMS environment: Concepts and algorithms. In *Proceedings of the ACM SIGMOD International Conference on Management of Data*, pages 404–412, Chicago, Illinois, June 1988.

[SLR89]   T. Sellis, C.-C. Lin, and L. Raschid. Data intensive production systems: The DIPS approach. *SIGMOD Record, Special Issue on Rule Management and Processing in Expert Database Systems*, 18(3):52–58, September 1989.

[Smi94]   K. Smith. Execution ordering for multilevel secure rules. In *Proceedings of the Fourth International Workshop on Research Issues in Data Engineering (RIDE-ADS '94)*, pages 98–104, Houston, Texas, February 1994.

[SPAM91]   U. Schreier, H. Pirahesh, R. Agrawal, and C. Mohan. Alert: An architecture for transforming a passive DBMS into an active DBMS. In *Proceedings of the Seventeenth International Conference on Very Large Data Bases*, pages 469–478, Barcelona, Spain, September 1991.

[SRH90]   M. Stonebraker, L. Rowe, and M. Hirohama. The implementation of POSTGRES. *IEEE Transactions on Knowledge and Data Engineering*, 2(7):125–142, March 1990.

[SSH86]   M. Stonebraker, T. Sellis, and E. Hanson. An analysis of rule indexing implementations in data base systems. In *Proceedings of the First International Conference on Expert Database Systems*, pages 353–364, Charleston, South Carolina, April 1986.

[Sto75]   M. Stonebraker. Implementation of integrity constraints and views by query modification. In *Proceedings of the ACM SIGMOD International Conference on Management of Data*, pages 65–78, San Jose, California, May 1975.

[Sto92]   M. Stonebraker. The integration of rule systems and database systems. *IEEE Transactions on Knowledge and Data Engineering*, 4(5):415–423, October 1992.

[Str87]   B. Stroustrup. Multiple inheritance for C++. In *Proceedings of the European UNIX User's Group Conference*, pages 189–208, Helsinki, Finland, May 1987.

[Str91]   B. Stroustrup. *The C++ Programming Language (2/E)*. Addison-Wesley, Reading, Massachuessets, 1991.

[SW92a]   P. Sistla and O. Wolfson. Triggers on database histories. *IEEE Data Engineering Bulletin, Special Issue on Active Databases*, 15(4):48–51, December 1992.

[SW92b]   K. Smith and M. Winslett. Multilevel secure rules: Integrating the multilevel and active data models. Technical Report UIUCDCS-R-92-1732, University of Illinois, Urbana-Champaign, March 1992.

[Syb]   Transact-SQL user's guide for Sybase, release 10.0. Berkeley, California.

[TC94]   D. Toman and J. Chomicki. Implementing temporal integrity constraints using an active DBMS. In *Proceedings of the Fourth International Workshop on Research Issues in Data Engineering (RIDE-ADS '94)*, pages 87–95, Houston, Texas, February 1994.

[Ull89]   J.D. Ullman. *Principles of Database and Knowledge-Base Systems, Volumes I and II*. Computer Science Press, Rockville, Maryland, 1989.

[UO94]   T. Urpí and A. Olivé. Semantic change computation optimization in active databases. In *Proceedings of the Fourth International Workshop on Research Issues in Data Engineering (RIDE-ADS '94)*, pages 19–27, Houston, Texas, February 1994.

[vdVS93]   L. van der Voort and A. Siebes. Termination and confluence of rule execution. In *Proceedings of the Second International Conference on Information and Knowledge Management*, Washington, D.C., November 1993.

[WC94]   J. Widom and S. Chakravarthy, editors. *Fourth International Workshop on Research Issues in Data Engineering: Active Database Systems*, Houston, Texas, 1994. IEEE Computer Society Press, Los Alamitos, California.

[WCL91]   J. Widom, R.J. Cochrane, and B.G. Lindsay. Implementing set-oriented production rules as an extension to Starburst. In *Proceedings of the Seventeenth International Conference on Very Large Data Bases*, pages 275–285, Barcelona, Spain, September 1991.

[WF90]   J. Widom and S.J. Finkelstein. Set-oriented production rules in relational database systems. In *Proceedings of the ACM SIGMOD International Conference on Management of Data*, pages 259–270, Atlantic City, New Jersey, May 1990.

[WH92]   Y.-W. Wang and E.N. Hanson. A performance comparison of the Rete and TREAT algorithms for testing database rule conditions. In *Proceedings of the Eighth International Conference on Data Engineering*, pages 88–97, Tempe, Arizona, February 1992.

[Wid92]   J. Widom. A denotational semantics for the Starburst production rule language. *SIGMOD Record*, 21(3):4–9, September 1992.

[Wid93]   J. Widom. Deductive and active databases: Two paradigms or ends of a spectrum? In *Proceedings of the First International Workshop on Rules in Database Systems*, pages 306–315, Edinburgh, Scotland, August 1993.

[Zan93]   C. Zaniolo. A unified semantics for active and deductive databases. In *Proceedings of the First International Workshop on Rules in Database Systems*, pages 271–287, Edinburgh, Scotland, August 1993.

[ZH90]   Y. Zhou and M. Hsu. A theory for rule triggering systems. In *Advances in Database Technology–EDBT '90, Lecture Notes in Computer Science 416*, pages 407–421, Springer-Verlag, Berlin, March 1990.

[Zlo77]   M.M. Zloof. Query-by-example: a data base language. *IBM Systems Journal*, 16(4):324–343, 1977.

List of Authors

1. Alejandro P. Buchman
   DVS-1
   Fachbereich Informatik
   Technische Hochschule Darmstadt
   Frankfurter Str. 69a
   64293 Darmstadt
   Germany
   buchmann@dvs1.informatik.th-darmstadt.de

2. Stefano Ceri
   Dipartimento di Elettronica e Informazione
   Politecnico di Milano
   Piazza Leonardo da Vinci, 32
   I-20133, Milano
   Italy
   ceri@elet.polimi.it

3. Sharma Chakravarthy
   Database Systems Research & Development Center
   E470 Computer Science and Engineering Building
   University of Florida
   Gainesville
   FL 32611-6125
   USA
   sharma@cis.ufl.edu

4. Umeshwar Dayal
   Hewlett-Packard Laboratories
   1501 Page Mill Road, 3U-4
   Palo Alto, CA 94304-1120
   USA
   dayal@hplud.hpl.hp.com

5. Piero Fraternali
   Dipartimento di Elettronica e Informazione
   Politecnico di Milano at Como
   Via Lucini, 3
   I-22100, Como
   Italy
   fraterna@elet.polimi.it

6. Nariain Gehani
   Database Systems Research Dept., MH 2C-220
   AT&T Bell Laboratories
   600 Mountain Avenue
   Murray Hill, NJ 07974-0636
   USA
   nhg@research.att.com

7. Eric N. Hanson
   CIS Department
   301 Computer Science and Engineering Building
   University of Florida
   Gainesville, FL 32611-6120
   USA
   hanson@cis.ufl.edu

8. H. V. Jagadish
   Computing Systems Research Laboratory, MH 2T204
   AT&T Bell Laboratories
   600 Mountain Avenue
   Murray Hill, NJ 07974
   USA
   jag@research.att.com

9. Jerry Kiernan
   IBM
   555 Bailey Avenue
   San Jose, CA 95141
   USA
   jkiernan@vnet.ibm.com

10. Stefano Paraboschi
    Dipartimento di Elettronica e Informazione
    Politecnico di Milano
    Piazza Leonardo da Vinci, 32
    I-20133, Milano
    Italy
    parabosc@elet.polimi.it

11. Spyros Potamianos
    Technical University of Athens
    Ippokratous 56
    Athens 10680
    Greece
    spyros@theseas.ntua.gr

12. Eric Simon
    INRIA
    78153 Le Chesnay
    France
    eric.simon@inria.fr

13. Michael Stonebraker
    Department of Computer Science
    617 Soda Hall
    University of California
    Berkeley, CA 94720
    USA
    mike@postgres.berkeley.edu

14. Letizia Tanca
    Dipartimento di Elettronica e Informazione
    Politecnico di Milano
    Piazza Leonardo da Vinci, 32
    I-20133, Milano
    Italy
    tanca@elet.polimi.it

15. Jennifer Widom
    Department of Computer Science
    Stanford University
    Stanford, CA 94305-2140
    USA
    widom@db.stanford.edu

Index